Meanings of Violence

Meanings of Violence

A Cross Cultural Perspective

Edited by
Göran Aijmer and Jon Abbink

Oxford • New York

First published in 2000 by
Berg
Editorial offices:
150 Cowley Road, Oxford OX4 1JJ, UK
838 Broadway, Third Floor, New York, NY 10003-4812, USA

© Göran Aijmer and Jon Abbink 2000

Berg is the imprint of Oxford International Publishers Ltd.

Library of Congress Cataloging-in-Publication Data

A catalogue record for this book is available from the Library of Congress.

British Library Cataloguing-in-Publication Data

A catalogue record for this book is available from the British Library.

ISBN 1 85973 435 9 (Cloth)
1 85973 440 5 (Paper)

Typeset by JS Typesetting, Wellingborough, Northants.
Printed in the United Kingdom by WBC Book Manufacturers, Bridgend,
Mid Glamorgan.

Contents

Notes on Contributors   vii

Preface: Violation and Violence as Cultural Phenomena   xi
Jon Abbink

Introduction: The Idiom of Violence in Imagery and Discourse   1
Göran Aijmer

1   The Enigma of Senseless Violence   23
    Anton Blok

2   'Criminals by Instinct': On the 'Tragedy' of Social Structure
    and the 'Violence' of Individual Creativity   39
    Nigel Rapport

3   Ritual, Violence and Social Order: An Approach to Spanish
    Bullfighting   55
    Alberto Bouroncle

4   Restoring the Balance: Violence and Culture Among the
    Suri of Southern Ethiopia   77
    Jon Abbink

5   Tolerating the Intolerable: Cattle Raiding Among the Kuria
    of Kenya   101
    Suzette Heald

6   Rethinking 'Violence' in Chinese Culture   123
    Barend J. ter Haar

7   Butchering Fish and Executing Criminals: Public Executions
    and the Meanings of Violence in Late Imperial and Modern
    China   141
    Virgil Kit-yiu Ho

Contents

8   The 'Tradition of Violence' in Colombia: Material and
Symbolic Aspects   161
Gerard Martin

Bibliography   193

Index   217

Notes on Contributors

Jon Abbink is an anthropologist and a senior researcher at the African Studies Centre (at Leiden University) and previously taught at the Universities of Nijmegen and Amsterdam. He did fieldwork in Israel and Ethiopia. His current interests are the history and ethnology of Ethiopia and Northeast Africa as well as ethnicity, culture and violence, and political culture in Africa. He published articles on the Beta Israel ('Falasha'), Ethiopian ethnology and African studies. Recent monographs are: *Mytholégendes et Histoire: l'énigme de l'ethnogenèse des Beta Esra'el* (1991); *The Me'en of Southwestern Käfa: material culture of an Ethiopian shifting-cultivator people* (1992) and *Eritreo-Ethiopian Studies in Society and History: a Supplementary Bibliography 1960–1995* (1996). Since March 2000 he is a Professor of African Ethnic Studies at the Free University, Amsterdam.

Göran Aijmer is Professor of Social Anthropology at the Faculty of the Social Sciences in the University of Gothenburg and sometime Director of The Institute for Advanced Studies in Social Anthropology (IASSA) at the same university. His research interests are wide with some emphasis on the theory of symbolism. He has conducted empirical investigations in various systematic fields – economics, religion and politics. One focus in his work is symbolic anthropology based on historical data. His writings have mainly been concerned with Central and Southern China, but he has also published on Southeast Asia and Melanesia. Recent monographs are: *Ritual Dramas in the Duke of York Islands: An Exploration of Cultural Imagery* (1997) and (with Virgil K.Y. Ho) *Cantonese Society at a Time of Change* (1999).

Anton Blok is Professor of Anthropology at the University of Amsterdam and Amsterdam School for Social Science Research. His main research interests are in history and theory of anthropology, symbolic and historical anthropology. He has specialized on the Mediterranean and Western Europe. Among his many publications are: *The Mafia of a Sicilian Village, 1860–1960* (1974, new edition in 1988); *Antropologische Perspectieven* (1978); *De Bokkerijders. Roversbenden en Geheime Genootschappen in* *de Landen van Overmaas, 1730–1774,* 2nd edn (English translation in preparation) and numerous articles.

Alberto Bouroncle is a member of the Research School of the Department of Social Anthropology at the University of Gothenburg and a former scholar of the Institute for Advanced Studies in Social Anthropology (IASSA) at the same university. His research interests have ranged from ethnomusicology to the history of civilization and he has conducted field work in the Andean areas of Peru as well as in Spain.

Barend J. ter Haar teaches social and economic history of China at the University of Heidelberg, where he is Professor of Sinology. He has published *The White Lotus: Teachings in Chinese Religious History* (1992) and *Creating an Identity: The Ritual and Mythology of the Chinese Triads* (1998), as well as articles on local temple cults, Yao culture, violence, and secret societies.

Suzette Heald is Professor of Social Anthropology at Brunel University and has extensive anthropological research experience in East Africa, especially Uganda. Her main publications include: *Controlling Anger: The Anthropology of Gisu Violence* (1986/98); *Anthropology and Psychoanalysis* (1989); *Praise Poems of the Kuria* (1991) and *Manhood and Morality. Sex, Violence and Ritual in Gisu Society* (1999). In 1998–99 she has been teaching and supervising a research project which she prepared at the University of Botswana.

Virgil Kit-yiu Ho is Assistant Professor in History in the Division of Humanities at the Hong Kong University of Science and Technology. A student of social history he specializes in the emergence of modernity in Southern China, especially in the city of Canton. He has also conducted fieldwork in rural areas in Guangdong Province. Together with G. Aijmer he published *Cantonese Society at a Time of Change* (1999), and is also the author of many articles.

Gerard Martin has been teaching sociology at the University of Lille III in France and is at present a research associate at Georgetown University (Washington, DC). His major research interest concerns the interplay between political and non-political, organized and disorganized forms of violence. His research focus has been on Colombia, where he carried out extensive fieldwork and taught at the National University of Medellín. He has published several articles on Columbia and is preparing a PhD thesis at the École des Hautes Études en Sciences Sociales in Paris. He is a member of the editorial team of the journal *Cultures et Conflits*.

Nigel Rapport is Professor of Anthropological and Philosophical Studies at the University of St Andrews. He has undertaken research fieldwork in England, Newfoundland and Israel, and his theoretical interests include individuality, consciousness and cognition, literary anthropology, symbolic interactionism, and discourse analysis. Among his publications are: *Talking Violence. An Anthropological Interpretation of Conversation in the City* (1987); *Diverse World-Views in an English Village* (1993); *The Prose and the Passion. Anthropology, Literature and the Writing of E.M. Forster* (1994) and *Transcendent Individual: Towards a Literary and Liberal Anthropology* (1997).

Preface:
Violation and Violence as
Cultural Phenomena
Jon Abbink

This book intends to throw new light on violence by offering a variety of studies on the 'versatility' of violent performance, and on the explanatory efforts to account for this.

Violence is a human universal: in no known human society or social formation is interpersonal aggression, physical threat, assault, or homicide and armed conflict completely absent or successfully banned. This may be trivial observation. But while phenomena of violence are pervasive in human society and are easily evoked in full dramatic force, the issue of how to explain what violence 'is' or does, remains one of the most thorny and challenging ones. At the same time these are becoming questions most frequently posed to (and within) social science, and to which instant answers and 'solutions' are demanded from wider, non-academic audiences.

The problem starts with *definitions* of violence. In this book we do not claim a uniformity of approach among the authors, but perhaps it can be said that the conception of inter-personal violence underlying the contributions in this book is based on the following four, minimally defining, elements: the '*contested*' use of *damaging physical force* against other humans (cf. Riches 1991: 295), with possibly fatal consequences and with purposeful *humiliation* of other humans. Usually, this use of force – or its threat – is pre-emptive and aimed at gaining dominance over others. This is effected by physically and symbolically '*communicating*' these intentions and threats to others.[1] Such a description of violence shows that it is always, by nature, ambiguous interaction.[2] This problem was already amply dealt with in the path-breaking collection of Riches (1986).

Apart from definition, another challenge for social science is to disentangle the study and explanation of violence from the public media discussion and popular opinion. Not that these are unimportant, but as they tend to demand instant moral response, judgement and 'taking a stand', one has to view them with reserve. This book intends to take a step back and look at what historical and cultural factors are at issue in situations and meanings of violent behaviour of either a personal or collective nature (This does, however, not entail a view that 'culture' – in whatever definition – is in any way explanatory of violence).

This collection of essays by historians, sociologists and anthropologists thus seeks to illustrate at least that, first, in studying phenomena of violence in their social and cultural effects, it is necessary to suspend moral and legal judgements while describing the empirical diversity of its manifestations; and secondly, the point that 'violence' is contingent and context-dependent, and thus not a straightforward urge in all humans wanting to come out. Violent actions are much more 'meaningful' and rule-bound than reports about them lead us to believe. Obviously, this understanding does not imply to ultimately suspend evaluations of violence altogether: we do not have to subscribe to the view that *tout comprendre c'est tout pardonner*, which in itself is a moral stance. Violence, though the defining image of our world, is infamy; and its dynamics consists as much of its exercise as of the attempts to refuse it. The social science approach is a child of the Enlightenment, and to many authors in this volume the best part of this philosophical heritage is the old Kantian idea of human emancipation and of broadening and democratising the human 'community of discourse'. But the point is that the theoretical implications of a view of violence that looks at its different cultural definitions and its situationality are still not sufficiently taken into account. Also in political theory, the issue of culture – i.e. the varying perceptions of the meaning of events and human agency – in the explanation of collective violence is usually bypassed, or only seen as secondary.

A relatively new point of view advanced here is that in many historical instances violence has the effect of a 'creative' or at least 'constituent' force in social relations:[3] deconstructing, redefining or reshaping a social order, whether intended or not. This is not meant as an evaluative statement as to its positive or negative value, but as an analytical one. It is only to call attention to the vital role of socially rooted and historically formed relations of power, force and dominance – also in an ideological sense – in defining social relations, effected through violent action. The various chapters in this volume therefore intend to examine the meaning of statements and acts of violence being 'creative' or 'constructive' in this neutral sense.

Most of the contributors in this book are social anthropologists, and on this account their job is to explore social and cultural contexts as well as and cognitive constructions (and implications) of phenomena of violence. This entails taking an essentially historicizing view. In turn, the historians who are represented here are strongly influenced by cultural approaches to issues of violence as found in social anthropology.

There are, obviously, many other approaches to violence the value of which we do not deny: ethological, criminological and psychological. These remain essential to put violence in a comparative perspective and to consider possible phenotypic predispositions of assertiveness or aggressive behaviour of humans,[4] as well as socialization processes (cf. Baumeister 1996). But as humans are historical and culture-bearing social beings engaged in relations of meaning-creation and symbolism, we have deemed it fit to explore the recurring questions about the degree in which historical and cultural contingencies of human social groups or societies shape violent behaviour and bring out these (alleged) predispositions. This is not easy: one meets recriminations of being 'partial to violence' if it is assumed that violence can have a 'meaning' or a creative effect. But such a view confuse the disciplinary idiom of social science with every-day language. Social science simply has the right and duty to use concepts and theories which are forged and used at one remove from everyday language — and the distance can be great. When we speak of 'meaning' it is not to advance a cultural-relativist view on the ('positive') meaning of violent performance for the perpetrators, but to refer to the *contexts* in which this performance is enacted and carries 'communicative messages'. For instance, as Zulaika has show in his exemplary study of Basque terrorism (1989), a whole range of implicit symbols and metaphors — and hence meanings — is present in the violent practice of Basque youth throwing bombs and liquidating innocent victims. But even the contexts of what is known as criminal violence such as random assault on the streets or football hooliganism often have their communicative messages. Hence, the obvious point is that one cannot explain violent behaviour by an immediate appeal to moral arguments, as one has to first explore the socio-cultural and historical contexts of violation — intimidation or transgressing behaviour towards other persons' physical and psychological integrity with harmful effect — and violence before one might appeal to moral or other factors.

This is not to deny that basic questions as to the psycho-biological nature of humans emerge at some point, especially when trying to describe and explain cruelty or extreme humiliating behaviour which appear to go beyond any instrumental or 'communicative' meaning. Here one perhaps touches upon the disturbing elements in the psycho-biological make-up of humans as social animals that derive physical and mental pleasure from inflicting terror and pain on others, bathing in feelings of superiority and detachment at that moment. These are perhaps still taboo issues in the study of human society, but no less important (cf. Cameron and Frazer 1994; Baumeister 1996). Numerous statements of historical and contemporary warriors, concentration-camp guards, terrorists and common criminals could also be cited which demonstrate their sense of ultimate power and excitement during the acts of torture, rape and killing. One might claim that to contain and canalize such a human disposition is, and always has been, one of the challenges of any human society or group in so far as it attempts to create a meaningful order; it has also contributed to draw identities and boundaries between groups.

It was noted frequently (e.g. McFarlane 1986, Bloch 1992, Harvey and Gow 1994, Krohn-Hansen 1994, Keeley 1996: 4) that the explicit theorizing of violence in social anthropology has been limited. This despite the fact that armed conflict or violent encounters were a favourite topic in ethnography: a large corpus on 'tribal warfare', ethnic conflict, personal violence, etc. is available since at least the 1940s. Neither has there been a lack of general historical and social theories giving central place to violence as a factor in the constitution of human society or in the emergence of state civilizations. And already in 1871 E.B. Tylor, one of the pioneers of anthropology, posited his rule of exogamy (with its theoretical implications): humans face the challenge to be 'killed out' or to 'marry in', i.e. to ally themselves with others in order to overcome the disposition to animosity and fragmentation among social groups.

The problem of violence and social order was also central to the first generations of grand theory sociologists like Spencer, Marx, Weber, Simmel and Durkheim. Obviously, Freud was also deeply concerned with the question of violence and his work has had a profound impact on twentieth-century theories (both social and psychological) on the subject (one example: Sagan 1974, 1979, 1985). In one of the most influential theories of the twentieth century, Girard (1972, 1983) has identified 'scape-goating' as a basic psychological mechanism of classification which is generating violence. Also in the sociology of important theorists like N. Elias and, more recently, A. Giddens and P. Bourdieu, the study of violence and its relation to 'social order' or cohesion are key issues.

Nevertheless, what is probably meant by pleas for more theorizing of violence is that a fundamental discussion in social science and anthropology on the 'constituting force' and the ontological status of violent behaviour (in the definition given above) should be radically extended, not in the least in view of its importance in human history and culture and in its quality as an assumed 'predisposition' in human behaviour. What this implies, however, is not clear. One cannot revert to a psychoanalytic model of violence and human aggression, given the decisive shaping of patterns of violence by specific historical and cultural conditions. For the same reason, one can neither explain all violence in terms of the evolutionary-biological (neo-Darwinian) paradigm (see Knauft 1991) which is focused on reproductive struggle and competition for survival and status, and tends to declare the rest epiphenomena, making social science analysis largely superfluous. For instance, the important monograph on homicide by Daly and Wilson (1988) fails on this account.

Interesting attempts to meet the challenge of theorizing violence in anthropology are to be found in recent studies by, among others, Riches (1986, 1991), Moore (1994) and Nordstrom and Robben (1996). They emphasize the constructed nature, the symbolism within which it is embedded, and also the destructive, traumatic effects of violence. But here – especially in the latter book – we often see a full turn towards phenomenological description and 'evocation' of violence. This indeed brings a very useful methodological point, because the views and commitments of perpetrators and victims are often not fully recognized and assessed, and because the horror and humiliation of violence can perhaps never be reduced into discursive accounts let alone adequate theories making it 'rational' and controllable. But a radical empiricist approach as seems to be offered in the latter book and in much of recent writing – however impressive, revealing and attentive to the victims the case-material may be – may reinforce a tendency to abdicate efforts of comparative explanation.

There seem, nevertheless, to be no cogent reasons to give up the search for more integrative explanations of the dynamics and socially re-ordering effects of violent action. Apart from its being rooted in the social nature of humans, there are seemingly certain socio-historical conditions which tend to generate or stimulate violence. While each discipline has its own distinct contribution to make to the study of violence – the new developments in criminal sociology, law, ethology, history, psychology and human evolutionary biology simply cannot be ignored – the challenge, however, is to integrate some of them into a larger whole and to reshape our perception of the nature and causes or relevant factors of violent behaviour. This change of perspective – which entertains the idea that interconnections are vital for understanding – is a long way from being accepted among social scientists. Especially anthropology – due to its holistic and comparative perspective and its interest in intersecting domains of human behaviour – should continue to search for such integrated views. Whether a general theory of violence or violent behaviour or violence is possible is, however, another question. This would embroil us into a discussion of theory and epistemology in general, and will not be taken up here.

While the case-studies in this book give evidence of the pervasiveness of violence in human society, they also demonstrate the need to understand its contingency, its historical variability and its cultural guises. There is no law stating that human societies will eventually generate the same amount and intensity of violence or the same measure of intimidation and cruelty. Although there is still a widespread popular image to the contrary, there is no easy hierarchy of 'more' or 'less civilized' societies either (see for the backgrounds of engrained violence in American society: Brown 1994, Duclos 1996).

Hence, the chapters in the present book, while referring to this problematic and pleading for a more holistic view of phenomena of violent performance, do not elaborate on the issue of whether such unified theories of violence are possible, or even necessary. What is suggested is that the enduring task of a social science approach – especially social anthropology – to human violence is to help shape an informed academic discourse and public debate on violence. It can do this by sensitively describing and demonstrating its historical forms and its discursive forms, revealing its cultural aspects and its social reproduction among humans, and in doing so contextually explain its variability and contingency. Any essentialized views of violence as inevitable and immutable in human nature – or, allegedly, in some societies or so-called 'cultures of violence' – can thus be rejected as explanatory non-starters. This underlying theoretical orientation is amply demonstrated in all of the cases described in this book – selected for their empirical novelty, their broad range, and their dealing with generative and constituent aspects of violent performance.

Notes

1. A case could be made to extend this use of the concept of violence to other beings (animals, especially the higher apes or primates, see Cavalieri and Singer 1993), as violence in this sense may not be 'typically human'. But this aspect will be excluded from the present discussion: apes do not live in a universe of verbal discourse and symbolism.

2. Actions like destruction of property or common resources, or sacrificing animals (and humans), or (accusations of) witchcraft pose problems of another nature, but because of their often being contested, they have clear elements of violence.

3. This point has recently also been made by Kurimoto and Simonse (1998: 10) in their overview of studies of age systems in North East Africa. They state that '. . .war and antagonistic relations are sometimes constructive or creative' (ibid.), and exist in conjunction with peaceful relations between those involved.
4. Although they remain very controversial; compare Blanchard and Blanchard (1984). See also Eibl-Eibesfeldt and Salter (1997).

Introduction: The Idiom of Violence in Imagery and Discourse

Göran Aijmer

In the social sciences one usually thinks of war, strife and violence as forces emerging from chaos. Violence is seen as 'meaningless', the violent act merely serving the analyst as a pointer indicating states of dysfunction and anomaly in the society under study. An outburst of harmful commotion is a symptom, something which is caused by other forces operating in society and which, because of its asocial nature and destructive constitution is seen, in social terms, as without any meaning of its own.

There are good reasons to look at violence from new perspectives. Ethnography and history give ample evidence that violence in its endless manifestations is part and parcel of human existence and in all likelihood a constituting element of human society used as a cement in processes of social aggregation. Everywhere history has been written in blood. And yet, violent action as we find it in a variety of forms – warfare, penalties, insults, feuding, assault, murder, rape, suicide, sports, and so on – remains in all its complexity one of the least understood fields of human social life.

Violence has several natures and whatever ontological grounding we may opt for in the human sciences, we will find violence appearing as an important ingredient of reality. It is a basic ethological phenomenon in human life on a par with phenomena like sexuality, sociality and domination. It is also a latent ingredient in the forming of social relationships and offers a strong foundation for the construction of power. It appears in iconic symbolism as an expressive device in the construction of possible worlds. In a discursive perspective violence is an intended, often calculated, sign in the flow of performative acts, with a capacity of representing a great number of objects and states.

To be the victim of violence is mostly a humiliating and frightening experience of physical or psychic pain; generally it is the recognition of this experiential level that has provided the starting point for social scientists trying to grasp the significance of the execution of violent acts.

Focus has been on the results of violation and the possible retracing of the causal mechanisms which have led to observed states of pain and devastation. But the many ambiguities that occur in the use of violence ought also to be considered in new attempts to grasp why peace seems only to exist as a contrast to the violation of peace.

We need new ideas and thoughts on violence. Let us briefly consider what possibilities are offered by a symbological approach. The symbological project is here seen as a conjoint study of cultural semantics, social pragmatics and operational functions.[1] The study of human production and understanding of symbols offers a platform and a structure of thought which synthesizes many achievements in a broad field of social and cultural enquiry. This platform should not be seen as a set of dogmas, but rather as an ongoing debate and a bundle of opportunities to promote interesting and radical studies of social life as symbolic construction. This introductory essay is a tentative endeavour in this direction, trying to point to some less frequently considered sides of the symbolic use of violence.

We have to make the theoretical positions for this endeavour somewhat more explicit. Different sets of ontological presuppositions will generate several theoretically distinct approaches, which each in its own way strives to account for its version of reality. The symbological approach sees these versions as discursive modalities and wishes, from an overarching meta-theoretical position, to bring the results of ontologically incompatible research together in an exploring synthesis. Insights in one realm can be activated in a different ontological order to build a more comprehensive understanding. We should thus take advantage of (rather than battle) different scientific ways of looking at the world, which each in its own way is suggestive, and allow them to co-exist inside some larger pluralistic framework without internal confrontation. Holism and comparison are essential features of the symbological project. 'Holism' must be understood as a scientific attitude – an analytical awareness that in a localized study, any ethnographic datum in focus may ultimately be related to any other possible ethnographic data. Holism in symbology is a question of an attentive disposition, not an issue of closed corpora of material. Furthermore, symbology is a comparative and generalizing proposition. It is in the matching of disparate findings, in the discoveries of parallels and similarities, and in the exploring of contrasts that we may make some headway in the synthesizing study of how human beings understand and handle violence in the stream of life.

The symbological approach is based on the meaningful juxtaposing of various items of social and cultural information, either drawn from some specific body of ethnographic data, or brought forward from several different ethnographies. It is an approach which looks for connections. It presupposes a general theory of human symbol-making. This attempt at sketching the outlines of a symbological approach to violence, will take its starting point in the proposal that the study of human activities as symbolic processes can usefully explore three essentially different and yet equally valid scientific perspectives. These 'orders' is each character-ized by a discourse of its own and a distinct set of ontological presupposi-tions for this discourse. Let us dwell very briefly and in the most abstract way on the characteristics of these three orders and then later expand the discussion into a topical concern with the human phenomena of violence and violation, and their semantic ambiguities.

In outline the three orders could be described as follows:

One perspective on human life would concern the symbolism of iconic codes and their use in the visionary building of possible worlds, forming the *imaginary order* of a society. By 'code' I merely refer to an expressive device (a sort of 'language') in a broad sense, symbols and the ways they combine to articulate messages. In this little understood field we deal with symbolic displays of strong expressive force, and yet of little communicative value. This is a realm of symbolism working outside language and thus without truthful reporting and referential meaning. What we deal with is iconically encoded information, well beyond what can be introspectively retrieved by a speaker's/thinker's verbally carried thought and linguistic competence. Language and imagery are entirely different sorts of codes, neither being instrumental for reaching into the other.

Images make manifest people's intuitive[2] cognizance as to what ultimately conditions social and personal existence. Imaginary manifesta-tions are visions of alterity and their construction is an exploration of realities otherwise unknown. Images are essentially separated from the world of everyday living in that they, as they become composed, create their own realities – they are grounded only in themselves. In imaginary construction symbols will be used to buttress symbols. They form unintended messages or motifs to which there is no author and which generally cannot be retold outside the imaginary event.

Needless to say, the circumstance that people cannot introspectively explore their own iconic symbolism, does not mean that they are not able in other ways to account for their images; certainly they talk about them, discuss them and form relevant opinions about them. But this discursive exploration of imagery is different from people taking cognizance, it is an attempt by way of intended cogitation and rational reasoning to come to terms with a universe beyond truth and argument. Such processes of commenting on the world are of course interesting in their own right and it is to them we must now turn.

So, there is another province to be explored by symbology, which we might call the *discursive order*. This enquiry will concern the intentional performative acts of men and women of a society, and their ongoing conversation about themselves and the world. The discursive order is clearly a wide and many-faceted field of social pragmatics and implies an attempt at coming to terms with indigenous discursively constructed and construed worlds. 'Discursive' should be understood as referring not only to a flow of communicative acts in which information is articulated verbally. Though language is vital and a dominant element of the process, social discourse also freely uses – often in combination – other forms for sensory communication like pictures, tableaux, smells, vocalizations and other sounds, tactility and the expressive use of time-space. Discursive analysis implies an accounting for human acts within an ontology which is a pragmatically construed universe emerging in the communicative interaction of an array of people using language and language-like types of codes.

Like the compositions of the imaginary order are expressing several possible worlds, the discourse of everyday life is a modal narration, telling many alternative stories. This is the theme which Nigel Rapport addresses in Chapter 2. Looking for discursive alterity as a dynamic factor in the ever-changing social landscape, Rapport sees the constant generation of possible alternative versions of everyday procedures as a mental activity challenging conventional social morphology – in social discourse thought-of modalities violate and threat what is given. This is a normal process of social creativity involving what Rapport labels 'democratic violence' – disrupting alternatives promoting new understandings and deeper communication. In contrast, discursive 'nihilistic violence', is intended to block comprehension and predictability by the introduction of various misleading markers. In Rapport's view violation is already a constitutive part of the dynamics of the discursive processes that build social structure.

It should be added that the two ontologically defined orders we have characterized so far, are all remotely rooted in yet another, the *ethological order*. This order is based in a realist ontology and implies a research strategy taking account of the fact that all human activities have a biological/genetic dimension. It also concerns the complex processes of thinking and remembering in the human brain, and ultimately the chemistry of the nervous system. The effects of violence – pain in physical and psychic forms – are clearly grounded in the ethological order. In fact, the purposeful achievement of pain is a constitutive feature of violence.

The syndrome of violence and pain is given symbolic shape in both iconic and discursive contexts; this can be elaborated in various ways, as for instance in the Christian notion of suffering as a path to blessing. In the Christian traditions, penitential people seek out various forms of self-inflicted violence as symbolic similes drawing their basic archetypal[3] meanings from the motif of the Passion. The antonymous relation binding together life and death is grounded in ethological realities which so provides material for both iconic symbolism and discursive construction. It is only then, as a symbolic image or as a discursive topic, death is turned into a violent category of existence. Not only is the wilful infliction of death an ultimately violent and immoral act, but the discursive use of death can with great effect be extended beyond physical death. The handling of a dead body, as Anton Blok points out in Chapter 1, could signal that biological separation from life does not bring an ongoing wilful execution of violence to an end. Calculated mortal violation is pursued far into death – funerals not being allowed, carcasses turned into exhibits and so continuously humiliated and desecrated. In contrast to physical death, social death may not be irrevocable, but the dead person could be symbolically resurrected as a praised martyr. Therefore, in the exercise of political power, also the social-symbolical killing of the dead may become of utmost importance.

Human beings never live in solitude, unless isolation is symbolic and thus contrasted with union. We need a sociological strategy to explore how agglomerates of people emerge in a landscape by the formation of groups as a response to prevailing tasks generated by environmental[4] circumstances. The environmental factor would encompass the likely existence of other groups in the terrain. Such studies may at first seem quite peripheral to our quest for a better understanding of violence, but might actually in the end be helpful. If violence is taken to be part of social symbolism, we need some sociological grounding for this claim and what is suggested here may carry us some way towards that goal.

In this sociological, or 'operational', perspective, 'groups' are conceived as agglomerations of people who are united solely in one particular task – a definition which paves the way for a comparative sociology of groups (Verdon 1995). It is in the operational world that practical social organization is founded. Furthermore, it is in the agglomeration of groups as a response to a topographical and social landscape that we may find the primary arenas for human politics, violent or not. What is of particular interest in our present context, looking at societies in this 'deculturized' way, is the fact that there are areas on the map in which we find groups organized around the exercise of violent terror, devastation being their formative task. Gerard Martin's account of guerrillas and militias in

Colombia bears witness of a situation in which one important sector of social organization in this way evolves around the calculated use of mass destruction and killing (Chapter 8).

It should be kept in mind that the three orders we have discussed here, are but dimensions of the indivisible person producing expressive symbolism. Needless to say, what has been suggested is in the nature of research strategies. We cannot expect unfolding violent events to be clearly tagged for easy classification in accordance with this or any other pre-conceived scheme.

Disconnected by their different ontologies, but seen together as a union of possibilities, these orders provide in this togetherness a new version of holistic thought, which in turn offers a spectroscopic view of the phenomenon of violence. What we need is an overarching proposition which allows a plurality of ontologies and yet promotes some sort of correspondence in description and explanatory endeavours. As long as contrastive versions of the world, not all reducible to one, are counte-nanced, unity is to be sought, not in an ambivalent or neutral common denominator beneath these versions, but in some overall organization embracing them. Once we break our habits to allow a pluralistic world view with no prior dogmatic commitments, we will become aware of novel analytical possibilities. We will gain a new freedom of movement between differently situated vantage points for a more complete and interesting accounting for the stream of symbolism in human life. Should we find points of connection where information from one order flows into another – and some brief suggestions in this direction has already been made – then we might find new ways of thinking about the ambigu-ities of human violence.

Violence is then is a phenomenon which can be found in the realm of iconic non-verbal symbolism. Why and how a particular image of violence has emerged are questions well beyond what possibly can be answered by way of historical enquiry – human beings will always have had access to non-verbal versions of the world; most likely this kind of iconic symbolism is in its essence pre-human, part of our primate background and reaching deeply into the ethological order. Typically, violence is an idiomatic instrument for separation and integration in iconically con-structed narrations.[5] We can be sure that the human body as a primary target for physical aggression and symbolic violence has always been there, so has pain and death. However, to formulate a binding connection between social environment and violent symbolism remains a hopeless task. In the course of history, there have always been 'befores'. What would be a more realistic working hypothesis is the proposition that the imaginary world maintains some relation with the ethological order, operational social organization and structures of production in that they are mediated and made interrelated by way of intentional human social discourse and so they often are made to converge and become structurally consonant. This hypothesis that symbolic imagery and ethologically founded structures are brought together in an ongoing discursive negotiation may help us see how the meanings of violence are transformed.

The construction and use of violent images is something which can also be observed, thought about and put to use by reflecting people. In the perspective of pragmatics, a given cluster of cultural imagery takes on a text-like appearance – images are being turned into accountable pictures and tableaux; through the pragmatic perspective we may open up means to understand how non-retrievable icons are strategically used in the stream of symbolism. What we must understand is that the social flow of performative acts also makes relevant use of available images. As a phenomenon with a place in the pragmatic world of minds in action, violent imagery reaches into discourse. Seen in this perspective images are also part of that world which is generated by intended performatives in the ongoing social conversation that bind humans together. Intuition is evoked and used by intention. By using words with reference to imagery, these words become capable, by implication, of carrying also archetypal, non-verbal meanings along as tacit understandings. As has been said before, people can discuss their imagery, oppose it, praise it and actually construct it. They can also attempt exegesis and analysis.

It has been suggested here that violence is a phenomenon which appears independently of what ontological presuppositions we allow in the metaphysical construction of realities to be investigated. It is a well-known mechanism in the ethological order where it forms part of processes of domination. It is a forceful element in the imaginary order, an iconic idiom incorporated into many different sorts of symbolic textures. In social discourse violence emerges as a sign with many references and endlessly purposeful for intended action. This threefold appearance in the stream of human symbolism is a primary factor creating ambiguities around violent phenomena. Furthermore, within each of the ontologically defined orders, violence has many sides and meanings.

The result of all this is that the scientific investigation of violence becomes a thing of utter complexity, evasiveness and ambiguity. This opaqueness must not refrain us from trying to come to grips with the social production of violation; rather, its apparent negative functions and meaningless applications should encourage us to pursue its other less obvious sides, not only for intellectual reasons, but also to counterbalance the simplicities of superficial and moralistic approaches. Ambiguity will be the great challenge in the symbological study of violence: the uses of war, strife and open violation are phenomena that possibly contribute to structure and so can be seen as formative in social interaction and for people's perceptions of this interaction. Violence as an idiom is given form, shape and meanings inside the institutions and conventions of society and once so conventionalized, it is turned into a formative force of 'construction through destruction'. Individual suffering may be turned into social blessing.

One example of this is found in Chapter 4 where Jon Abbink describes how among the cattle herding Suri in Southern Ethiopia, violence is domesticated and shaped into a controlled presence in various social institutions. The main iconic use of the idiom of violence is the killing of cattle in sacrifice. The archetypal meanings which are intuited in an instance of sacrifice seem to be present – as implications – also in the discursive use of violence in established liturgies for extraordinary events, like duelling, purification, blessing of cattle raiders, and bodily decorations. The supervised infliction of pain is characteristic of such occasions, but this is not seen as something gruesome by the Suri. The violent events are part of the construction of group and inter-group relationships and, in fact, Suri violence as a symbolic idiom is a constitutive feature in the construction of their society. Likewise, among the agro-pastoral Kuria in southern Kenya, described in Chapter 5 by Suzette Heald, violent cattle rustling was part and parcel of the construction of a society characterized by demarcated age-sets.

To say that violence is used for social blessing is of course not to deny its frightening and fearful aspects, nor is it to aestheticize about the cruel sides of life, but rather to direct analytical interest towards what is less obvious and less well known. Violence, whether iconic or discursive, exists as an experienced reality and is not to be understood by way of some *a priori* definition, but through its incorporation in the streams of human life.[6] We should aim at deconstructing the uses of violence in imaginary orders, explore its force in whatever form it appears in social discourse, while at the same time remain aware of its ethological grounding. Symbological research on violence should be attempts at exploring both its archetypal semantics and its pragmatical, intended meanings, thereby turning its superficially opaque appearance into a transparent meaningfulness, a formative force in human interaction.

That violence is inherently part of domination is something which is well known and has a solid foundation in ethological studies. Still, we must not be mislead by socio-biology. To say that violence is to be found in all primate societies, in no way explains how it emerges among human beings. A genetic predisposition for aggressive domination may be there, but knowing this cannot alone help us understand how violence is institutionalized for exploitation, control, or social blessing.[7] In fact, violence can only exist under conditions of reflexive and wilful control, and possible preventive counteraction – Nature sees no violence, only purposive aggression. It is in the symbolic control of the force of aggression that violence gets a moral foundation – is transformed into a morally loaded idiom. From a symbological point of view, the process of domination in human societies is a very complex affair, which cannot be reduced to biological orders of ranking.[8] What remains of interest here is the fact that human societies not only use direct violence to uphold their hierarchical orders, but that they also resort to abstract forms of symbolically constructed violence – targeting persons and communities by exposing them to humiliation; generally symbolic force and physical forces are, in a manner of speaking, intertwined in the performative act, the former supplying the meanings to be absorbed by the latter – a relationship that is pointed out by Anton Blok in Chapter 1.[9] This symbolic transformation of physical aggression into violence – by its incorporation in the conventions of social life providing it with meaningful shapes and uses – is something not well known.

To grasp the occurrence of violent phenomena we should pursue a comparison of human societies in the meta-theoretical perspective of plural ontologies. This very ambitious scheme can only be achieved step by step. A possible way to start is to approach ethnographic information in a topical fashion. Taking the holistic view we need some promising entrances into a symbolic world containing violence as an idiom, to see it empirically manifest–conventionalized, institutionalized and monopolized in performative action. A topical approach will allow us to discover and compare it in several empirical contexts and juxtapose the archetypal messages involved in the construction of imaginary textures and in iconic narration. It will help us focus on the meanings of discursive violence. It will also contribute to an increasing understanding of the ethological logistics of violent practice.

A comparative and contrastive approach to the domestication of violence in terms of the institutions of the 'state', promises to be revealing in several ways. The articulation of the state through the use of institutionalized violence can take many paths. Such studies would include ideologies expressive of destructive violation as legitimate instruments for achieving and maintaining power. We may expect that such ideologies are informed not only by endless precedence, but also by available imagery. The rhetoric of the state concerning its sovereignty and territoriality over time, will draw together images and history, while at the same time it tags strategically both time-less images and discursive depictions of the past with new situationally opportune meanings.

It is somewhat trivial to point out that the violent imagery of the state would incorporate discursive martial activities, including the use of uniforms, drills, parades and displays. The uniform communicates danger as well as style and beauty, the drills are choreographed for assumed effectiveness and staged also to appear threatening for those who are defined as outsiders. Military shows are intended to be visually pleasing in their displays of potential violence.

In a sense it could be said that military parades form political rituals and seen in a more general perspective, a component of violence is very common in symbolic politics. Rituals, of course must be understood as both discursive and imaginary phenomena in that they are constituted by iconic displays conveying archetypal meanings, while the acts involved at the same time have a degree of intentionality and so also can be seen as performatives. Ritual semantics is thus a question of twofold meanings — archetypal and discursive — and involves two different ontologies.

In his essay on the emergence of the Iberian forms of bullfighting, Alberto Bouroncle (Chapter 3) demonstrates how violence was incorporated, given shape and was institutionally used in the formation of the state of Spain. Rustic, village-based rituals, in which bulls were fought to inflict bleeding — the drawing of taurine blood being a way to obtain a blessing of fecundity — were transformed into a public and elegant butchering of the animals. Bouroncle shows how the Iberian aristocracy, mobilized by their Old Christian ideology, in the years to follow their successful crusade against the Moorish domains, dramatized warfare into a show of violence where mounted knights by special privilege fought a fierce but soul-less enemy beast. Playing on people's cultural intuitions of the archetypal meanings of taurine blood, death, fecundity and violence, the political ritual of aristocratic bullfighting brought in crowds of spectator commoners as essential participating elements in the ritual construction. Bullfighting created a discursive model in terms of an idiom of violence, a model for an understanding of the nature of power and the possession of power. This political ritual came to form an arena throughout Spanish history in which power relations between various segments of society were negotiated and renegotiated. The most remarkable feature of this process was the rise of the assistant footman to become the hero of the celebration, the *matador*, whereas the part of the knightly horseman was reduced to the relative unimportance of the *picador*.

Introduction

If Spain forms an example of the state emerging around a spectacle of violence, China provides us with an example of how the state in its ideological articulation has shunned all expressions of violence. Barend ter Haar's *longue durée* study of the development and transformation of ideological élite discourses in China provides us with an extremely interesting case of the growth of an official rhetoric of *Verfremdung* from all kinds of violence in favour of literary activities, the study of philosophy and the cultivation of the liberal arts. Starting in ancient times in a situation dominated by internal war and strife, we find a contemporary set of ideals in which the martial arts were the official virtue. The later growth of a civil bureaucracy was accompanied by a marginalization of the military career and also by an ever increasing distancing among the civil literati who governed China from the ability to handle arms. Official weapons became decorative and heraldic forms of insignia, while strategic thinking became limited to the playing of various board games. The cultivation of peaceful occupations among the élite ruling the country did, however, never arrest the state in its exercise of power from using extreme forms of violence with little concern for human suffering. The discourse of alienated elegance provided the rulers with a tradition that was constituting its own symbolic reality – one with a different story line than that which was told in practical politics in a vast and populous country of frequent upheaval. The two discursive modalities were always parallel, but given different emphasis at different times, always vesting the notion and exercise of violence with a fundamental ambiguity – an understanding oscillating between one of despise and one of effectiveness.

Gerard Martin's study of anarchic violence in Colombia (Chapter 8) offers a radically different case in that we here find a very weak state with few and powerless autonomous institutions, which historically have failed to monopolize violence to endow it with a politically and morally legitimizing shape. Instead we encounter a situation in which politics is war and where one finds various social networks in everlasting struggle, networks which crystallize as operational groups for terrorizing and marauding. Martin argues that Colombia has developed a tradition of violence, with a normal condition of a chronic but moderate level of violent activities, but also seeing periods of deep intensification of social devastation. The discourses surrounding socio-political developments vary according to current degree of intensity and are formed on the bases of varying experiences; violence is thus situationally ascribed differing meanings, which again will refer back to some extent to the symbolic hardness and aggressiveness of everyday life. This is a country where politics implies polarization without reconciliation and where there is a lack of legal institutions, which in some ritualized fashion could negotiate kinds and degrees of necessary retribution. Under the conditions of a weak state there is always the risk of an endless chain of vengeance, because to vengeance there is no end. The judicial procedures that exist under the varying conditions provided by different states, deserve further attention since the process of law implies the open or covert exercise of violence. Much of legal procedure and jurisdiction in many societies has been constructed in order to create an opportunity for transcendental power to intervene and make itself known through institutionalized violence; a legal system fosters a rhetoric of the state as a moral polity, against the standards of which people will be judged. Still, as Anton Blok and Virgil Ho point out (Chapters 1 and 7), it is in the discourse of the legal institutions that the social classification of violent crimes takes place, implying a negative ranking of harmful acts. The re-negotiation of such classificatory schemes will reflect changes in current discourses of power and styles in society. Legal court procedures often take on a dialectics of prosecution and defence, and it is in a discursive battle between these two forces that 'truth' is ultimately made manifest.

Penalties, and their ambiguities, provide very interesting (if gruesome) material for analysis. The exercise of violent punishments and public humiliations are almost universally thought to be effective social mechanisms for keeping people in order. A more unorthodox view of some such displays of violent sanctions is that what is released on each occasion of a corporeal punishment, may be construed as a manifestation of some supreme force, which in this way extends into mundane life. The presence of such divine benignity in a society may be intuited as something desirable, even if it can be known only in the blunt exposure of violence. Public executions in front of enthusiastic crowds have been common in both traditional Europe and China – where they are still staged; to be present at such a gathering of spectators suggests an attempt by those so assembled to appropriate something of what is lost in another's violent death.

These ambiguities that are part and parcel of publicly inflicted death, form the field of enquiry that is addressed by Virgil Ho in Chapter 7. Ho shows how the violent discourse of execution throughout China's modern history has drawn on imaginary narrations, taking archetypal meanings out of their iconic contexts and by reintroducing them into discursive construction, has rendered every case of capital punishment into a gruesome *tableau vivant*. Each execution forms a drama with a story line that puts what is actually taking place into a metaphysical perspective, in which violence is turned into socio-political blessing. The state is just instrumental in a cosmic search for balance of negative and positive forces. Anton Blok has pointed out (in Chapter 1) that in Europe, what happened around the scaffold may have been construed as a type of sacrifice. This anthology offers two examples of societies which are not organized centrally as states or state-like polities, but in which violent acts contribute to the structuring of social reality. Both are found in Eastern Africa. The Suri of Southern Ethiopia locally have a reputation of being a society which, both internally and in its relations with other surrounding peoples, is marked by frequent violence: inter-ethnic attacks, ambushes, robberies and killings. In his account of the Suri (Chapter 4), Jon Abbink shows how central leadership on an elementary level in this small-scale and relatively traditional society without much stratification, makes use of expressive violence. Violent behavioural patterns are constitutive of social communities and a necessary inversion of peaceful social relations between them and other peoples in the landscape, whenever social distance is required. However, violence is not simply an advantageous trait. Suri values and ideals certainly reflect a complex violent imagery, but at the same time they also voice a pervasive sociality within and beyond their society, suggesting that both are inextricably linked. This shows the ambiguity of violence as a category of social action – it both constitutes and undermines.

Among the Kuria who inhabit Southern Kenya, violent cattle raiding has of tradition been a constituting device for the construction of basic social and political relationships. Suzette Heald (Chapter 5) argues that among the Kuria, the cattle raider represents the cultural ideal of masculinity, the bedrock upon which family and social relations are constituted. But at another level, the raider represents the deviant and negative potentialities of violent theft. It is argued that the Kuria see the heroic raids as related to a cultural semantic complex of many contradictions, which pulls both towards and away from the exercise of violence. The traditional social landscape was construed as one of violent exchanges.

The cultural construction of individuals takes place within a prerequisite social community. Among the Suri we note that an endowment of violence is an aspect of the construction of the male gender (Chapter 4). This force is seen as quite unproblematic. To become a man involves a long period of socialization in which young boys learn to suppress fear and are encouraged to face the spilling of blood and inflicting of harm. So violence is made active in various stages and crucial moments of the life-cycle. In this way violence is both domesticated, embodied and made instrumentally useful. Similarly, among the Kuria (Chapter 5), violent cattle raiding among the young men is an approved of activity in consonance with Kuria ethos. Raiding forms a network of negative exchanges in the social landscape and in the wake of this, some regional integration is accomplished in terms of an idiom of violence. In Kuria tradition men prove themselves by exposing themselves to danger while stealing cattle.

From the perspective of the present concern with the complexities of violence, these two empirical examples point to a wider category of life cycle contexts – rituals of birth, initiation, marriage and death – in which components of violence are of crucial importance in the construction of the individual. In later years new attention has been focused on a long-standing anthropological problem, the accounting for initiations and other rites of passage – rituals which often contain considerable amounts of violence. It has been argued that to create a social and moral person from a natural person, violence has to be exercised in the form of symbolic death and bodily mutilations. This discussion has also brought attention to how initiations, and the violence they contain, can be used metaphorically for a wide range of other phenomena which, subsequently, are intuited as acts of violent separation of what is natural from what is social (Bloch 1992).

The argument could be extended by a further consideration of the symbolic idiom of violence as an organising device in society. In an anthology like this it is impossible to cover but a few themes, but there are hosts of other topics which insist on our attention for future explorations. The relevance of war and struggle as metaphors for other social phenomena is one such feature. It is also well known in studies of religion that violence and violent death, for example as exercised in sacrifice and martyrdom, are central components in a great many religious systems and should be dealt with both in iconic and discursive perspectives.

Looking in another direction, we will recall that Claude Lévi-Strauss has drawn attention to a widespread cultural dichotomization between Nature and Culture. In our present concern with violence as an organizing and expressive force, one may rephrase this basic opposition in terms of society as being embedded in nature. Members of a society seek out the possibilities to conquer nature and to appropriate its life-giving forces. Examples of this are found in European and Chinese forms of hunting, whether in fenced-off game parks – domesticized tracts of nature – or in the non-inhabited wilderness. In his survey essay, Anton Blok points to the pleasures of hunting in northwestern European society (Chapter 1). In the Netherlands (as elsewhere), hunters justify their sport in terms that suggest that they really are agents of nature, helping to keep animal populations within ecological control. These arguments are supported by a certain life-style. In the Germanic tradition, the hunter makes himself part of nature, entering the forest dressed in green and with feathers in hat (appearing as a non-human predatory being), to take part in and of nature's own violence. In public debates, however, hunting is seen as human violent interference with nature. Civilized people should not show that they enjoy violence and killing. In another example, British fox-hunting, the same arguments are at hand. Still there is a difference here in the articulation of the hunter's exercise of hunting. If the German huntsman leaves culture to penetrate nature, his British counterpart remains without interruption in culture.[10] In British fox hunting it is the exercise of cultured and socially controlled violence – the salon brought into nature – and the aestheticized (but killing) violence of the participants, as mediated by hunting hounds, which makes it possible to draw forces of vitality from nature.

Another obvious topic, which is discussed by Blok, is sport as a socially approved violent contest. The public enthusiasm for sport in modern societies may be understood not merely as an interest in the competitive release of energy, but also in outbursts of violence in controlled forms in accordance with accepted rules. In Europe violence organized in arenas attended by spectators, from ancient times and up to today, has included devices for drawing life force from death and, in the absence of death, from defeat – the moral destruction of the opponent. Abbink's (Chapter 4) account of duelling with wooden poles between young men forms a contrast in that the outcome does not really matter – a good pole fighter has no particular long-term advantage in Suri society. The duelling seems more of an exposition of competitive violence as such and it is the heroism of fighting that counts. It also offers traditional authority an arena to manifest itself in that the pole matches require experienced referees.

The social use of violence has two sides. Violence may be seen as a basic socio-cultural phenomenon, a sort of constant around which societies organize themselves in various institutionalized forms. It could also be seen as an idiom which is employed to express a wide range of other social phenomena. Violence exercised in a society is both iconic, discursive and ethological in nature, and this ontological complexity turns it analytically evasive and socially extremely ambiguous. In many violent rituals the targeted person is not really destroyed, but benefits from the violent treatment he or she is exposed to. Such semantic ambiguities are also reflected in the part the symbolic idiom of violence plays in social and cultural dynamics. In the cases presented in this omnibus we find the basic ambiguities of socially institutionalized violence at work. Alberto

Bouroncle (Chapter 3) shows how a transform of martial violence becomes a political ritual in which power relations have been negotiated in the long-term development of the state. Ritual violence provides stability, but the ritual liturgies surrounding violence are changing as part of a changing political discourse. Abbink's study (Chapter 4) of the Suri is a story of an escalation of traditional violence, an increase that is in part consequential of the modernization project of the state. Traditional rituals and customary law can no more achieve what they were designed for in bygone days. Apart from faulty state policies, there are ecological pressures of droughts and rapidly increasing population which contribute to the dissolving of traditional morals. There are also features of modernity like tourism, modern education, video shows, automatic rifles and criminal activities, all with an impact on the construction of Suri norms. They have turned to a much less inhibited use of force leading to more numerous killings. One feature is that the ceremonial duelling with poles has undergone notable changes, and the frequency of these contests has increased significantly while the traditional referees are vanishing. Wooden poles are complemented with Kalashnikovs and formerly accepted, socially meaningful action is being transformed into a violence which is heralding the emergence of new social structures.

Among the Kuria increasingly violent cattle thefts have changed their character from being a negative cement and the symbolic means for male articulation of socially constructive heroism, into wide-scale criminal activities. There are several factors involved: a new wealth originating in tobacco planting, but also the emergence of a new meat market which is by and large supplied by networks of organized crime. Young men cannot any more be controlled by internal moral institutions, but link up with the market demands and its criminal agents. The escalation of theft of cattle and its accompanying fighting and killing, is removing the traditional moral support for the thieves and invites new measures of defence and lynching of intruders (Chaper 5).

The two essays on China (Chapters 6 and 7) seem at first glance contrasting. Ter Haar's study shows how the political élite for centuries have cultivated a lifestyle of increasing refinement – perhaps not so different in essence from a parallel civilizing process in Europe (Elias 1978) – displacing martial idioms of violence as means for an articulation of power. Government was literate and dependent on sophisticated use of language. Ho shows how capital punishment in traditional China was dramatized in a demotic operatic fashion, turning the attending official from a lofty literate and bureaucrat into a representative of Imperial divinely justified power, appearing not unlike the judges of the ten

Buddhist hells. Leaving his *yamen* to supervise an execution, the magistrate, in a sense, also left behind the Imperial civilized government and instead became part and parcel of a cosmic battle between gods and godlings on one side and attacking demons on the other. A dehumanized, and so demonized, culprit was executed in an act which was blissful for the realm. The particular place of institutionalized violence in Imperial China as an antonym to literary cultivation – militarized or ritualized, but nothing in itself but a necessarily sinister support for righteousness – has turned violence into a conservative factor in the dynamics of Chinese society. Modern public executions and their concern with impurity bears witness of a lingering robust structure of meanings, for centuries accompanying violent death.

The Colombian situation, again, exploits violence as a conservative and retarding factor in the construction of political and social life. Social relations outside of the family seem to be constituted so that they always incorporate a possibility of violation. Periods of latent or moderately executed violence are at times replaced by periods of general devastation, Colombian society oscillating between two antonymously related states of affairs (the peaceful end never being accomplished before the swing back sets in). Violence not only forms an idiom for political action, but also in a most real way constitutes the changes that occur, its social dynamics being its potential for intensification of itself (Chapter 8).

A symbological approach of a type sketched out in the beginning of this Introduction might be helpful in several respects in the study of violence and acts of violation. Accepting several views as to what constitutes reality we could develop a plurality of enquiries, the results of which could be matched through a study of the interfaces between ontologically defined orders, for instance how imaginary phenomena are handled within the realm of discourse and how discursive conventions may drift into the world of iconic symbolic construction. In Christian societies, violence and suffering are key elements in their symbolic imagery, death and resurrection being a major theme in all sorts of iconic narrations. Violence offers the path leading to life, or rather to a super-life. There is the ambivalence here that suffering through the exercise of violence may purify the individual in martyrdom and transcendental life, but it may also be a penalty of infernal origins, suffering caused rebounding on the immoral causing agent. How are such ambiguities put to use in discursive contexts?

It seems, for instance, that Iberian bullfighting connects with this iconic motif in two ways. The ritual killing of a bull releases new life forces to be appropriated by those present. It also is a comment on morality in

Göran Aijmer

which an immoral beast is killed to preserve a pure ideology. Who should be seen as vested with the righteousness to conduct the ritual, and how the killing should be choreographed, are matters which have been disputed and negotiated throughout the intertwined histories of Spain and bullfighting. Hunting, on the other hand, connects only more remotely with the death/life transformative force. It is only when the prey is discursively ascribed anthropomorphic features that hunting becomes a moral problem, and so hunters develop symbolic forms of hunting which in various ways can handle what is essentially a discursive ambiguity, which in turn draws on imaginary semantics. Whenever we find examples that public executions were construed as a form of sacrifice, we should look further into the interfaces between the discursive and the imaginary orders. The Colombian case of permanent warfare invites to further reflections on Christian discourses in an environment of violence beyond negotiation and the part played in those negotiations by the fuzzy semantics of violent death as a gate to blessed life, alternatively to eternal suffering.

In traditional Chinese demotic religion violence is produced by demonic forces and must be controlled by counterviolence, exercised in rituals of exorcism. Demonic violence is also part of the Buddhist eschatology in which a dead person passes through ten hells, to be judged and consequently tortured. These penalties correspond directly to the dead person's deeds in life. Pictures and tableaux in popular temples tell people of this story. The imagery of violence in traditional China seems to have conveyed a message of transformative force as part of an unresolvable cosmic duality. We may guess that iconic motifs in various ways are brought into religious, judicial and political discourses, providing tacit assumptions of the nature of violence and its works in the world. A deconstruction of the cosmic idiom of violence may also contribute to a further discussion of the civilizing process among the Chinese gentry and its explicit movement towards refinement, away from contrasting violent vulgarities. Aesthetics is not only a grammar for the iconic construction of imagery, but also a controlling agent through the imagery it regulates.

In the two African cases, which seem to exemplify widespread processes of change, it might lead to an expanded discussion, if we could be better informed as to what made cattle so 'valuable' in the imagery of continuity in pastoral societies. Recent research in some other areas of the continent, like among the Himba of northern Namibia (Wärnlöf 1998), point towards strong links between cattle, men, graves and ancestry and the circulation of life force over time. Perhaps there will be new openings for studies into pastoral cultural semantics.

Violence as a systematic field has been surveyed in various perspectives (e.g. Riches 1986) and in this anthology also Anton Blok (Chapter 1) offers an overview of the lingering problems. Such mappings will always remain useful as violence, of course, is a far too open and abstract notion to be discussed 'in its own right'. It needs locating historically and in certain relations and structural systems of power. The empirically orientated contributions in this volume strive in this direction. In contrast, this introduction has been looking at violence as a general symbolic phenomenon, an idiom appearing in iconic and discursive codes as part of processes of expression and communication. Such an abstract discussion runs the risk of superficiality and some propositions may, at first glance, even seem trivial. Empirical examples serve more as pointers than as evidence. However, the broad theoretical proposition launched here – that our scientific discourse is modal and comprises several realities which in turn produce alternatives in modal narrations – may open up new perspective on the human use of violence as manifesting and representing meanings in both conventional and idiosyncratic acts. It is not tried to define violence in terms of victims as unwilling recipients and illegitimacy. Violence has no conditions, it is a phenomenon of the world offering itself to human use. When employed it may be destructive and this is no doubt the more common way it is used. It may also be that violent acts are received voluntarily providing the recipient with extraordinary qualities and blessings. Some small-scale human groups have learnt to master outbursts of violence by avoidance[11] while others incorporate it in the form of warfare, anthropophagy and sorcery in their systemic construction of society.[12] Victim and executor may have very different views as to what goes on in acts of violation. Semantically violence is filled with evasive ambiguities. This introduction does not offer a theory of violence stipulating the conditions for violent acts. Rather, it suggests ways of 'reading' violence as it occurs in the world. A symbological approach promises to provide insights which are complementary to what more conventional types of sociological and psychological studies could possibly offer. And promises, however vague, should not be neglected.

Notes

I wish to thank Barend ter Haar whose thoughts on Chinese society have been very seminal with regard to some of the basic ideas on violence which inform this introductory essay. I also wish to thank Jon Abbink for comments. The responsibility for what is said here remains with the author.

1. See further Aijmer, forthcoming, *The Symbological Project*. This brief introduction is not the place for an extensive presentation of symbology. What is essential in the present line of thinking is the notion of ontology and the idea of plural ontologies and their bases in human cognition. To me ontologies are grammars and so specifications of ways of identifying and marking the boundaries of particulars. Ontologies contain their own practices and fix appropriate forms of discourse and methods. They are always prior to the phenomena (cf. Harré 1998: 47) and relate to information processing in the human brain. This is in marked difference from the use of ontology favoured by Bruce Kapferer (1988: 220 ff.) which assumes that meaning in ontology does not precede the reality of experience but is inseparable from it and simultaneous with it. Being reiterated phenomena in history and context they become particularistic systems of meaning. To Kapferer ontology is synonymous to a mode of being (p. 79). So one can find an individual ontology, a capitalist ontology, a scientific ontology, a mythic ontology, one for the State, one for evil, another for power, and so on: there is an ontology for every possible situation. According to Kapferer you can have an ontological commitment (as monks may have, p. 82). Ontologies have logic and they are part of realities, models for and models of at the same time. In my parlance this idiosyncratic use of the word ontology come close to something like symbolic idiom. My own argument is differently grounded – for better or worse – but this should be said as Professor Kapferer in a friendly comment has suggested that what is being said in this introduction, with its obvious limitations in scope, recapitulates what was achieved by his own work of 1988. For the reasons cited above, I would argue that our positions are rather different.

2. 'Intuitive' (and so 'intuition') is here used to point to a kind of knowledge that is not readily retrievable by linguistically carried cogitation, and therefore cannot be accounted for by introspection.

3. I borrow this term from Humphrey and Laidlaw (1994) as a characterizing name for 'meanings' in iconic messages and motifs. Needless to say, this use of 'archetypal' has nothing to do with Jung and Jungian psychology.

4. 'Environmental' has here a very broad frame of reference, and should not be read as confined only to physical phenomena.

5. See Bloch's (1992) extensive discussion of these features.
6. The fact that the contributors of this anthology in various ways use working definitions of violence, does not provide counter-arguments against my general proposition. It is perfectly justified to characterize in some abstract way a field you wish to discuss – as long as the definition is not thought to say what violence is essentially.
7. Against sociobiological and materialist interpretations of social violence, see Howell and Willis (1989), Robarchek (1977; 1979; 1989; 1991); Robarchek and Denton (1987). In favour of materialist and socio-biological analysis, see for instance Chagnon (1988) and Daly and Wilson (1991).
8. As has been argued by, for instance, Russell and Russell (1968).
9. Another way to phrase this would be that the symbolism of violence is manifest and known only in performative acts of violence, and that the two aspects are empirically inseparable.
10. I am aware that there are other traditional modes of appropriating life in nature in Britain, then generally called 'shooting' or 'stalking', and which are more along the Germanic line of tradition.
11. It has frequently been pointed out that not all human societies are violent – there are, for instance, the counter-examples of the Semai (Thomas 1958, Dentan 1968, Robarchek 1977, 1979, 1989, 1990, 1994; Robarchek and Dentan 1987), the Buid (Gibson 1986, 1990), and the Chewong (Howell 1984, 1988, 1989). But it remains very clear from these ethnographies that they know violence and behave accordingly. You cannot avoid violence unless you know it.
12. For example, Aijmer (1997: ch. 31–3).

1

The Enigma of Senseless Violence
Anton Blok

'Violence is often called irrational. It has its reasons, however [. . .]'

Girard, *Violence and the Sacred* (1977)

The Problem

The comparative study of violence suffers from several handicaps. The most important is the dominant conception of violence in modern societies in which the means of violence have long since been monopolized by the state. Precisely because of the stability of this relatively impersonal monopoly and the resulting pacification of society at large, people have developed strong feelings about using and witnessing violence. They are inclined to consider its unauthorized forms in particular as anomalous, irrational, senseless and disruptive – as the reverse of social order, as the antithesis of 'civilization', as something that has to be brought under control.

The pacification of society and its acceptance as 'natural' lie at the basis of both scholarly and popular accounts of violence: if focused on the actual use of violence at all, the emphasis falls on the instrumental, most obvious aspects of violence.[1] The cultural dimensions of violence – its idiom, discourse and meaning – receive less attention.

Discussing violence in Northern Ireland, McFarlane notes that 'there is rather little discussion of violence per se in anthropology' (1986: 192). The reluctance of scholars to commit themselves to the study of violence is also evident in the historiography of the French Revolution: in her article 'Beheadings' Regina Janes (1991: 7) argues that historians have systematically declined to discuss and explain popular violence.[2]

Another telling example of this avoidance behaviour is provided in one of the most famous pieces of the anthropological literature. In a footnote at the end of his essay on the Balinese cockfight, Geertz mentions the mass killings on the island at the end of 1965 in a single sentence: 'in two weeks of December 1965, during the upheavals following the unsuccessful coup in Djakarta, between forty and eighty thousand Balinese (in a population of about two million) were killed, largely by one another – the worst outburst in the country' (1973: 452 n 43). It would take more than twenty years before an historian-anthropologist explored these events and the wider context in which they took shape (Robinson 1995).

We want to understand violence primarily in utilitarian, 'rational' terms, in terms of means and ends. The question what violence signifies, 'says', or expresses is at best of secondary importance. In this way, historically developed sensibilities serve as a standard in comparative research and are responsible for distorted views of both violence and society.

This may help explain why we speak of 'senseless' violence in cases where easily recognizable goals and obvious relationships between means and ends are absent. These dominant perceptions and representations of violence are all the more remarkable because modern societies include several domains in which unlicensed violence is part of everyday life and, what is more, far from disreputable.

Rather than defining violence *a priori* as senseless and irrational, we should consider it as a changing form of interaction and communication, as a historically developed cultural form of *meaningful* action. Frequently used qualifications such as 'senseless' and 'irrational' reflect a western bias and indicate how often cases of violence are divorced from their context. Without knowledge of their specificness and circumstantiality, without a thick description of those cases, they cannot but appear as 'senseless' and 'irrational'. Ironically, then, these qualifications close off research precisely where it should start: with questions about form, meaning and context of violence.

The phrase 'senseless violence' has recently attained general currency in newspapers, in particular in comments on cases of street violence and violent incidents in and around places of entertainment. Some commentators even propose to get rid of the expression altogether because its use implies that violence can also be 'meaningful' when all violence is 'senseless' by definition. I agree with Noel Malcolm who writes in a recent review article that 'the phrase "senseless violence" is a peculiarly empty piece of huffing and puffing. However repugnant deliberate violence may be, the one thing it is not is senseless' (Malcolm 1998: 7).

Widely different forms of violence routinely labeled as 'senseless' or 'irrational' are governed by rules, prescription, etiquette, and protocol. Ritualization characterizes any number of violent operations, including sacrifice, hunting, bullfights, butchering, charivari, duelling, wars, judicial torture, public executions, the killing of sacred kings, tyrannicide, feuding, vendetta, ethnic cleansing, and organized crime.[3] In all these cases, more is at stake than an instrumental move towards a specific goal. If there are any goals involved, they can only be reached in a special, prescribed, expressive, indeed *ritualized* way.

Details and Context

We take two cases of serious delicts that received some attention in Dutch newspapers: the so-called parking place killing in Leiden at the end of April 1991 and the killing with a knife of a train conductor in Frisia in early May of the same year. In both cases important information about details and circumstances of the events was not reported in the newspapers. For example, we do not know what kind of verbal and non-verbal exchanges preceded the killings. In the first case, the ethnic identity of the offender was not revealed until much later, during the trial, when he turned out to be a young Turkish man. In the second case, the suspect was a young unemployed Moroccan.[4] Time and place, gender and age, cultural background – all these aspects were of course vital details and contextual aspects of these cases. This also goes for the nature of the confrontations themselves. Consider gaze, gesture, posture and verbal exchange. To what extent are we dealing with offensive or disparaging attitudes and remarks and other forms of symbolic attacks on the person and violations of his territory that may have triggered the violent and fatal response?

In general very little about the details and circumstances of violent encounters is reported in newspapers. Distortion of events and context seriously hampers understanding and obstructs grasping any sense or meaning. Since violent events are represented only fragmentarily and largely out of context, it is not surprising that people define them as 'senseless'.

It is well-known that many cases of homicide result from insults. We also know that sensitivity to insults varies with context and that some people are more sensitive to them than others. When inflicted in public domains, insults can be experienced as a serious form of verbal violence. This is particularly true in cultures with a strongly developed sense of honour, as anthropologists have demonstrated for Mediterranean communities.[5] For a man, the use of violence is the best way to obtain satisfaction for stained honour and to restore his reputation of manliness; 'the ultimate vindication of honour lies in physical violence' (Pitt-Rivers 1977: 8).[6]

But this does not tell us enough about the context of the examples mentioned above. Both cases involved men from minority groups in confrontations with members of the autochthonous population. This element may have reinforced the existing tendency toward and sensitivity to condescending, arrogant and provocative behaviour.[7] Distortion of the context – through under-reporting and ignoring important ethnographic details, particulars about events and circumstances of such delicts – can only produce defective perception and misunderstanding. These journalistic practices may help explain the popular and erroneous conceptualization of violence in terms of 'senseless' and 'irrational' behaviour.

Examining accounts of violence confronts us with a paradox. The emotional value attached to violence in modern societies prejudges and colours research and stands in the way of identifying the reason for and meaning of violence. Comes to mind Hildred Geertz' criticism of Keith Thomas' book on the decline of magic. She blamed him for an uncritical use of indigenous categories as analytical tools (Geertz 1975, quoted in Tambiah 1990: 22–3). In comparative studies of violent delicts a preoccupation with the classification of violence often dominates the participants' own classifications. The emphasis on numbers leaves little room for the careful study of cases. Moreover, we are concerned with prejudices that dovetail with a public opinion more interested in the increase or decrease of violence – in prevention, policy and control – than in ethnographic detail, form, meaning and context of violence, which includes more than occasional references to the age, gender and occupational or ethnic background of the offenders.

Rather than look at violence through essentialist or naturalist spectacles, it makes more sense to consider violence as a cultural category, as a historically developed cultural form or construction. How people conceive of violence and the meaning it has for them depend on time and place, vary with historical circumstances and also depend on the perspective of those involved – offenders and victims, spectators and bystanders, witnesses and authorities.

What we call the 'bullfight' is not defined in Spain as a fight but as a spectacle called *corrida de toros* (the running of bulls) in which the *torero* has to demonstrate in a stylized fashion his courage, daring, *gracia* and manliness (Hemingway 1977; Pitt-Rivers 1983; Marvin 1986). Dutch society is divided over the issue of hunting and whether it involves acceptable violence: the *weidelijke* or 'decent', 'self-respecting' hunters, who strongly ritualize their relationship with game, on the one hand, and the larger public that, not bothered by much knowledge about the subject, rejects any form of hunting, on the other (Dahles 1990: 14–15 *passim*; Thomas 1983: 160 ff.; Elias 1986).

That we have to consider violence as a cultural form or construction is also obvious from changing classifications and the definition of everyday crime. Street robberies, including snatching purses and handbags from women and elderly people, counted for a long time as theft, but was recently redefined as a violent delict. Interviews with convicts with long prison terms suggest that burglars have a code of their own and often differ with judicial authorities over the definition of violent delicts. In earlier days, violence against persons, including manslaughter, was considered less abominable and punished less severely than crimes against property, some of which were defined as capital crimes. Today the law considers violence against persons as a more serious delict than crimes against property (van den Brink 1991: 101). These shifts of meaning, which neatly fit the drift of the civilizing process described by Elias, can also be detected in the discourse on rape. Recent discussions on rape within marriage and in other contexts, including so-called 'date rape', reveal that we are again concerned with actions or aspects of actions that, for many people, have obtained a different meaning and that are now also formally defined as violent crimes.[8]

Rape illustrates the importance of meaning because it shows how meaning depends on the context. So-called 'undesired intimacies', or sexual harassment (violations of privacy) at the workplace and elsewhere concern social action that one would not accept from A, but might desire from B.[9] About such aspects of the context of micro-behaviour Goffman has reported extensively and admirably in *Territories of the Self*: 'The very forms of behaviour employed to celebrate and affirm relationships – such as greetings, enquiries after health and love-making – are very close in character to what would be a violation of preserves if performed between wrongly related individuals' (1971: 57–8).

In his treatment of ceremonial violations in his earlier essay on deference and demeanour Goffman already points out the possibility of inversion that all rituals include: 'The idiom through which modes of proper ceremonial conduct are established necessarily creates ideally effective forms of desecration, for it is only in reference to specific proper ties that one can learn to appreciate what will be the worst possible form of behaviour. Profanities are to be expected, for every religious ceremony creates the possibility of a black mass' (1967: 86).

Doing and Saying

Anthropologists have found it useful to distinguish between instrumental (technical) and expressive (ritual, symbolic, communicative) aspects of human behaviour.[10] The former involve expediency and practical reason, the relation between means and goals. The latter involve meaning: what do these practices 'say', what do they express? The emphasis is on cultural form rather than on means and ends. Both aspects are important and closely connected. It may be useful to see this relation in terms of a continuum: some actions are more instrumental, other actions are more expressive.

All social action, however, has potentially something 'to say'. In street robberies, for example, the instrumental aspects seem dominant. Yet it would be wrong to ignore the symbolic import, the meaning that these operations have for both the victim (fear, humiliation, the loss of a loved object) and the offender (position, status, prestige, reputation in his own group). These are important matters and constitute precisely what symbolic action is all about. It is the task of cultural anthropologists to focus on what Leach (1964: 12) calls the 'aesthetic frills' – how people operate and give form to social action and explicate the meanings implied.

The analytical distinction between instrumental and expressive aspects of social action can be especially helpful in the study of violence. If the use of violence can be primarily understood in terms of symbolic action, this does not imply, of course, that we are dealing only with 'symbolic' violence. What it does imply, however, is that the effective use of physical force very much depends on its symbolic form. Like all performances, it turns on how it is carried out: it depends on the message, on what people want to say, to communicate. Hence the ritualization of violence. Although violence may be primarily directed at the attainment of specific ends, such as wounding or killing an opponent, it is impossible to understand these violent operations in terms of these easily recognizable goals alone. There are often more effective ways to obtain these results.

Liquidations in the world of the rural *mafia* in Sicily were often carried out by sawed-off shotgun, the weapon formerly used for hunting wolves. Hence the name *lupara* for this disfiguring and humiliating mode of killing. *Post mortem* mutilations of victims and dressing them up in grotesque ways also had specific meanings as had feeding corpses to pigs. *Lupara bianca* denotes elimination of opponents without leaving any traces. This more recent form of liquidation still permits mourning but excludes funeral rites and, therefore, underscores desecration and humiliation. From Antiquity up to the present day, from Hector and Antigone to the anonymous victims of Srebrenica, we can detect the enormous value people attach to the integrated body and a proper burial in the numerous cases of dead bodies being mutilated and proper burials denied – both in the practices of official criminal law and in forms of popular justice. The symbolic import, the point of these cases lies in the very absence of ritual (see Blok 1995b: 153–76).

The church robberies in eighteenth-century Overmaas (the hinterland of Maastricht), for which the so-called *Bokkerijders* were held responsible, not only involved the violation of sanctuaries, but also included further profanations such as the theft of ceremonial objects and celebration of a black mass (see Blok 1995b; 1998). The point of the bullfight is not that six bulls are killed and sent to the butcher, but how these dispatches are performed – how the *matador* faces the bulls, has them run, controls them, and so on.

As stated above, ritualization characterizes a majority of violent operations. This ritualization is not only evident from rules and prescriptions, etiquette and protocol but also from specifications of time and place, the presence of special persons in special outfits, the use of a special vocabulary – in short from their formalized, theatrical character. In all these instances more is at stake than the mechanical move towards a specific goal. If there are goals involved, they can only be reached in a special, prescribed, indeed *ritualized* fashion.

Violent action involves major transitions, including crossing the boundaries between life and death. Special precautions serve to avoid or remove pollution (Gernet 1981: 265–6). One can detect in the ritualization of violence attempts to avoid moral responsibility for killing 'fellow' human beings. Special names for opponents and victims, like animal names ('dogs', 'cockroaches' and the like), offensive nicknames and other abusive terms serve to dehumanize them, set them apart from ordinary people and remove them from the moral community. Special times and places locate the action outside the moral community. Alcohol and drugs serve to exempt executors and offenders from moral responsibility for killing human beings.

We should therefore hesitate before defining violence as 'senseless' or 'irrational'. Moreover, the reason for and meaning of violence are also implied in the sanctions that come into play if the perpetrators commit errors or fail in the performance. People set great store by committing violence in a prescribed, formalized, theatrical fashion because deviation from protocol and scenario implies pollution and therefore often results in disqualification: the executioner who fails is punished himself (lynched by the spectators); the hunter who fails to observe the rules of *weidelijkheid* is excluded from his milieu; the man who refuses to give or demand satisfaction in a duel loses his membership in the 'good society'; the burglar who uses violence against victims is branded by his peers as an amateur; the football hooligan who uses unmanly means of fighting is looked down upon by his friends; the bullfighter who performs the prescribed moves without *gracia* or without taking risks — 'coming out before coming in' as Hemingway puts it in *Death in the Afternoon* — is scoffed at, called *asesino* (murderer) by the spectators.

Why the use of violence is so often ritualized and so unmistakably a cultural form is a problem in itself. Avoiding pollution and the issue of moral responsibility for killing fellow human beings have already been mentioned. This interpretation ties up with what Meuli and Burkert say about the *Unschuldskomödie* (comedy of innocence) in sacrificial and hunting rituals in ancient societies. In these cases one can see attempts to create a distance, to avoid and remove pollution, attempts at reconciliation with the victim and, ultimately, to justify and legitimate violence.[11] Bloodshed is associated with transitions, the crossing of boundaries between life and death, this world and the next, culture and nature, and the like, which invariably imply pollution. For all these reasons, one can expect that the use of violence is commonly surrounded by ritual.[12] This is also why the use of violence can have a 'purifying' effect in vindication, as 'washing the stains of honor' by 'taking blood for blood' testifies (see Blok 1996).

That violence is symbolic action obviously applies to sacrifice. But it also applies to terrorism, which at least sometimes acquires the character of ritual sacrifice, as Zulaika argues in his study of political violence in the Basque country.[13] Terrorism is usually represented as irrational and senseless, especially when the victims are innocent and selected at random. A worse interpretation is hardly possible. The terror under the Zulu king Shaka has often been depicted as arbitrary and irrational; on closer inspection, however, there was method in Shaka's pitiless massacres (see Walter 1969: 131–2, 133–77). This early nineteenth-century king and his European biographers understood already what long puzzled twentieth-century social scientists (cf. ibid.: 171). Zulaika recalls Aron's definition of terrorism as violence whose psychological effects are in no way commensurable with its physical results. He argues that what characterizes terrorism is the manipulation of the psychology of violence by inspiring fear among potential victims. Terrorism and ritual sacrifices share a fundamental feature: the victim (who encapsulates and embodies the aim and meaning of the action) has to be innocent. The innocence of the victims is implied in the randomness of terrorist attacks. But we also know that many victims of Basque terrorism were by no means randomly selected.

The ritual character of public executions has recently been emphasized by various scholars and hardly requires further discussion. A few comments are in order. To define death on the scaffold and banishment of convicts as 'laborious' is to miss the point: a formalized, dramatic form of social communication concerning the removal of pollution. The ceremonies that accompanied the punishments, or of which the punishments consisted, cannot be understood in merely technical terms, of the mere physical elimination of criminals. Alongside their magico-religious import, public executions were 'spectacular' in more than one sense. They presented a warning aimed at deterrence as clearly specified in the sentence: 'to inspire fear and set an example'.[14]

In what happened in and around the scaffold earlier scholars saw a ritual sacrifice. This point of view receives further attention in Girard's studies of the role of the scapegoat in collective violence (von Amira 1922; Girard 1977; Hamerton-Kelly 1987). Although public executions largely disappeared from modern societies in the nineteenth century, their form still holds a strong fascination for contemporary audiences as executions *in effigie* and the toppling of statues of hated rulers demonstrate. These practices are clearly expressive, communicative and magical. Iconoclasm and public exhumation, the carrying around and display of corpses and further profanations of remains are usually directed against persons who themselves have become icons of a hated regime, an oppressive form of life, a dark epoch.[15]

Violence as Meaningful Action

The main point of this essay is that violence should not be dismissed as 'senseless'. On the contrary, it should be understood primarily as symbolic action, that is as *meaningful* action. This is perhaps most evident in the emphasis on ritual and ceremony, status, identity and group membership. Violence makes statements and it is the task of anthropologists to decipher them. They are greatly helped in this because violence often has the character of theatre and performance in which things are 'said' as much as they are 'done'.[16]

Ritual is no less prominent in 'everyday violence'. Football hooliganism in England and elsewhere in Western Europe also abounds with symbolic activities and ritual performances. Confrontations between fans of different clubs provide young men (often from working-class background) with occasions to demonstrate their aggressive masculinity. Dunning and his collaborators, who studied the phenomenon in Great Britain, mention the repertoire of *symbolic demasculinization* and *ritual denigration* in the encounters between groups of supporters. They argue that hooliganism is rooted in the working-class subculture where fighting and open aggression are appropriate and desirable in certain situations and serve as a means to acquire status and prestige (Dunning *et al.* 1986: 170–8; cf. Stokvis 1991; Bromberger *et al.* 1995: 221–95).

The time and place of football vandalism are also symptomatic of its ritual character. It occurs on days and in locations that are unusual – on holidays and weekends and in stadiums, special trains and busses. Ritual plunder by crowds has also been noted as an integral part of rites of passage, such as at the death of bishops and popes in early modern Italy. Charivari or 'rough music' was, until recently, quite common in rural Europe. It provides another example of ritualized violence in which unmarried youngsters played a salient role (Davis 1975: 152–87; Ginzburg 1987; Le Goff and Schmitt 1981; Blok 1989a; Rooijakkers 1994).

Ritual is also obvious in the violent struggle between Catholics and Protestants in Northern Ireland. Retaliation killings are rarely simple eliminations. Time and place are important. Sometimes opponents are shot dead in the presence of their wife and children. Territory can be so crucial that one scholar refers to *spatial formations of violence* (Feldman 1991: 17–45). Ethnic violence in the Balkans is not only a matter of physical harm and destruction. It also involves social and cultural destruction. The most grisly form of symbolic violence is 'ethnic cleansing'. This expression is revealing because it shows once more how strongly the use of violence involves legitimation and the construction of an object defined as polluting that has to be purged. Also elsewhere, like in Sri Lanka and South Africa, ethnic violence shows in all its details that much more is at stake than the physical elimination of opponents. Tambiah, who explored the ethnic war between Sinhalese and Tamils in Sri Lanka, writes: There occurs an increasing 'theatricalization' and an accompanying ritualization and polarization, in the escalating contents of violence between ethnic, religious, linguistic, or political minorities on the one side and the majority collectivities and established governments on the other (1990: 116).

What is at stake in all these tests of strength is epitomized in the classic European duel: honour, identity, pride and meaning – and the group membership implied in them. What can be deployed and sacrificed for them, Simmel summarized long ago as follows: 'To maintain honour is so much a duty that one derives from it the most terrible sacrifices – not only self-inflicted ones, but also sacrifices imposed on others' (1983: 405).

One cannot explain and understand violence in terms of practical goals only. To justify hunting to their numerous critics, Dutch hunters point to their responsibilities for the preservation of game, the protection of agriculture and the conservation of nature in general. They emphasize the alleged utilitarian, instrumental, functional, practical aspects of their profession rather than the meaning and function that hunting has for them. Obviously, it is difficult to discuss these elements of a life style and to explain how and why hunting also involves performance, sociability, entertainment and excitement.[17]

The discussion on violence is dominated by these taboos. Civilized persons may not show that they enjoy violence. In the course of the civilizing process a growing number of social practices have been defined and classified as violent and consequently proscribed and hidden behind the scenes, especially activities related to lust and pleasure, including sexuality, hunting, animal fights and duelling.[18] This may be why there has been little interest in the stylization of violence, the meaning and shifts of meaning for people involved in them – as if, for example, interest in these matters were also inappropriate.[19] There are many literary and forensic cases, however, that illustrate the complexity and ambivalence of incest and rape. The discussion of violence has run into a contradiction: on the one hand people pretend to know what violence is; on the other hand and under pressure from increasing democratization and civilization, they define and mark new areas of human action as violent.

Violence is not an unchanging, 'natural' fact but a historically developed cultural category that we have to understand primarily as symbolic activity, as meaningful social action. To define violence as senseless or irrational is to abandon research where it should start: exploring meaning, interpreting symbolic action and mapping the historical and social context of activities defined as violent. It is the task of the anthropologist or historian to find out what violence 'says' about honour, reputation, status, identity and group solidarity. The codes can be rather complex, but, fortunately for the researcher, there is much redundancy in ritual sequences (see Leach 1966: 404; 1976b: 10–11). Violence is interwoven with masculinity and the human body often serves as a cultural medium, as a source of metaphorical material to symbolize power relations. As Campbell writes of Greek pastoralists: 'There is no more conclusive way of showing that you are stronger than by taking away the other man's life' (1964: 318). In her article on decapitations and parading severed heads on pikes during the first years of the French Revolution, Regina Janes notes: 'While severed heads always speak, they say different things in different cultures . . . Cross culturally, taking and displaying an enemy's head is one of the most widely distributed signs of victory' (Janes 1991: 24, 47). As Keeley (1996: 100) notes, the 'popularity of this practice is probably explained by the obvious fact of that the head is the most individual part of the body'.

Violation of reputation, humiliation, subjection – all these shows of strength are expressed most clearly through the medium of the human body: shaven heads, stigmas, brandings, mutilations, decapitations, exhumations, displays of corpses and denial of decent burial. In this regard, violence in ethnic confrontations, caste wars, tyrannicides, iconoclasm, or public executions shows striking similarities. By and large, and beyond infinite local variations, physical violations speak a uniform language, as Ranum points out in his essay on tyrannicide in early modern Europe. Both the violation and the vindication of honour are often represented in the idiom of the human body: the stained honour which can only be vindicated, 'cleansed', or 'washed' with blood. The symbolism of the human body and the related issue of honour and identity loom large in violent confrontations. They raise the issue of family resemblances and cultural uniformities, which, next to our focus on cultural specificity, deserves close attention in a world that is becoming increasingly interconnected.

Notes

Dutch versions of this essay appeared in H. Franke *et al.* (eds), *Alledaags en Ongewoon Geweld*. Groningen: Amsterdams Sociologisch Tijdschrift/ Wolters-Noordhoff, 1991, pp. 189–207; and in H. Driessen and H. de Jonge (eds), *In de Ban van Betekenis. Proeven van Symbolische Antropologie*. Nijmegen: SUN, 1994, pp. 27–45. An English version was presented at the 5th Biennial EASA Conference held in Frankfurt/M., 4–7 September 1998, in the section 'Wordviews and Violence'. For editorial advice I am grateful to Rod Aya.

1. The social sciences have usually been more interested in social order than in violence and chaos – a bias that is closely connected with the pacification of western societies: the means of violence have long since been monopolized by the state and have in most part moved 'behind the scenes' (cf. Elias 1978: 191 ff.; Blok 1995a).
2. This is a strong statement which does not do justice to the work of the English social historian Richard Cobb (*Les Armees Révolutionnaires, Reactions to the French Revolution*, etc.).
3. On sacrifice, see Girard (1977), Burkert (1983), Hamerton-Kelly (1987); on hunting, see Howe (1981), Bromberger and Lenclud (1982),

Elias (1986), Dahles (1990); on charivari, see Le Goff and Schmitt (1981), Blok (1989a) and Rooijakkers (1994); on plunder, see Ginzburg (1987) and Blok (1995b); on football hooliganism, see Dunning *et al.* (1986), Stokvis (1991) and Bromberger (1995: 229–95); on feuding, see Boehm (1987); on the Sicilian *mafia*, see Blok (1988) and Gambetta (1993); on duelling, see Kiernan (1988), Billacois (1986), Elias (1986: 44–119), Nye (1991), McAleer (1994) and Frevert (1995); on terrorism, see Walter (1969), Zulaika (1988), Douglass and Zulaika (1990) and Feldman (1991); on tyrannicide, see Ranum (1980); on public executions, see Linebaugh (1975), Schild (1980), Gernet (1981), Spierenburg (1984), von Dülmen (1984) and Blok (1989b; 1995b); on war, see Koch (1974), Meggitt (1977), McNeill (1982) and Keeley (1996: 59–69); and on judicial torture, see Langbein (1977). Collective violence during revolutions is often less spontaneous and more 'directed' than has generally been assumed; see Aya (1990).

4. On this hypocrisy and self-censorship for fear being branded as politically incorrect or racist, see the article by K. van Zomeren in the Dutch newspaper *NRC-Handelsblad* (17 August 1991) on the trial and the deliberately distorted reports in two leading Dutch dailies. Publicity on the ethnic background of offenders was still a controversial subject when this essay first appeared (cf. Bovenkerk 1991).

5. For a summary of the literature, see Gilmore (1987). The related code of honour among aristocrats is discussed in Elias (1983: 94 ff.); Pitt-Rivers (1977: 1–17); and Nye (1991).

6. The relationship between honour and violence is explicitly addressed in Campbell (1964); Bourdieu (1979); Blok (1981); Jamous (1981); Nye (1991). Pitt-Rivers in anthropology and Goffman in sociology have, independently of each other, drawn on the fundamental insights of Simmel.

7. For an inventory and discussion of the repertoire of offensive performances, see Goffman on 'territories of the self' and 'remedial exchanges' (1971: 28–61, 95–187). About the person as a ceremonial object and the symbolic actions related to this sacredness, see Goffman's famous essay on deference and demeanor (1967: 47–95) and his book *Stigma* (1963). Cf. Simmel (1950: 320–1) on discretion, distance, honour and the 'ideal sphere': 'Although differing in size in various directions and differing according to the person with whom one entertains relations, this sphere cannot be penetrated, unless the personality value of the individual is thereby destroyed. A sphere of this sort is placed around man by his "honor". Language very poignantly designates an insult to one's honour as "coming too close": the radius of this sphere

marks, as it were, the distance whose trespassing by another person insults one's honor' (1950: 321).

8. Cf. N. Gibbs, 'When is it Rape?' (*Time*, 10 June 1991). Gibbs refers to Estrich (1987) and Brownmiller (1975), who argues that rape is not a sexual but a violent crime. Attitudes in the Netherlands are also changing. In September 1991 the Dutch government initiated a four-year publicity campaign to help change the sexual behaviour of boys and men in order to diminish sexual violence against women. Current ideas about sexual violence had been investigated before. Forty per cent of those interviewed define all intimacies carried out against the will of partners and others as sexual violence. Thirty per cent prefer to restrict the use of this term to rape and assault.

9. Because the concept of 'undesired intimacies' would wrongly imply that one is concerned with intimacy, some prefer the term 'sexual intimidation' (*NRC Handelsblad*, 19 October 1991), which links up with the current term 'sexual harassment' in English. The expression 'undesired intimacies', however, best captures all the uninvited advances and passes short of sexual intimidation. These terminological changes alone suggest that violence constitutes a cultural category and refers to historically developed practices, representations, perceptions, and attitudes that are closely bound up with (although not reducible to) the largely unplanned shift in the balance of power between the sexes in favour of women. These developments illustrate modern anthropology's belief that culture makes people as much as people make culture.

10. Cf. Radcliffe-Brown (1952: 143); Leach (1964: 10–4; 1966; 1976b: 9). For a slightly different appreciation of the distinction between expressive and instrumental behaviour, between 'saying' and 'doing', see Rappaport (1979: 175 ff.); Geertz (1980: 120, 134–6); and Tambiah (1985: 77ff., 123 ff.).

11. Cf. Meuli (1975, II: 952 ff., 1004 ff.); and Burkert (1983: 35 ff.). Some scholars view the so-called *Henkersmahlzeit* (last meal of the condemned) an attempt at reconciliation. See von Hentig (1969). In a French documentary on deer hunting shown in Aix-en-Provence in the fall of 1997, a man who had shot a deer lifted its snout and placed a brief kiss on it.

12. See Meuli (1975, II: 952); and Burkert (1983: 22–34 *passim*). On the ritual pollution of warriors in Antiquity, see Redfield (1975: 222). For a modern variation, see Zulaika (1988: 86–101). On prototypical territorial violations that entail ritual pollution, see Goffman (1971: 50–2).

13. Cf. Zulaika (1988: 206, 326) and Douglass and Zulaika (1990: 225), who emphasize the innocence of victims in sacrifice: 'Some societies resort to the institution of drawing lots to assure the ritual innocence of the victim. To kill someone for an offense is an act of justice; to kill someone to placate an angry god is a ritual sacrifice in which the innocence of the victim has to be made patent through random selection'. Cf. Walter (1969: 133–77) on Zulu terror under Shaka. See also Burkert (1983: 35–48); Girard (1977: 314); and Simmel (1983: 405). Unlike English and French, the Dutch language retains in the word 'slachtoffer' (victim) the connection with the concept of sacrifice.

14. For discussions of seventeenth- and eighteenth-century public executions in the Dutch Republic, see Spierenburg (1984); and Blok (1995b: 153–76). For Germany and England, see von Dülmen (1984); and Linebaugh (1975). Gernet discusses public executions in Ancient Greece and observes: 'The victim of *apotumpanismos* is *exposed* as an object of public indignation and cruel laughter. The victim is also an *exemplum*, since agony is more telling than a dead body' (1981: 267).

15. For sixteenth and seventeenth-century examples, see Ranum (1980); for the ritual killing of the Dutch politician Johan de Witt and his brother in The Hague in 1672, see Rowen (1978: 61–84). For our time, recall the fate of Mussolini. Some years ago, Haiti was the stage of *post mortem* profanations of the remains of the tyrannical president François Duvalier, who died in 1971. For the exhumation and desecration of the remains of *religieuses* and ecclesiastics during the Spanish Civil War, see Lincoln (1985). More recent and less harsh examples of these forms of symbolic violence are found in the iconoclastic wave in Eastern Europe after the fall of communist regimes.

16. Hence the term 'performative action' for ritual. For ritual as performance, see Rappaport (1979: 176–97); and Tambiah (1985: 77ff., 123–66). Ritual action does not only 'say' something, but also 'does' things, brings them about. This implies a further refining of the distinction between instrumental and expressive aspects of human behaviour.

17. Cf. Dahles (1990), who describes how hunters justify their activities to themselves (in terms of *weidelijkheid* or ritualization) rather than to a critical outside world (in terms of social usefulness). For a candid report on hunting, see the interview with a young Dutch hunter, a student of the University of Amsterdam, in *Folia Civitatis*, 4 October 1991. It is significant, however, that the title of the interview, 'Hunter

replaces lynx and wolf', again highlights the utilitarian aspects of hunting. In the densely populated Low Countries, hunting is a flourishing business. Of the total area of the Netherlands, about 75 per cent is open to hunting, which occurs on many fields virtually all year round. The number of hunters (almost exclusively men) has increased during this century from about 7,000 in 1900 to 20,000 in 1950 and over 30,000 at present. See Dahles (1991: 13–14), who also notes that the image of hunters has become more negative over the past few years. The same applies to fox hunting in England. Popular resistance against hunting in the Netherlands is growing: over 90 per cent of the Dutch population is in favour of abolishing all hunting and parliament has recently (September 1997) proposed new laws that would restrict hunting to just a few species of animals.

18. See Elias (1978); Blok (1995a); and Thomas (1983). For the growing sensitivity to domestic violence, see Brinkgreve and van Daalen (1991).

19. Kiernan's book *The Duel in European History* (1988), for example, is a study against rather than about the duel. The author shows little understanding of the meaning and context of duelling and totally ignores the anthropological and sociological literature on honour. In his book, one looks in vain for thick descriptions of famous duels like Nabokov offers in an extensive note to his annotated edition of Pushkin's *Eugene Onegin* on the duel fought on 27 January 1837 near St Petersburg between the poet and his challenger, Baron Georges Charles d'Anthès, a protégé of the Dutch ambassador Van Heeckeren (see Nabokov 1975, II, 2: 43–51).

2

'Criminals by Instinct':
On the 'Tragedy' of Social Structure and the 'Violence' of Individual Creativity
Nigel Rapport

'[D]ivine inventiveness is inherent in all of us (. . .). But do not forget it is the power of destruction as well as creation.'

Edmund Leach, *A Runaway World?*

'[A]ll of us are criminals by instinct. (. . .) [A]ll creativity, whether it is the work of the artist or the scholar or even of the politician, contains within it a deep-rooted hostility to the system as it is.'

Edmund Leach, *Custom, Law and Terrorist Violence.*

Prognostic

In his Introduction to this volume, Göran Aijmer hypothesized on the possibly constitutive relationship between violence and society. Paradox-ical as it may seem, ethnography shows violence to be intrinsic to everyday social relations: as instrument and as idiom. Violence acts and violence speak, and while it may seem, by definition, to exist beyond the habitual, orderly and routine, nevertheless its dramatic presence occasions an impulse towards the order of social practice and cultural imagery being re-formed.

If there is a processual relationship between violence and the orderly, then the relationship is also characterized by ambiguity. It is in the nature of all human behaviour, that, as the Berkeleyan motto has it: 'To be is to be perceived' (*Esse est percipi*); as Bateson sums it up: 'All "phenomena" are literally "appearances" ' (1972: 429). Hence, violence is in the eye of the beholder, and its influential role in ritual, sport, punishment and statecraft can only be understood through it being appreciated to be a meaningful 'experienced reality' (see Introduction).

In this chapter, I approach the ambiguity of violence and the processual relationship between it and socio-cultural order in terms of another processual relationship: that between individual creativity (or *poesis*) and social structure. My intent is both descriptive and prescriptive. I want to arrive at a position where I can differentiate between 'democratic violence' and 'nihilistic violence'. There always is the violence in the everyday inasmuch as there always is individual creativity existing within, beneath and through social structure. Given the ambiguity of violence as a behavioural and symbolic form, there is room for a social scientific, even a moral, accommodation of the democratic kind within the ambit of the apparently orderly, habitual and routine. The paradox of the disorderly within, beneath and through the orderly, must be given due space in the anthropological account of human being (cf. Rapport 1993).

In *The Anxiety of Influence*, Harold Bloom (1975) argued that the history of poetic traditions could be seen to proceed in terms of a continuous misreading of prior poets and existing poetry – through caricature, parody, distortion, misrepresentation and wilful revisionism – by those currently living and writing. He described this misreading as 'an act of creative correction', which was necessary for clearing an imaginative space in which one could write oneself, 'create one's own voice' (1975: 30). For to write with the voice of another, to write variations on extant poems or to accept someone else's description of oneself, was merely to execute a previously written narrative and to take one's place within a previously determined schema. In 'strong poets', this instilled the great anxiety that their indebtedness to the past might mean that they would fail to create themselves; and it was to allay these fears that such poets wrestled persistently with the work of their 'strong precursors'. Hence, strong poets spent their lives acknowledging and yet appropriating their own contingency. They might be situated in all manner of social, historical and cultural forms of life but they were nevertheless capable of telling the story of their situatedness in words never used before, thus escaping from inherited descriptions. Their formula was: 'where my precursor's poem is, there let my poem be' (1975: 80). Poems arose, in short, out of poets' melancholy at their lack of priority, at their not having begotten themselves, and yet out of a sense of priority being possible. In the words of Oscar Wilde (1913: 205): 'A truly great artist cannot conceive of life being shown or beauty fashioned, under any conditions other than those that he has selected'. In sum, to imagine was to misinterpret, and all new poems were antithetical to – in violation of – their precursors. The history of poetry, Bloom concluded, was a history of the influence of the past and yet of its creative appropriation through the 'capable imagination' of 'strong individuals' in the present (1975: 5).

In this chapter I should like in similar fashion to create a way for myself by rewriting the writing of mainly anthropological others and in the process suggest the outlines of a developmental relationship between social structure and individual creativity. I shall conclude that the '*violence*' – the departure-from-order, the un-order, the dis-order, the out-of order (Stanage 1974: 229) – which this creativity represents can be admitted (even celebrated), democratized, and differentiated from *nihilism*, by promulgating a distinction between form and meaning: between a formal behavioural civility in which all participate, as distinct from the meanings of such behaviours in terms of which individual participants may violently (creatively) differ.

'You are your creativity'

The above epigraph comes from Edmund Leach (1976a), alluding to the imaginative operations of the human mind and its 'poeticism': its untrammelled and unpredictable and non-rule bound nature (cf. 1976b: 5). But let me rather begin the argument of this section with an intriguing comment of Gregory Bateson's (1972: 126). Extrapolating from processes of schismogenesis among the New Guinean Iatmul, Bateson concludes that each human individual can be conceived of as an 'energy source'; here is something capable of and prone to engagement in its own acts, being fuelled by its own processes (metabolic and other) rather than by external stimuli. Furthermore, this energy is then imposed on the universe in the process of creating order.

Bateson's commentary was, of course, to be taken up by Laing, and his definition of a person as 'an origin of actions', and 'a centre of orientation of the objective universe' (1968: 20). But I should instead like to extrapolate back in time from Bateson (and back from Bloom) to a number of pronouncements of Nietzsche's on the priority of individual action over reaction, on the individual who uses his imagination for the conscious purpose of self-creation.

'We invent for ourselves the major part of our experience', Nietzsche begins in *Beyond Good and Evil* (1990), and we do so, he continues, by rearranging that which (socially, culturally, naturally) confronts us in the world, reinventing its language of description and relationship, and so stamping our own impress on what is and what is to come. It is, indeed, the essential and inherent nature of the individual to be self-caused and free, to exhibit self-control and to achieve self-determination. As God is recognizably dead, we can claim to serve no higher purpose, and it is through self-creation, not through contacting or manifesting something bigger than oneself, that we may reach 'redemption'.

Nietzsche (1990) described such self-creation in terms of a major human drive which he called 'the will to power', and he painted a portrait of the ideal exponent of this drive which he named the 'overman' or 'superman' (*Uebermensch*): humanity's hero, whose individuality is not contained by the terms of an inherited language-game, who more than all others epitomizes a fully developed, mature, autonomous, 'powerful' individual, violating the arrangements, the controls, the determination of others by transcending them. He creates his own mind by creating his own language, and so makes himself original ('Be yourself! Be unique! Be original!').

I would prefer to see self-creation willy-nilly as part of the human condition: not so much a willing of power which some individuals possess to a greater degree than others (and to others' detriment), but rather a willing of meaning, of understanding, which all individuals practice and whose inevitable consequence is overcoming – in the sense of going beyond, failing to become completely commensurate with – precedent meanings and understandings. As Rorty phrased it (in the context of seeking to reconcile the writings of Nietzsche with those of Mill, and demonstrate how the egoistic and aesthetic philosophy of the first and the public-minded and liberal philosophy of the second could be made to work together in the life of one person), we can see in the brazen need of the *Uebermensch* or strong poet to boast that he is not a copy, or replica, merely a special form of an act and a need which everyone has. Here is 'the need to come to terms with the blind impress which chance has given him, to make a self for himself by redescribing that impress in terms which are, if only marginally, his own' (Rorty 1992: 43). Even to track down the causes of one's being, to confront one's contingency, is to create oneself – if one describes oneself in new terms, new metaphors. For now, one's idiosyncrasy is more than a specimen of a type already known, and 'the length of one's mind' is not set by the language others have left behind (Rorty 1992: 27).

'This one fact the world hates: that the soul becomes . . .'

In the *Uebermensch* is born 'existentialism's ego', according to Shweder (1991: 41), and it is there that I would now turn, in particular to Sartre, to glean further insights into how the creativity of the Nietzschean self-inventing individual can be expected to manifest and express itself. 'Being precedes essence', Sartre famously begins (1957): each human being makes himself what he is, creates the essence of himself and his world. Of course he is born into a certain socio-cultural situation, into certain historical conditions, but he is responsible for the sense he makes out of them, the meaning he grants them, the way he evaluates and acts towards them; between the given and what this becomes in an individual life there is a perennial (and unique) interplay. Moreover, he is always able to remake this sense, meaning, evaluation and action; he can negate the essence of his own creations and create again. In short, he might be surrounded by the 'actual facts' of an objective historico-socio-cultural present, but he can transcend their brutishness, surpass a mere being-in the-midst-of-things, by attaining the continuous possibility of imagined meanings. His experience cannot be reduced to objective determinants (cf. Kearney 1988: 225–41).

Imagination is the key in this portrayal: the key resource in consciousness, the key to human existence. Imagination is an activity in which human individuals are always engaged and it is through his imagination that an individual creates and recreates the essence of his being (makes himself what he was, is and will become). As Sartre put it, imagination has a 'surpassing and nullifying power' which enables individuals to escape being 'swallowed up in the existent', frees them from given reality, and allows them to be other then what they are made (1972: 273). Because of imagination, human life has an emergent quality, characterized by a going-beyond: going-beyond a given situation, a set of circumstances, a status-quo, going-beyond the conditions that produced it. Because of imagination, the human world is possessed of an intrinsically dynamic order which human individuals, possessed of self-consciousness, are continually in the process of forming and designing. Because they can imagine, human beings are transcendentally free; imagination grants human beings that 'margin of freedom outside conformity' which 'gives life its savour and its endless possibilities for advance' (Riesman 1954: 38).

Imagination issues forth into the world in the form of an ideally 'gratuitous' act, gratuitous inasmuch as it is seemingly uncalled for in terms of existent reality: unjustifiable, 'without reason, ground or proof' (*Chambers's Dictionary*); in Woolf's words, 'something useless, sudden, violent; something that costs a life; (. . .) free from taint, dependence, soilure of humanity or care for one's kind; something rash, ridiculous' (1980: 180). For here is an act which, in its gratuity, surpasses rather than merely conserves the givenness in which it arises, which transcends the apparent realities of convention, which seems to resist the traditional constraints by which life is being lived. The gratuitous act appears to come from nowhere and pertain to nothing; it is more or less meaningless in terms of the sense-making procedures which are currently instituted and legitimated; it is beyond debt and guilt, beyond good and evil.

Finally, then, the gratuitousness of the creative act of human imagination makes it inherently conflictual. The ambiguity, the indeterminacy, of the relationship between individual experience and objective forms of life – the dialectical irreducibility of socio-cultural conceptualization on the one side and conscious individual imaginings on the other – means that the becoming of new meanings will always outstrip the present being of socio-cultural conditions. In the process of creating a new world, existing worlds are often appropriated, reshaped, reformed, in a word, violated. Thus, between imagination and what is currently and conventionally lived there will be a constant tension – '. . . the world hates . . .', as Emerson has it in my epigraph (1950: 179; also cf. Wilde 1913: 169). For while what is currently lived is itself the issue of past imaginative acts of world-creation, and dependent on continuing individual practice for its continuing institutionality, inevitably, present imaginative acts will be moving to new possible futures. To turn this around, the continuity of the conventional is an achievement and a conscious decision (not a mindless conformity) which must be consensually worked for – and superficially – imposed.

EXCURSUS 1

In Acts of Meaning, *Jerome Bruner argued that not only is there a human 'predisposition' to organise experience into* narrative *form, to render experience as narrative, but also that there is a constant human readiness to rewrite such narratives, to write new narratives, and so render experience (the world) otherwise. Willy-nilly, existing narratives attract variant readings. Even though contained in those (possibly widely shared) existing narratives is a sense of what the world is and how it is properly ordered, even though we posit in narrative our sense of the normative, still human narratives – symbolic constructions of the world in collective, institutionalised systems of signification – remain in essence 'open, undetermined, uncertain, subjunctive, vague' (1990: 51). Hence, in the writing and telling of narratives is assured not only a human knowledge of the normative but also a knowledge of breach and exception, of alternative ways of being, acting, striving, which we can envision. Our narrational predisposition, Bruner concludes, 'is a perpetual guarantee that humankind will 'go meta' on received versions of reality' (1990: 55). For while, in one sense, we might be creatures of our historical condition, possessing cultural languages and social selves, in another sense we are autonomous agents, with the reflective capacity to escape and re-evaluate and reformulate what culture has on offer and so be other than we are.*

EXCURSUS 2
In Migrancy Culture Identity, *Iain Chambers argued that* writing *embodied a paradox: the writing project was ambiguous in being both imperialist and revolutionary. To write was to establish a dominion of perception, power and knowledge; and to write also involved a repudiation of dominion: an attempt to reveal an opening for ourselves in the inhabited world by extending, disrupting and reworking it. By opening up a cognitive space, writing entailed permitting a certain distance to develop between ourselves and the contexts that had erstwhile defined our identities. Hence, while starting from known materials – a language, a lexicon, a series of discourses – writing none the less afforded a move, a travelling, a transition, to something more: 'an unforeseen and unknown possibility' (1994: 10).*

EXCURSUS 3
In The Language Myth, *Roy Harris argued that innovation in linguistic usage, the 'renewal of language', was a continuously creative process involving individuals in interaction. Indeterminacy – of what was meant, of what was interpreted, of what will be invented – was the rule not the exception, and underlay all acts of communication. Past linguistic practice did not determine present or future linguistic possibilities because individuals would continually adapt the linguistic fund to their current requirements. Hence, an Archimedean point of linguistic reference outside the continuum of creative activity was a myth; the language being practised at any one time was highly varied and characterised by inconsistency rather than a standard idiom. 'If language is a game', Harris concluded, then 'it is a game we mostly make up as we go along (. . .) in which there is no referee, and the only rule that cannot be bent is that players shall improvise as best they can' (1981: 186).*

'Metanoia (. . .) connotes a change of mind envisaging new moralities'

The essence of being human, Edmund Leach wrote, is to resent the domination of others and the dominion of present structures (1977: 19–20). Hence, all human beings are 'criminals by instinct', predisposed to set their creativity against current system, intent on defying and reinterpreting custom. Indeed, it is the rule-breaking violations of 'inspired individuals' which ever leads to new social formations and on which cultural vitality depends. And yet the hostility of creativity to systems – as – are means that its exponents are likely to be initially categorised and labelled as criminal or insane – even if their ultimate victorious overturning of those systems' conservative morality precipitates a redefining as heroic, prophetic or divine . . .

Returning to anthropology from the above excursi, and extrapolating not back in time from Bateson to Nietzsche but forward, as it were, to those who wrote anthropology after Bateson, and trying to pick up the same thread of ideas relating social structure to individual creativity, the orderly to the violent, Leach seems a good point to start. Victor Turner, of course, would be another (1969: 109; 1974: 169, 231–8, 268–9). Abstracting from the ritual practices undertaken in the liminal period of Ndembu rites of passage, Turner could understand the entire symbolic creation of human worlds as turning on the relation between the formal fixities of social structure and the fluid creativity of liminoidal '*communitas*'. Drawing on Sartre's dialectic (1957) between 'freedom and inertia',[1] Turner theorised that society be regarded as a process in which the two 'antagonistic principles', 'primordial modalities', of structure and creativity could be seen interacting, alternating, in different fashions and proportions in different places and times. Creativity appeared dangerous – anarchic, anomic, polluting – to those in positions of authority, administration or arbitration within existing structures, and so prescriptions and prohibitions attempted precisely to demarcate proper and possible behavioural expressions. But, notwithstanding, ideologies of 'otherness' (as well as spontaneous manifestations of otherness) would erupt from the interstices between structures and usher in opposed and original behavioural proprieties for living outside society (ritually if not normatively) or else refashioning in its image society as such.

However, it is perhaps to Kenelm Burridge, from whom the epigraph to this section comes, that I might best turn. Theorising, like Bateson, on the basis of his New Guinean fieldwork, Burridge, in *Someone, No One. An Essay on Individuality*, posited a processual relationship between social structure and individual creativity. If 'persons' are understood as those who embody categories of thought and behaviour which are prescribed by tradition and so realise a social order, while 'individuals' are those who create anew, Burridge begins, then most people are 'individuals' and 'persons' in different respects and at different times (1979: 5–6; cf. Harré and de Waele 1976: 212). As persons are products of material (sociohistorico-cultural) conditions, and live within the potential of given concepts – feeding on and fattened by them, killing for and being killed by them – so individuals exist in spite of such concepts and conditions, seeking the disorderly and the new and refusing to surrender to things as they are or as traditional intellectualizations and bureaucratizations would wish them to be. For to become an individual is to abandon self-realization through the fulfilment of normative social relations (to transcend the truth of established moralities, established accounts of what is right and proper), and to concentrate one's individual intuitions, perception and behaviour instead on the dialectical relationship 'between what is and what might be' (1979: 76).

Each 'spatially bounded organism', moreover, is able (in terms of both opportunity and capacity) to become both; so that 'individuality' might be how one identified the practice of moving to the status of being individual. What individuality does, in effect is to transform the person, a social someone, into a social no-one – an 'eccentric' at best.

However, if others are willing to accept for themselves – as new intellectualizations, a new morality – the conceptual creations of the 'eccentric' individual, then his move from someone to no-one culminates in him becoming a new social someone, a new 'person'. That is, persons are the endpoint of 'heroic' individuals, individuals who have persuaded (or been mimicked by) others into also realising new social conditions, rules, statuses, roles; for here, individuality dissolves into a new social identity.

Indeed, Burridge concludes, the cycle of: from someone to no-one to someone, is inevitable, and constitutive of our very human being. While its expressions may vary, individuality is a 'thematic fact of culture', the universal instrument of the moral variation, the disruption, the renewal and the innovation which are essential to human survival (1979: 116). Different material conditions may eventuate in situations which variously allow, encourage or inhibit moves to the individual, moments of creative apperception. But over and above this, individuals' creativity means that they continually create the conditions and situations which afford them their opportunity. From hunters and gatherers to pastoralists to subsistence agriculturalists to peasants to village people to townsfolk to city-dwellers, new intellectualizations are always being offered – whether courtesy of (!Kung) story-tellers, (Aborigine) Men of High Degree, (Cuna) shamans, (Nuer) Leopard-Skin Chiefs, (Hindu) Sanyasi, (American) hippies, or whatever. In short, there are ever individuals who are determined to be 'singletons': to interact with others and with established rationalizations in non-predefined ways, to escape from the burden of given cultural prescriptions and discriminations, and so usher in the unstructured and as yet unknown.

Since Burridge wrote, anthropology has begun filling in the gaps in the ethnographic record of relations between structure and creativity, everyday order and its violation. For instance, defining creativity as 'human activities that transform existing cultural practices', activities that, courtesy of a 'creative persona', emerge from traditional forms and yet move beyond them and reshape them, a recent volume, *Creativity/ Anthropology* (dedicated to Victor Turner), brings together cases of 'creative eruption' from different parts of the world (Rosaldo, Lavie and Narayan 1993: 5–6).

Here we find Shostak supplementing the !Kung story of Nisa with those of Jimmy, the creator of a thumb-piano repertoire which was subsequently adopted by a large percentage of the population; N!ukha, a pioneer in a new woman's drum dance which was to give women an increasingly more direct and significant role in healing; and Hwan//a, whose intricate patterns of bead-weaving and innovative musical composi- tions for voice and instrument express and mourn the might-have-beens of her personal life. All three individuals evince the creativity that flourishes in !Kung life and the value placed upon it, we hear, and also the thriving individuation of personality (1993: 54–69).

From Barbara Babcock, meanwhile, we learn of Cochiti Pueblo woman, Helen Cordero, whose 'Storyteller' doll pottery reinvented a moribund traditional form and engendered a revolution in Pueblo ceramics, thus transforming the life of her pueblo and innumerable other people's outside (1993: 70–99). Here, Babcock advises us, we meet one of those whom Ruth Benedict defined as 'gifted individuals who have bent the culture in the direction of their own capacities' (1932: 26). For Cordero's pottery has objectified an individual cast of mind in an accessible material form or structure, 'materialised a way of experiencing', so as to comment on and expand the premises of Pueblo cultural existence. Now women's roles in general (in terms of mobility and economics and communication) have been reshaped; now they re-present, appropriate and interpret (for outsiders as well) discourses of Pueblo culture in which they were traditionally displaced.

Similarly, through James Fernandez (1993: 11–29), we meet Ceferino Suarez, a versifier from village Spain (also sculptor and musician), whose insightful, resourceful, ironic and lively search for and assertion of a social identity which was adequate to his individual persona – despite the disinterested, frustrating and constricting socio-cultural categories surrounding him – evidence a 'play of mind (. . .) that transcends the materials out of which it arises' (1993: 12). Now, as returned emigrant from Cuba, he has come to presume the wherewithal to speak for, orate to, and pass moral judgement on, his Asturian community as a whole (1993: 21):

> Attention, noble audience!
> If you can be attentive:
> This is your servant
> And proud to be so,
> Finds himself charged
> From very distant lands
> With the highest authorization,
> And by the most sacred document,
> To pair up the villages
> By means of marriage.

'Creativity/anthropology'

The new structure to which individual creativity gives rise soon petrifies, however. In Simmel's terms (1971), in gaining independence from their individual creators, structurings of the world congeal into fixed, objectified, generalised, institutionalised cultural forms. And yet, all the while, the creative impulse, the active drive to individuality, goes on. Hence, it is creativity's fate ever to find itself constrained and stultified (at the least threatened by) structure which is inappropriate to its needs – even a structure of its own one-time creation. Notwithstanding, Simmel concludes, this tension between the forms of social life and its creative processes provides the dynamic of cultural history This is something ethnographically evidenced from, for example, England (Rapport 1993) to the Admiralty Islands (Schwartz 1978) to Africa (Fernandez 1978) to Truk (Goodenough 1963).

For Burridge, the very same dynamic pertains to the world and writing of social science (1979: 75). Individual creativity provided the apperceptions which made an anthropological world-view possible, but then routine anthropological analysis has come to fix, objectify, generalise and institutionalise its socio-cultural object: it ever transforms individuals into persons, events into categories, and the continuous vicissitudes of life into a constraining and stultifying, logical and orderly structure (cf. Rapport 1994: 255ff.). Only a new drive to individuality then challenges the ideological appropriateness of this version of social reality – and so the cycle goes on.

For Simmel, the distress and damage caused by fixed structural forms amounts to a 'sociological tragedy' (1980: 36). Burridge, meanwhile, finds relief in a quasi-spiritual certainty that individuals can nonetheless be counted on continually to perceive a 'real truth of things', whether in social life or in social science (1979: 74; cf. Jorgensen 1994: *passim*).[2]

In writing a course for myself between Nietzsche, Simmel and Sartre, between Bateson, Leach, Turner, Burridge, and Fernandez *et al.*, it has seemed that the violence of individual creativity has remained a sub-merged strand in anthropological perspective, drowned out by the demands and rigours of social structure. Maybe this is to be expected. The charisma of creativity will ever be routinised and institutionalised, Weber advised – new cultural forms ever congeal (Simmel); *communitas* ever become normative (Turner) – in the process of it being apperceived and apprehended by others (anthropologists included). Nevertheless, it seems to me that unless we work to keep creativity ever a part of our anthropological world-view, in a dynamic dialectic with structure, then our vision will be not simply impoverished but severely impaired (cf. Riches 1986: 25).

What it comes down to is our anthropological attitude towards structure, what it represents, and how it is to be represented. Social structure, especially in its 'deep' French manifestation (Durkheim, Lévi-Strauss, Godelier), but also its 'conventional' Anglo-Saxon one (Radcliffe-Brown, Fortes, Gellner), has been seen as a more or less *sui generis* mechanism which determines relations between elements of a society – indeed, to an extent determines those elements (their being and behaviours) as well (cf. Park 1974: *passim*). Here are individuals buried under a vast weight of collectivities (cf. Brittan 1973: 171). A Nietzschean/Sartrean (/Simmelian) perspective would correct this through an appreciation of structure as 'discursive idiom' (Jackson 1989: 20). Here, instead, is structure understood as a shared language which forms the basis (the form) of individual interpretation, which articulates, mediates and typifies individual experience, but cannot be taken at face value as encompassing, capturing or determining that experience (cf. Parkin 1987: 66; Rapport 1990: *passim*). Social structure is the form within which individuals create meaning, beneath which flows individual consciousness and beyond which the significant content of individual lives is experienced.

There are two corollaries of this. First, social structure is not *sui generis* and does not exist through inertia, but depends on the continuing, conscious, concerted activity of different individuals to intend, produce and sustain it. Language, for instance, 'is rooted in individual specificity: in the finally irreducible personal lexicons, meanings, ideolects of individual speaker-users' (Steiner 1975: 46; cf. Holy and Stuchlik 1981: 15–16). Second, social structure does not inexorably give rise to homogeneity, stability, consistency or communication. As a discursive idiom, a fiction, it is always subject to creative interpretation, to individual manipulation and re-rendering, to 'alter-cultural action' (Handler and Segal 1990: 87).

The latter phrasing comes from Richard Handler and Daniel Segal's illuminating work on the ethnography of the novelist, Jane Austen, and the social-scientific insights underpinning it. For Austen, we hear, social rules (and the norms and institutions with which they accord) can be seen less to regulate conduct or ensure the reproduction of an established order than to give communicative resource, significance and value to the pragmatics of different individuals' world making, their 'serious play'. Rather than taking the rules of conventional etiquette and propriety literally or normatively, her heroines and their partners treat these structurings as matters for meta-communicative comment and analysis – and thereby displacement – in the construction of an individual and a situational order. In Austen's work, Handler and Segal sum up (1990: 3), it is the 'fiction of culture' which is celebrated, and the creative potential (the capacity and proclivity) of alter-cultural individual world-making: world-making which is not merely intra-paradigmatic (Geertzian) – which plays constructively with extant forms and makes interpretations within a prior cultural framework – but whose re-interpretations 'go meta'. How much more realistic, they ponder, might not an anthropology be which similarly pointed up the enduring human condition to render all social rules ultimately contingent?

Diagnostic

Leach would depict the creative violation of present social structures as 'the very essence of being a human being' (1977: 19). Nietzsche, Sartre, Camus, Bloom, would agree that doing violence to current norms is fundamental to individual creativity; while Woolf describes the violence that the gratuitous act of individual imagination gives onto. What I intend in this final section is to extend the notion of form versus meaning which I have introduced above in order to suggest a way in which this violence and violation might be approached as 'democratic', and differentiated from a type of violence which is, by contrast, 'nihilistic'. My argument will be that while the term 'violence' is commonly associated with the breakdown of civil order and exchange, with the extreme breach of mediums of civility between people (cf. Stanage 1974: 232), nevertheless by distinguishing between the outward *form* of civil exchange and its inward *content*, one can reach a point of accommodation between the violence of universal and ubiquitous individual creativity on the one hand and the civility of social structure on the other.

Social structure, I have argued, is a set of discursive idioms in terms of which individuals meet, for the purpose of expressing, constructing, fulfilling and extending their personal world-views (cf. Rapport 1993: *passim*). Meeting in terms of common, shared, often formulaic behavioural forms (verbal and non-verbal), individuals are able to make meaningful interpretations of their worlds and selves of great personality and diversity. In the days of the Culture and Personality debates in anthropology, Anthony Wallace spoke of 'the organization of diversity' which social structure entailed (1964: *passim*). Hence, Wallace continued, individuals in any one society will not be found 'threaded like beads on a string of common motives'. Rather, they may interact in a stable and mutually rewarding fashion, and organise themselves culturally into orderly, expanding, changing societies in spite of their having radically different interests, habits, values, customs, and despite there being no one cognitive map that members share. Indeed, the 'mazeway' of each individual, the mental map of plans, techniques, people and things, the organised totality of meanings which each maintains at a given time and which is regularly evoked by perceived or remembered stimuli, may be unique. Each individual may possess a complex cognitive system of interrelated objects which amount to a private world, and may rarely if ever achieve 'cognitive communality' or mutual identification with another. What *is* necessary for individuals regularly to engage in routine interactions with one another is mutual predictability: for them to have developed a capacity for mutual prediction whereby the specific behaviour of one is highly likely to eventuate in the specific response of another, and so on. That is, individual A knows that when she perpetrates action a1 then individual B, in all probability, will perpetrate action b1, which will lead to her doing a2, etc. Meanwhile, individual B knows that when he perpetrates action b1, individual A responds with a1, which he follows with b2. In other words, individuals A and B need not concur on when precisely the interaction begins and whose action is perpetrated first – on who acts and who reacts – never mind concurring on the content of their interaction. Rather, Wallace's image of the orderly relationships which constitute stable socio-cultural systems is of what he calls 'equivalence structures' or sets of equivalent behavioural expectancies. Individuals can organise themselves, integrate their behaviours into reliable and joint systems, without developing uniform cognitive maps or possessing equivalent motives but instead by learning that under certain circumstances others' behaviour is predictable, and can be confidently interrelated with actions of their own. And Wallace calls such joint systems, 'contracts': something which individuals establish for the mutual facilitation of their separate strivings and which amount to structured wholes.

What is crucial in the above is expectability. However different and diverse the interpretations of individuals who partake of the contractual relations of exchanging common social forms – however creative and new – so long as each can predict, each can expect, certain behaviours from the other, then the relationship is able to continue, the diversity can continue, the individuality can continue. Expectability means that each is able to continue to find the behaviour of the other understandable, meaningful. Even to the extent that *had each understood the actual meanings of the other*, then they might have felt violated. A 'democratic violence' I would like to describe, then, as one which does not deny or negate the possibility and ability of fellow-interactants to go on interpreting and meaning as they choose, even as the meanings which each construes in the interaction might be found to violate the others'. 'Democratic violence' enables individual creativity to live beneath a deceptive surface of social structural calm and within a form of behavioural norms which individuals continue to share. If the *sine qua non* of the social contract is individuals' possession of mutual expectations which allow them to orient their behaviour to one another in a particular relationship or kind of relationship, then the stability of such expectations is not threatened by a violent diversity of individual interpretations which do not breach the civil surface of the exchange.

A 'nihilistic violence', on the other hand, I would describe as behaviour which deliberately or unintentionally disorientates others in the relationship such that the latter's acts of prediction and interpretation are made impossible. Nihilistic violence breaches the surface of civil exchange, breaks the shared forms of behaviour, such that orientation towards it by others, and their development of stable expectations with regard to it, is prevented (cf. Johnson 1982: 8).

In this depiction, violence per se might be morally neutral, a fact of the individual (creative) interpretation of social exchange (cf. Marx 1976: 110). It is, as Aijmer has introduced it, 'a sort of constant' around which the social is organized (see Introduction). Furthermore, violence need not be tied only to particular behaviours and excepted from others: violence does not correspond to brutality or physicality or the absence of empathy; violence is not precluded by the presence of empathy or the expression of love, for instance, (cf. Rapport 1987: 191–3). Rather, it is violence of a nihilistic kind to which others cannot adapt, behaviour which others cannot expect or predict and find meaningful in some way; only nihilistic violence makes mutual expectation and diversity impossible. For such violence denies the possibility of a civil relationship of mutual predictability and orientability by violating any practicable norms of exchange. This denial may take a variety of forms and degrees. Random sounds, silences and actions will preclude viable interactions of a routine and ongoing kind, and hence deny others the opportunity of making sense, of making meaningful interpretations of the particular exchange. But then maiming or killing will preclude viable interaction and meaningful interpretation henceforward and in general. Hence, a sliding scale of nihilistic violence may be instigated, the severity adjudged in terms of the intended or received injury to others' ability to make sense, to create meaning, at that time and henceforth.

Distinguishing between democratic and nihilistic violence in this way, between a (democratic) violence encompassing diverse individual meanings and a (nihilistic) violence negating common forms of exchange, seems to me a way to alleviate the 'tragedy' of social structure: to accommodate and celebrate individual creativity, while not advocating individual 'instinctual criminality' necessarily be given free expression.

Notes

1. As Leach drew on Camus's 'essential rebellion' (see Camus 1956).
2. Likewise, Marilyn Strathern is stoical, if less dogmatic. For her, the writing of social reality (anthropological and other) can remain innovatory, always polemical, while its true cumulative achievement is 'constantly to build up the conditions from which the world can be apprehended anew' (1990: 19).

3

Ritual, Violence and Social Order: An Approach to Spanish Bullfighting

Alberto Bouroncle

When Emile Durkheim (1912) divided religious phenomena into two fundamental categories – beliefs and rites – he was convinced not only of the close relationship between religion and society, but of the major role played by ritual in the creation of ordered social life. Rituals were considered as occasions in which the ties of identity, belonging and solidarity were reinforced through an elaborated ceremony presented in a dramatized form, in which feelings and emotions were shared. Furthermore, to Durkheim rituals were of crucial importance, not only to create but even to maintain ordered social life by resolving the contradiction of a 'structural pair of opposites' (individuals and society). Through rituals, individuals and society come together by inculcating affective feelings and exercising control due to its promotion of consensus and its psychological and cognitive consequences.

The model of ritual as a means of social control has played an important role in the development of modern theories of ritualization and was to generate the most influential theses related to this notion. Two of these theses approach rituals in its rather 'positive' role by stressing the archetypal character of ritual as a representation of the sacred order of the world and a model for successful social action. The other two analyse ritual from its 'negative' or repressive aspects, focusing on ritual as a mechanism that channels or represses outbursts of asocial violence to avoid any menace to social unity. In the first group, we found Durkheim's thesis of ritual as the sacrament of social solidarity, and the model developed with different methods and results among others by Geertz (1971), Turner (1984), Douglas (1973), Lukes (1974), Bloch (1989) and Bourdieu (1977), of ritual as defining social or cultural reality. In the second group Max Gluckman (1962) and Victor Turner (1969) have developed the thesis of ritual as a means of channelling conflict, while scholars like Girard (1977) and Burkert (1983) have been focusing their studies of ritual as the repression of human violence to allow ordered social life.

Despite the popularity of Durkheim's approach among modern researchers, his model of ritual has been criticized for the excessive importance it attributes to solidarity as the core of ritualized practices. Lukes (1975) points out that the Durkheimian notion of ritual as a place for social integration and consensus is too limited to deal with the complexity and range of political or state rituals. He asserts that collective effervescence does not necessary unite the community, but strengthens the dominant group.

The limits of the thesis of ritual as the definition of social or cultural reality which considers ritual forming ideal relations and structures of values, are marked by the lack of explanation relating to how ritual controls. Ignoring the strategic role of ritual as a means of social control, this approach considers ritual a rather magical mechanism that transforms normal human experiences into the 'super-real'. It shadows the role and importance of the particular types of social negotiation in which rituals are an effective way to define reality.

Although the exponents of the theory of the channelling of conflict address social and structural problems rather than psychological, their general approach contradicts this point of departure and looks at the individual as an entity controlled by social processes. Their concern is to show how ritual integrates the social and the individual: yet they do not seem specially interested in the exercise of power and how rituals force people to coexist in a relation that implies domination and subordination.

The thesis of ritual as repressing psycho-social instincts and needs uses psychoanalytic elements including guilt, desire and the idea of an original sin in the form of a collective murder, stressing the importance of a latent social aggressiveness. It constitutes the base for a theory of ritual sacrifice as the central act of a system generated by primal violence. Thus the ritualized killing of a substitute is itself a substitute of the violence that threats social order. It is hard, however, to accept Girard's theory of violence as being the result of a merely psychological process, independent of culture but generated and created by (culturally created) ritual.

Despite the importance of these approaches to the study of ritual, none of these theoretical models seems to embrace the complexity of the term. One of the main problems seems to be the obsessive search for the ultimate binary opposition, a consequence of the stress put on the role of ritual as a resolving agent in the basic conflict between individuals and society. The emphasis given to the identification of a particular, or a group of, basic oppositions, made them unaware of the role of rituals as a strategy for establishing power relations. That is, an arena for social intercourse with convergence and contradiction among individuals, classes, institutions, foreign elements (among others) in which every change in the balance of power has an effect on ritual.

One of the major critics of the approaches that privileges the study of 'structural opposites' in the analysis of rituals, is Catherine Bell. Bell condemns the tendency, quite common among social anthropologists, to look for just binary oppositions, not only expressed in the opposition between thought and action, but also in other constellations like diachrony and synchrony, or society and individual, on the assumption that ritual serves to unify those poles. She argues that most theories of ritual 'function to resolve an initial bifurcation of thought and action . . .' (Bell 1989: 6).

Bell points out the need to focus on ritual as a practice profoundly dependant of its circumstances, and as such, understood in its appropriate, changing, context. As a mechanism of social control, ritual is not only strategic, but also manipulative and expedient; it constitutes an instance for the negotiation of power relations – inherent to ordered social life. The very fact that in every social group rites are used in different ways and to different degrees, shows the need to specify what type of society or community is likely to depend on this specific form of control and why. It means that only an endless number of pairs (or triads or whatever) of opposites, or allies, may be studied as interacting in ritual through history.

The distinction between power understood as implicit social control and power as explicit acts of political coercion was to generate an opposition between symbolic power (related to ritual and ideology) and secular power (associated with repressive institutions). As a strategy of power, ritualization has specific limits, what it can do and how far it can extend. The psychological mechanisms of ritual are insufficient devices to defend social order from physical menaces, to carry out an offensive manoeuvre[1] or to control outbursts of physical violence directed against the established social order or its members. These limits, inherent to ritual control, made possible certain forms of intercourse between the spheres of symbolic and secular power in order to control society. Rituals may inspire or direct physical or political actions but they do not constitute physical or political actions. Of course ritual could eventually prevent, channel or even repress some cases of asocial violence, but to preserve ordered social life it is necessary to count on a secular power consecrated to exercise social violence to maintain social control. Thus the right of the secular power to exercise social violence has to be justified by the force of symbolic power by sharing a *Weltanschaung*, sanctioned by some kind of ritual consensus and ruled by a code. In other words, social violence may have a ritual counterpart, in which the participants not only negotiate and confirm their legitimacy and status, but express their ideology and reflect the balance of power in a certain historical context in a given society. Although scholars and participants seem to recognize symbolic and secular power as different entities, the relationship appears unclear and the study of Iberian bullfighting will provide material to discuss the viability of such a differentiation.

Among the scholars interested in ritualization as a means of social control but who did not feel obliged to search for structural pairs of opposites, we find Arthur Hocart and Georges Dumézil. Studying royal kingship in Melanesia, Hocart (1971) was to pay attention to the relationship between rites and myths as ideological representations that justify not only the social structure but the exercise of violence within society. He points out the importance of sacrificial rituals in Fiji not only as recreating the order of the world but confirming the role of the military chief as defender of this 'sacred' order. Georges Dumézil (1968), on the other hand, analyses myths and epic literature, showing the presence of an Indo-European scheme of three functions that relate the ways in which old rituals consecrate the military, cast in its role as creator and defender of society. This epic mythology was transformed over time into history to strengthen the symbolic power of the guardians of social order.

In this attempt to put into profile the role of bullfighting in Spain, the stress will be given to the strategic and symbolic character of the *fiesta* to achieve the creation of a new social order. By presenting and discussing the origins and symbology of bullfighting as national ritual, the historical circumstances of its adoption, the changes introduced in its practice, its relationship with the different social actors and its role as arena of specific power negotiation, this article will try to understand the outstanding role of bullfighting in the unification, pacification and establishment of social order in Spain.

The Origins: From Rural Capeas to Chivalric Bullfighting

During the twentieth century most specialists have considered bullfighting a ritual more or less related to the notion of an archaic, bull-related cult extended in time and space throughout the Iberian peninsula. Cossio (1945) stresses the particular success of the *bos taurus* species in its multiplication throughout the Iberian peninsula. He believes that it must have been the Arabs who spread this race across northern Africa and Spain. These animals, selected in Egypt for their bravery, may have come together with the merino sheep and exploited in half-savage fashion in southern and central Spain.[2] The fame and bravery of these bulls was so widespread that Greek mythology tells us how Hercules had to steal cattle from what is now the province of Cadiz.[3] If, in addition, we consider the representation of bulls found in the caves of Altamira, the notion of bullfighting as the ancient liturgy of a bull-related religion has not only been appealing, but convincing. Furthermore, the documented presence of the bull as a powerful symbol throughout Spanish history, and the regularity of bull-related rituals, well-established in the Catholic calendar, suggests a long process of syncretism which would run from the 'sacred' drawings of Altamira to the bull considered as the unequivocal symbol of a modern European country.[4]

Despite the arguments that consider bullfighting as the result of the development of an ancient and sacred ritual with the bull as its central figure, there is no evidence to connect the modern spectacle of bullfighting with the cult of a bull-related divinity. An enormous stretch of time, the lack of documented links, and a number of unanswered questions separate the Palaeolithic cave paintings of Altamira, the bull-related spectacles of Roman dominated *Hispania* and the modern spectacle of bullfighting. Mitchell (1991) rejects the arguments that sustain the Roman origins of bullfighting, pointing out the archaeological discoveries in Soria that show an important number of knives, axes and bullhorns dated to one hundred years before the arrival of the Romans (300 BC). Even if in Roman times bull cults from Hispania evolved to become the worship of Bacchus or Dionysus, these animals did not seem to be as representative of the country as they appear to be now. The bulls were, of course, part of the well-organized institution of the Roman circus and certainly used in public spectacles together with lions, tigers, leopards, stags, boars, bears, elephants and even hippopotami, as well as human gladiators and convicts fighting each other or against hungry beasts.

During the sixteenth and seventeenth centuries, many Spanish theologians, most of them converted Jews, opposed the celebration of bullfights, arguing that these were directly descended from pagan Rome. However, these arguments reflect more the political confrontation within the Spanish Church than historical fact. The evidence presented by Cossio (1951) shows, on the contrary, that the predecessor of modern bullfighting, that is bullfighting on horseback practised by the aristocracy, was a derivation of the ancient capeas, practised in small villages, away from the Roman arenas. Nicolàs Fernández de Moratín (1777) also denies the Roman origins of bullfighting. He argues that bullfighting started as a demonstration of skills and bravery practised in Spain since the eleventh century, and that such practices were of Arab origin.

Although mentioned in a number of mediaeval texts as *correr los toros*, the *capea*, considered as a fertility ritual, was practised far away from the aristocratic courts and its celebration is not particularly rich in historical documentation. As Mitchell asserts: 'Although *capeas* have been going on in Spain for longer than anyone can remember, it is not to the historians that we can look for information about them' (Mitchell 1991: 27).

Different from *encierros*, which are the running of bulls through the town streets, as at the famous 'San Fermin' in Pamplona, a *capea* still takes place in any enclosed place of a given town or village. Unlike the official bullfighting, ruled by the Ministry of Interior, a *capea* does not present strict limits of time, neither a team of specialists to execute the ritual. Furthermore, in these popular *fiestas* almost any *suerte* or technique is possible, from dragging the bull with a rope, fixing rockets or torches to his horns or blowing darts at the beast. Most of all, what gives *capeas* their special appeal, is the crowd and its composition. In such ritual celebrations, local personalities, surrounded by people of all conditions, confirm their identity. Patronising the *fiestas* and watching them from honoured places, the town's elite found in these celebrations a perfect opportunity to enhance their status.

What makes this old tradition different from modern bullfighting is in essence that in a *capea* everyone is a potential actor in a drama in which the bull is always the protagonist. The well-defined role of the bullfighter and his quadrille as ritual executers of the National Feast, do not have an equivalent in *capeas*. In these popular celebrations men or women, many times encouraged by the effects of alcoholic drinks, may play a central role. However, both *capeas* and official bullfighting fill a role as a stage for social recognition that provides a showcase for popular concepts of honour and valour. Furthermore, the danger implicit in the celebration of these rituals may cause serious injury and even the sudden death of its participants.[5]

The Spanish scholar Angel Alvarez de Miranda (1962) analyses a number of Spanish tales that give account of the efficacy of the bull to cure female infertility. Alvarez found connections between this kind of tales and certain rituals or *capeas* that used the bull as a symbol of extreme sexual power.[6] Probably the most important of these rituals is the so-called '*Toro de Bodas*' (Wedding Bull), a ritual celebration that called for the bride and groom to force darts into a bull that their friends had tied to a rope. The apparent meaning of this ritual would be the evocation of the sexual power of the bull, spilling his blood ritually. The couple stain their clothes and their bed sheets with the bull's blood, appropriating the sexual strength of the animal. To Alvarez, the custom of the 'Wedding Bull' was transformed gradually into a form of gallant knightly tournament reserved to the aristocracy.

Another Spanish scholar, Manuel Delgado Ruiz (1986), has also paid attention to *capeas*. He builds his theory on the arguments of Alvarez, giving weddings and especially the nuptial night a central role in the symbology of bullfighting. To Delgado, what happens in a wedding night with a groom is the same thing that happens to a bull in a *corrida*. He becomes a victim of his libido, and as he consummates his marriage is symbolically castrated, domesticated and absorbed by the 'matriarchal community'. The bull as symbol of wild masculinity must be neutralized so that social order will be maintained.

In more recent years, Timothy Mitchell (1988, 1991) has approached Spanish rituals and bullfighting in particular. Concerned with the range and popularity of Spain's violent rituals, Mitchell stresses the ingredient of strong emotion as the core of Spanish popular celebrations. He points out the character of the *fiesta* as an event directed to provoke communal ecstasy through some kind of rupture with the normal world. In cultures that have not been contaminated by 'modern' ideas, the expression of this ecstasy will tend to be less inhibited in order to channel the largest amount of violent rupture latent in society. To Mitchell the 'problem of order' is assumed by traditional rituals through channelling aggression into deviance-punishing systems of ritualized collective violence.

The arguments of Alvarez de Miranda give enormous importance to the play element in the development of bullfighting, alleging that people simply forgot the power of fecundity in this ritual. However, his argument about the 'wedding bull' being transformed into a violent ritual as well as a stage for gallant love and matrimonial arrangements is of importance, as it indicates the role of bullfighting as an arena of negotiation and cultural modelling of the world.

Following Alvarez de Miranda, Delgado points to the sexual connotations of bullfighting. Delgado stresses the role of ritual as a socialising agent directed towards dangerous sexuality (and asocial aggressiveness) in young males in a society ideologically controlled by women. Besides this somewhat dubious characterization of Spanish society, the problem with this approach is that it concentrates on just one aspect of bullfighting, as a ritual that inculcates community norms. Delgado ignores the mechanism by which ritual deals with particular types of power negotiation that generate relations of domination and subordination. Furthermore, Delgado's hypothesis dismisses the generally accepted view of the Spanish family – implying the father as the dominant figure and men as the dominant sex.

The limits of Mitchell's approach, on the other hand, are related to the use of René Girard's concept of *violence originelle*, that stresses the repressive role of ritual to channel the asocial instincts produced by an 'original' collective guilt. In this perspective violence is the result of a purely psychological process that, paradoxically, is generated and controlled by a cultural creation: ritual.

In the Spanish case I will concentrate on the process that consolidated bullfighting into the Spanish national ritual during the second half of the war of *Reconquista* (roughly from the incitement represented by the Arab dominion and the arrival of the millennium, until the era of the Catholic Kings). This process transformed an old fertility rite in which the bull was rarely killed, into a *fiesta* in which the knights turned the bull into an antagonist. When in their reconstruction they changed rite into fight, these cavaliers needed a dramatic victory (the killing of the bull) as an epilogue.

As a ritual identified with the dominant elite, bullfighting will require an analysis in terms of a mode of action that does not have a direct effect on persons, as punishment or raw violence does, but indirectly by structuring the possible field of action of the participating individuals. Ritual will also be considered as the symbolic place in which this dominant elite negotiates the relations of power and the exercise of social violence. Thus, when analysing the ritual of the brave bull, it will be considered as different from physical determination, rather as an arena for particular types of power negotiations exercised over free subjects with the potential for struggle or confrontation within the limits of the ideology. The idea is to clarify the role of rituals as especially effective ways of acting. It may explain how the production of ritualized agents is a strategy for the construction of particular relations of power effective in particular social situations.[7]

The Adoption of Bullfighting and the Creation of a New Social Order

In the year 711 AD Don Rodrigo, the last Visigothic sovereign of Spain, was defeated by the Arabic army of Tarik, who crossed the straits of Gibraltar and within five years had conquered the whole peninsula, except for a few barren mountains in the north. In 753 the Umaiyad, Abd al-Rahman, arrived in Spain to create and unify the Cordoban monarchy, whose northern frontier ran from the Ebrus to the Tagus and from Coimbra to Pamplona. Arabic Spain, first dominated by Damascus, was under the lead of Abderraman I declared an independent Emirate. In 929 a descendant, Abderraman III, converted the domain into the Caliphate of Cordoba.

Many historians have sustained that close contact between the peoples of the Iberian peninsula had led to a mutual tolerance among the three main communities of Christian, Jews and Moors. According to this version of the *convivencia*, dissident minorities were tolerated within the territories of each community, to a degree that makes it possible to consider racial or religious divisions irrelevant.[8] However, there is a difference between the practice of tolerance and the principle of toleration. Obviously this ethnic coexistence had its basis in the political and military balance maintained by the three communities. When this balance was upset by the outstanding Christian advances that followed the defeat of the Moors at Las Navas de Tolosa, the social structure that supported the *convivencia* began to fall apart.

Although a number of scholars that support the idea of a peaceful and harmonious *convivencia* have argued that the notion of 'crusade' was largely absent from the early periods of the *Reconquista*, it is difficult to obviate the role played by religion in the fight for the Reconquest of the peninsula. After the fall of the Roman empire in the fifth century AD, Christian Spain as well as the rest of western Europe had entered a dark age of economic decline and instability that lasted until the arrival of the first millennium and the revival of the eleventh and twelfth centuries. The greater prosperity based on agriculture and trade and the trinity of politics, economics and religion was to be reflected not only in the great religious buildings of the age – churches, cathedrals and monasteries – but also in the spirit of Christendom. The impulse of the crusades, considered not only as military expeditions but also as pilgrimages, like the German groups during the *Völkerwanderungen*, constituted a movement of people searching for new lands to inhabit. The expression of this revival in Spain is marked by the sudden popularity of the cult and pilgrimage to 'Santiago Matamoros' (Saint James the Moor Slayer) in Compostela. The Jacobean myth worked as a dynamic factor in Spanish life in the middle ages and was a decisive factor in the remarkable success in the war of Reconquest, the product of a new political, economic and religious alliance, based on the ideology of 'full blood'.[9] Such was the impact of Santiago that Anwar Chejne (1987) considers that the role of Santiago in the Iberian peninsula was similar to the one fulfilled by Mohammed in the Islamic world.

It is in this context that bullfighting emerges to constitute a main symbol of these men consecrated to warfare in the name of Christendom. The spearheads of the Spanish crusaders, formed basically by the knights of the military orders, the brotherhoods and the Church, were not only the vanguard of the Reconquest but, because of the ambiguous character of this religious-military organization (oriented towards religious, military and civil ends), they worked as active peacemakers, becoming an armed aristocracy vested with the privilege of the use of social violence. The adoption of bullfighting during the Reconquest by the men carrying the responsibility to attain social order, may have served to negotiate their particular power relations and to inculcate among the participants the values and ideology behind it.

This chapter will analyse the remarkable position of Spanish bullfighting as the result of a socio-historical process in which the ritualized and public fight of the brave bull constituted not only the symbolical manifestation of a political force, but became an important vehicle in the establishment of a new social order. This new order was the product of an emergent society controlled by the alliance of the Crown, the Church and the aristocracy combined, and in warfare against 700 years of Moorish dominion in the peninsula. The *Reconquista* (Reconquest) was to culminate in 1492 with the siege of Granada and the definitive expulsion of Moorish civilization from the Iberian peninsula. Despite the success of the campaign, the inherent fragility of the new alliance was evident. The vulnerability of this partnership, a product of its heterogeneous character and the challenges posed by ethnic conflict, religious intolerance and an extremely unequal distribution of wealth, may have helped the rise of a ritual that symbolizes and glorifies the values and goals of the new political coalition. Thus through the symbolical power of bullfighting, the alliance was able to unify the dispersed kingdoms of *Iberia* under the 'ideology of full blood' and create the basis for a new social order in a process that reached its peak during the age of the Catholic monarchs, expelling the last bastion of Muslim Spain and opening up the era of Spanish hegemony.

Although it remains impossible to demonstrate the existence of a premeditated plan oriented towards the creation of a national ritual, the analyse of the process of appropriation and the following changes introduced in the traditional practice of fighting the brave bull, suggest the outstanding part of bullfighting in the construction, pacification and establishment of social order in modern Spain.

Full Blood

A brief review of the history of Spain since the first efforts to recuperate the peninsula from the Moors[10] shows the initial fragility of Spain's national structure; this is well reflected in the constant changes in the balance of power and the lack of success in unifying its national strategy. Thus when the demographic pressure on the independent kingdoms demanded migration towards the south, without a unifying force that could challenge the Moorish dominion, the irruption of the cult of Santiago and the adoption of bullfighting may have helped to create the conditions for the new alliance. This initial period of instability and chaos was partially given order by the alliance of the Castilian monarchs, the Catholic Church and the Christian nobility in the thirteenth century. One of the main ideological arguments to strengthen this alliance was the concept of 'purity of blood' or 'full blood'. According to this notion only Old Christian Spaniards were qualified to live and enjoy all the privileges of the Spanish nation, and the measures to ensure this new ideal of life were obviously directed against the remaining communities of Arabs and Jews that constituted an important part of the Spanish population. The fact that the ideology of 'full blood' became so appealing among Spaniards may be explained by the absence of a feudal system that was creating enormous differences among the citizens in other parts of Europe. It made possible the relative ideological equality between the nobles and the members of the lower classes, all of them defined as Old Christians. The need of soldiers to fight the crusade against the Moors increased the sense of relative equality among all 'real' Spaniards.

The new alliance proved to be a successful one, as was shown in the council of Lyon assembled in 1274, where the kingdoms of Castile, Aragon and Portugal, the most important states of Iberia, could look back on a recent history of crusades that stood in sharp contrast to the run of disasters that their contemporaries had experienced in the Holy Land and Romania.[11]

The chain of success in the war of Reconquest has made of the military vocation not only an attractive career open to anybody, but an outstanding mechanism for ambitious people to scale in the social hierarchy. However, this military success also generated a new attitude that began to put into profile the differences (among Old Christians) between nobles and plebeians, fighting side by side but separated by privileges that included the practice of bullfighting. Thus at the end of the thirteenth century the military orders and some armed brotherhoods stipulated that any candidate to become a knight, and as an extension to fight brave bulls, had to demonstrate all four grandparents to have been of noble birth. These restrictions, inherent to the practice of bullfighting, that assigned to the plebeians the role of assistants, may be considered as an attempt to structure the field of action of Spanish society. Thereby the relative openness of the Spanish army and its role providing a door of access to the Spanish hierarchy was broken: one had to be noble, not only to be a knight, but to fight bulls. As a result of this strategy, the military nobility of more recent origin, a consequence of the favours of Henry de Trasta-mara, emerged as a model for successful social action and their rapid accumulation of revenues and seigniories were to make them arbiters of the Castilian political situation in the fifteenth century.

The creation of Spain as a result of the union of the Crowns of Castile and Aragon in 1469 implied an attempt to reduce the power and influence of the aristocracy. In 1480 at the *Cortes* or parliament of the realm, held in Toledo, earlier conceded grants to noble families without sufficient cause were revoked. These economic measures, together with the razing of castles and the development of the armed brotherhoods to protect the population against the power of the aristocrats, were to provoke political confrontations. But these economic measures never achieved the intended decrease in the social and economic power of the aristocracy. The Cortes of Toledo certainly ordered the return of grants made since 1464, but all grants made before 1454 were explicitly confirmed; this meant that all the sources for the most important profits made by the Castilian nobility were left untouched. In fact the Catholic Kings seem to have been more concerned with pacification than with reformation, and this attempt to compromise inevitably led to an implicit agreement between the Crown and the aristocracy. This process followed the general trend in western Europe, where the rise of new monarchies was based on agreements with the feudal nobility in a stand against the urban middle classes. The results of this policy in Spain are of direct concern here, because these were events in which the crusader ideology incarnated in the military orders, the armed brotherhoods and the aristocracy led to the rise of the Spanish Inquisition and the definitive appropriation and re-shaping of the *capeas* to become the national ritual of bullfighting.

After the tacit agreement between the Crown and the aristocracy, the Crown lost its role as arbiter among the different communities of the nation, identifying itself with the one class that was considered essential to its own existence. The particularity of this new situation was that the ideas of the nobility were not confined to them as a class, but permeated all of the Spanish society. The peculiar structure of Castile, in which institutional feudalism had never taken root, partly because of the demands made on society by the constant struggles against the Moors, resulted in the complete absence of a servile peasant class. So even though noble and peasant were at opposite ends of the social ladder, each was as free from feudal obligation as the other. Particularly after the elimination of the more dynamic section of the urban middle class, the Jews, there remained little to separate a lord from his peasant. Henry Kamen (1983) suggests that the apparent familiarity between classes, and a theoretically open social mobility, may explain that the lower classes came to accept the ideals of their 'betters', the practice of chivalry, and the idea of honour which sprang from this. Nevertheless, in a society in which it was theoretically possible to move up and down the hierarchy without any stigma being attached to oneself, new forms of social control were applied to maintain the privileges of the noble minority. Thus due to the practice of chivalric bullfighting, popular at all levels of society, the privileged class of noble warriors on horseback not only expanded its violent ideology in times of warfare, but because of the restriction in its practice, bullfighting was able to create a symbolic representation of the ideal constitution of Spain, with the brave knights at the peak of the structure. The enormous popularity of bullfighting may have been decisive in the fact that the ideology and practices of the aristocrats found a ready home in the imagination of the Spanish peasants and labouring men.

One of the most important consequences of this military way to scale the hierarchy and become wealthy was the growing disdain for manual labour as a result of an unfortunate yearning for nobility.[12] The concept of honour bred a reactionary anti-capitalist and anti-labour outlook which even if it was certainly not peculiar to Spain alone, attained an influence equalled nowhere else. By and large the lower classes identified themselves with the 'crusading' spirit of the nobility. They too were heirs of the Reconquest, they too had been Christians before the entry of the new Jewish and Moorish converts into the faith. As Cervantes put it, through Sancho Panza: 'I am an Old Christian, and to become an earl that is sufficient' to which Don Quixote answers: 'and more than sufficient'. Thus bullfighting, by structuring the choreography of action of the individuals, not only blocked the path for peasants to the highest ranks of the hierarchy by excluding them from the role of bullfighters, it also confronted them with the minorities like the converts, by raising the distinction between Old and New Christians.

The first great measure of 'self-defence' raised by the old Christians against *conversos* was to exclude them from any participation in public administration after the disturbances at Toledo in 1449, in which they were accused of celebrating certain secret Jewish rituals, and were attacked by the mobs. It was resolved that no convert of Jewish descent might have or hold any office or benefice in the said city of Toledo, or in its territory or jurisdiction, and that the testimony of converts against Old Christians was not to be accepted in the courts. Besides a prohibition against the practice of their traditional professions as attorneys, landlords, pharmacists, physicians, surgeons or slaughtermen. The *conversos* were also prohibited to wear gold, silver, coral, pearls, or any precious stone.

They were not allowed to ride horses or possess weapons, both necessary elements for someone aspiring to become noble — and to practise bullfighting.

Despite the number of measures against heretics introduced during the first years of the Inquisition, the general social level of the converts remained unchanged and many of them were able to claim upwards into the higher ranks of the ruling classes. The paradoxical persistence of *conversos* in Spanish life may be attributed firstly to the tendency of the Habsburgs to chose as their closer advisers men who were not of the old aristocracy and, secondly, because of a long tradition that made *converso* families very generous to give their sons and daughters to the Church, to be brought up in the religious orders. By the mid-sixteenth century it was reliably reported that a majority, if not all, of the Spanish clergy resident in Rome seeking ecclesiastical preferment, was of Jewish origin. Thus the *conversos* still had a powerful voice in Rome from which they tried to defend themselves by attacking the ritual of the Spanish knights, the fighting of the brave bull. To them bullfighting was a spectacle directly descendant of pagan rituals practised in Roman times. Pope Nicholas V, under the title *Humani generis inimicus*, denounced the idea of excluding Christians from office, simply because they belonged to a particular race. But the prohibitions against the converts represented powerful forces, which could not easily be suppressed.[13]

The Military Orders and Bullfighting

The process of appropriation of the traditional bull-related rituals known as *capeas* was a phenomenon closely related with the war of Reconquest, a crusade against Moorish hegemony in the Iberian peninsula. In this context, one mediaeval institution played a core role in the spectacular success with which Christian Spaniards were able to defeat a powerful enemy: the institution of the military orders.

The thought of Christians devoting their lives to warfare in the service of God may seem a paradox. Nevertheless, in mediaeval times there were men consecrated to battle; these men were known as the brother knights of the Military Orders, noblemen vowed to poverty, chastity and obedience, who lived a monastic life in convents which at the same time were barracks waging merciless war on enemies of the Roman Church. In the Spanish case, as in many others, it also became a way to climb in the social hierarchy.

The three original and greatest Military Orders were considered to be the Templars, the Knights of St John and the Teutonic Knights, but there were scores of less well known associations of monk-warriors. These orders were created in the twelfth century to tame a brutal warrior nobility by establishing a body of knights obedient to the Church to counterweight the power of the lords and to provide the Roman Church with storm-troopers to 'eradicate pagan slavery' and to defend the Holy Land. Desmond Seward points out the efforts of St Bernard of Clairvaux who '... took over the new templar concept of soldiers under religious vows and synthesized knight with monk, producing a strange vocation which unconsciously substituted Christ for Wodan, Paradise for Valhalla. Again the syncretic genius of Catholicism harnessed a pagan hero-cult just as once it had metamorphosed gods into saints and converted temples into churches – transforming the ideal into a spiritual calling whose followers sacrificed their lives for Christ not only in the monastery but in the battlefield ... while retaining much of the Germanic war-band, by adapting the monastic organization they became the first properly staffed and officered armies since the Roman legions.' (Seward 1972: 4).

In Spain the brethren of Calatrava, Alcantara and Santiago constituted the spearhead of the Reconquest, consolidating the Christian advances by destroying the Muslim civilization of Cordoba and Granada. On the vast and lonely plateau where no peasant dared settle for fear of Moorish raiders, the monkish frontiersmen ranched herds of cattle and sheep, a practice that later on would expand to the new world in the form of the *haciendas*. The chief Iberian orders had been founded in the late twelfth as a means of providing assistance for the hard pressed urban militia, based in the organization of the brotherhoods in the cities. Following the Benedictine rule[14] they formed the living Christian frontier holding the Guadiana basin against the Almohad threat: the orders of Calatrava, Santiago, Alcantara and Montesa. Such was the warlike spirit of those military orders, that the brotherhood of Santiago chose the ferocious motto *Ruber ensis sanguine arabum* (may the sword be red with Arab blood).

Since their apparition in the war of Reconquest, the military orders had proven more useful in garrisoning strongholds and resettling border areas than in providing troops for the Christian field armies. This was to encourage the Castilian monarchy to grant them enormous estates in La Mancha and Extremadura, as well in parts of Andalusia and Murcia, regions largely known for their tradition in the celebration of bullfights. High officers of the military orders were magnates who dominated small villages or towns and who promoted their relatives into positions of power and prestige. A master was able to bring massive patronage to his entourage, including lordships and lucrative posts. As military chiefs the masters of the orders were used by their relatives and sponsors to win favours by granting benefices, intimidate their enemies with their soldiers, and in general give them unlimited opportunities for advancement.

The knights of the military orders cultivated their estates with *mudejar* slaves, but also exploited the barren *mesetas* in true Cistercian style. Both the nature of the terrain and the relatively few settlers who had come from the north, encouraged the orders to develop the pasturage potential of their new lands. They actually owned and used some of the best pastures for ranching cattle, horses, goats, pigs and sheep, all in a semi-domesticated fashion, driving them into the high sierras during the summer. The master of the order of Santiago was *ex-officio* treasurer of the Mesta, a confederation of sheep ranchers which constituted the richest and more powerful corporation in mediaeval Spain. At the decline of the military orders, Spanish landowners, the heirs of these knights, were to develop the model created by their ancestors, the *hacienda*.

Despite their enormous services to the Reconquest of the Peninsula and their support to the Crown, the Castilian monarchy was well aware of the dangers of making these very large grants to the aristocrats, especially to those related to the three more important military orders – Santiago, Calatrava and Alcantara. Thus the Crown was to take steps to control and stop them from abusing their power. One of the sovereigns who made efforts to limit the power of the military orders was Alfonso X. With royal protection he supported the various arrangements that secured the Castilian towns the right to the seasonal migration of their flocks to the grasslands of La Mancha and Extremadura, controlled by the military orders. This constituted a clear answer to the attempts of the military orders to prevent northerners sharing their winter grasslands, the landscape in which the brave bull was being raised in a semi-wild fashion.

One of the most formidable results of the presence of the orders on the borderline between Christian and Muslim Spain during almost three centuries, was the generation of a new kind of epic. The popularity of the so called *Romances Fronterizos* (Romances of the Frontier), which depicted the border with Granada as a theatre of chivalric holy war, was to generate a connection between the crusade and the enforcement, not only of religious orthodoxy, but of the ideology of full blood. This ideology was made manifest by the militant Christian warriors, who helped to establish not only physical, but cultural, aesthetic, religious and ideological borders.

The characterization of frontier life during the long process of Reconquest, and especially during the second half of the fourteenth century, remains a matter for discussion. Professor Angus MacKay (1977) has emphasized the role played by the life on the frontier in the process of acculturation, noticeable in the acquisition of new military techniques taken from the enemy. The frontier settlers on both sides adopted similar tactics of rapid raiding, executed by a lightly armed and highly mobile cavalry – a model that reappears in bullfighting on horse-back – against whom defensive systems of scouts, warning beacons and widely scattered fortified places were employed. MacKay has also pointed to the existence of peace-keeping mechanisms: the magistrates (*alcaldes* among Christians and Moors), and expert scouts (*rastreros*) who dealt with frontier incidents or complaints. This picture of life in the Spanish-Moorish borderlands is not acceptable for all Hispanists; Professor C.J. Bishco (1990) has highlighted the important role of the frontier towns, whereas the aristocracy and the military orders were deadlocked, waging an intermittent 'private war'. To Bishco, by painting this warfare in the colours of the chivalric mores, replete with splendour and courtesy, the authors of the *Romances Fronterizos* mythologized a situation in which frontier hostilities had the effect of restricting the agricultural economy in much of Andalusia and Murcia, making the impact of famine and plague here more severely felt than anywhere else in the peninsula. In addition, the borderline remained, as during the best part of the Reconquest, a place where obscure members of the lesser nobility were able to achieve wealth and renown by fighting Moors and bulls.

As a Sort of Conclusion

It has been suggested that the revival of crusading enthusiasm in fifteenth century Castile represented the spread northwards of border habits, attitudes and the accompanying ideology, through the popularity of the Romances of the Frontier. This chapter suggests, to the contrary, that it was through the practice of the violent and mortal ritual of chivalric bullfighting that the aggressive ideology of the Old Christians became the basis for the creation of Spain. The ritualized fight of the knight and the brave bull turned into the representation of a new social structure that needed to be expressed in violent contrast with the values of former (or foreign) cultures and ideologies.

As it was mentioned, the Christian knights possessed huge pastures where the brave bulls were bred. They dominated the military tactics of light armoured cavalry, so influential in the display of chivalric bullfight. But, and this is most important, in the pauses between battles and religious duties, the Spanish crusaders were engaged in chivalric games with such devotion that it conquered not only the hearts of kings and plebeians, but also the hearts of the authors of the early Spanish epic tradition. Thus, this chivalric joust became the symbolic embodiment of the ideology of the frontiersmen, based on the principles of the Old Christian warrior.

The role of the military class in the creation of Spain is outstanding. They constituted not only the spearhead of the movement that expelled the Moors from the Iberian peninsula, but were able to create an ideology that has survived centuries of political and social convulsion. The secrets of their success are many, but one of them may be found in the appropriation by the armed aristocracy of an ancient ritual of fertility turned into the knightly – and deadly – practice of bullfighting on horse back. The explanation of the stunning ascent of bullfighting from a local celebration to a national symbol seems to lie in the enormous popularity it enjoyed at all levels of the hierarchy and in the dramatic effect of the killing of the bull – or the death of the bullfighter – on the minds of the participants. The violent framework in which the symbolic negotiation of power took place allowed bullfighting to become the expression of the right order, creating a moral world in which the followers were recompensed and transgressors relegated. Thus, bullfighting became the point of reference for successful social action.

Incarnating the military ideology of full blood, bullfighting served not only as a showcase for the dominant aristocracy, it also defined the roles so assigned to other social actors through particular types of social negotiation. Thus this violent celebration turned into a specific form of articulation of political authority; the arena for bullfighting was also an arena for the negotiation of power. Despite the outstanding role of the military aristocracy in the development of bullfighting, the National Feast was to survive the class that adopted it. Of course, bullfighting did not remain static in that process and a number of changes, the products of specific power negotiations, were continuously introduced in the celebration of the *fiesta*, in later years celebrated by *matadores* on foot. However, the presence of death, introduced by the military orders, appears as one of the key factors in the effectiveness of this ritual, suggesting that violent rituals could be more efficient in the exercise of control, just because of the dramatic culturally loaded effect achieved by the presence of blood and death.

In this particular attempt at deconstructing ritualized violence, it is possible to recognize the organizational force of bullfighting. By creating a symbolic world based in the aggressive ideology of 'full blood', the National Feast not only supplied a meaning to the exercise of power but furthermore demonstrated the essence of successful social and political action. As the result of a process of symbolic negotiation in which different factors and actors contributed to the creation and maintenance of a nation in which violence supported political unity and social continuity, bullfighting incarnates the double nature of violence as a destructive and constructive power in society.

Despite the constant changes in public bullfighting which have occurred for almost a millennium, the passion for the *fiesta* is very much alive in Spain. So it seemed to have been the case until recently with the complex of the aggressive ideology of full blood and its linked idea of the exclusiveness of Spain that survived up to our times, provoking enormous and dramatic consequences. Thus, the ambiguous role of violence in the creation of ordered social life is expressed in the National Feast, where the apparently useless and violent fight and killing of the brave bull appears to be a decisive factor in the consolidation and unification of a heterogeneous country. On the other hand, because of the reactionary ideology it represents, it has helped to perpetuate the idea of 'two Spains' in conflict, which is said to have characterized Spanish history ever since the retreat of the Moors.

Notes

1. Despite Bloch's (1992) argument on the fact that ritual 'so easily furnishes an idiom of expansionist violence . . .' some kind of military organization will be required to achieve its realization.
2. Cossio considers the *bos taurus* as related to half-wild bulls found in different places throughout Europe, like Scotland and Switzerland, where they were used to fight against one another. This race was probably developed in Egypt just to celebrate spectacles that involved fighting bulls.
3. Julio Caro Baroja (1981) mentions Diodoros' account concerning the fact that the descendants of the cattle that Hercules stole from the Tartesic king Gerion were considered sacred animals.
4. In 1994, the Socialist government was obliged under massive protests to declare as 'National Patrimony' the enormous silhouettes that represent the brave bull, used to advertise a well-known brand of sherry. These gigantic bulls are placed along motor roads all around the country. A new law which prohibited advertisements along motor roads was jeopardising their future.
5. Between 1786 and 1962, at least 153 young aspirants – that is people

involved with regulated bullfighting – died of wounds inflicted by bulls; this number does not include incidents which occurred during the performances of *capeas*, nor the accidents which occurred among the spectators.

6. The castration of the majority of the domesticated bulls puts into profile the sexual power of the brave bull.

7. The idea of *capeas* and regulated bullfighting as creating a moral world is reinforced by the figures compiled by Pérez Díaz (1974) for the beginning of this century. He found that the number of illegitimate births in regions with traditional bullfighting (The Basque country, Catalunya and both Castiles) was much lower than in regions without such *fiestas* (Galicia and the Canary Islands).

8. According to Sánchez Albornoz (1977), the assumed harmony between northern Spain and Muslim Spain never really existed.

9. The 'body' of St James had been discovered in Galicia and, as Santiago Matamoros, he had come down from Heaven to lead the faithful – his shrine at Compostella became the greatest pilgrim centre in Western Europe and his war a crusade long before the Franks marched on Jerusalem.

10. The reconquest of Spain lasted for eight hundred years. By the eleventh century, five Christian kingdoms had appeared: Galicia (together with Portugal), Leon, Castile, Navarra and Aragon.

11. The fourth crusade (1202–04), originally intended as an attack on Egypt, ended with a massacre in Constantinople, the fifth (1217–21) passed through Egypt and Syria without results, the sixth crusade (1228–9) obtained the peaceful cession of Jerusalem – lost definitely in 1244 – and the seventh crusade (1248–54) led by Louis IX of France, proceeded to Egypt, where the king was taken prisoner and forced to return to the city of Damieta and kept for ransom.

12. As in Dumézil's tri-functional scheme, we find in Spain an alliance of military functions and the holy monarchy directed against the class of producers. The fact that most of the poor farmers were involved in military action made Jews and Moors the obvious target in the process of achieving absolute control over the country.

13. It is interesting to consider the fact that Catholic Mass was never considered to be a ritual by which the alliance of Crown, Church and aristocracy found it possible to negotiate power or to impose their ideology. Many reasons for this could be suggested, such as the international character of the Catholic Church, or the division within the Spanish Church between Old and New Christians. On the other hand, the fact that a weakened papacy was transferred to Avignon,

leading to the Great Schism (1378–1417), provided another reason for a confrontation between aristocracy and Crown.

14. The Benedictine rule, written by Benedict of Nursia in the 530s – a relatively short document of 73 chapters – formed the basis of Christian monastic organization. The primitive rigour of the rule was re-established in the eleventh century under the influence of St Bernard and the Cistercian order.

−4−

Restoring the Balance
Violence and Culture among the
Suri of Southern Ethiopia
Jon Abbink

'This country is spoiled now . . . there is nothing to be said anymore.
Suffering, we will perish; this country has become dark.'

(Last 1995: 153)

Violence as a Problem

Violent action is social behaviour and can be more fully understood in a
theoretical perspective which sees humans as social animals with a
capacity for symbol manipulation and social construction of 'meaning'.
This capacity is a dimension of human behaviour which enters into the
very definition of reality itself by both subjects and observers. When this
perspective is combined with a sociological-historical theory based on
Weberian ideas about power and legitimacy, it might also be able to deal
with the *ambiguity* of the manifold social actions that in most societies
can be labelled as violent.[1] Ambiguity refers here to the very divergent
evaluation of action based on harmful physical force. Few if any societies
are consistently 'pacifist' in rejecting all violent action: in some conditions
it is seen and experienced as necessary, inevitable, justified, or even
psychologically rewarding.

In this chapter I examine the construction and expression of violence
among the Suri (or Surma) of southern Ethiopia, a pre-literate, non-
industrial society of agro-pastoralists at the margins of a state society.
This group does not share our (Hobbesian) model of man (being here
similar to the related Mursi people, as claimed by Turton 1994a: 21).
While in general terms the Suri cannot be called 'more violent' than, for
instance, people in Western industrial society, theirs is a setting within
which the workings of some elementary rules of violent behaviour in

face-to-face relations, and between groups who know each other very well and are strongly dependent on each other, might be observed. The Suri case could hence tell us about this cultural, symbolic dimension of violence in small-scale non-stratified societies, and make us doubt the often-heard statement that violent behaviour is usually meaningless and irrational. It can on the contrary be claimed that it is nearly always 'meaningful' (cf. Blok 1991, and above). In some respects, violence can be an 'organizing principle' in society, not only in moments of crisis but also to structure a part of human experience and values. Whether the Suri or related groups can be said to have a 'culture of violence' is a debatable point. This concept has questionable analytical value, and carries the danger of essentializing a group tradition which is in reality fluid and adaptive. It is, however, a term in the local discourse used by their peasant neighbours victimized by their raids.

David Riches (1991: 295) has succinctly described violence as: '. . . contestably rendering physical hurt'. This refers to social interaction whereby intentional harm is done, and where the views of perpetrator and victim (and witnesses) are the issue of dispute, these parties being conscious of the problematic aspects and of different views on the (il)legitimacy of the harm done. The definition (compare the Preface, above) points also to the fact that violence, even in its most crude and apparently aimless forms, always has an aspect of 'communication' – be it as a statement of social protest, intimidation, terrorizing, or of self-assertion – and thus of certain cultural representations or values. Violence is also 'rupture', immediate and challenging action, demanding a response. It may in all cases be tied to questions of social honour and of the integrity of the person or the group as these concepts are defined on a personal or cultural level.

The communicative, or 'performative', definition of violence *à la* Riches was perhaps meant as a step toward a theoretical framework and as tool for a more adequate ethnography of violence, assuming its universality but also seeing the culturally quite varying degrees of defining or contesting some social behaviour as 'violent'. But the definition excludes several forms of action which we would call violence from an outsider's point of view, e.g. when rendering hurt or intimidating persons, or for that matter, animals, is *not* in a particular culture seen as contestable (yet). For instance, Bloch's description (1992) of the sacrificial rite as being 'violent' (the shedding of blood through killing, with the purpose of 'appropriating' some other being's life force) will not count as such in many cultures.

Here we intend to follow the wider or 'weaker' conception of violence, along Bloch's lines. It is too restricted to only speak of violence when bloodshed among humans and destruction of the social order are involved. The challenge is to look for the cultural roots and antecedents of violent response in order to trace how 'aggressive', 'destructive' and 'murderous' violence of people could at all emerge. The local people and the representatives of the Ethiopian state in the area which will described here say that the Suri violence (i.e., what they see as their disregard for life and property, their raiding, their ambushing and killing others) '. . . is simply in their culture'. Does such a statement make any sense? To answer the question the loose conception of violence is needed, which emphasizes that violence consists of the human use of symbols and of acts of intimidation and/or damaging – potentially lethal – physical force against living beings to gain or maintain dominance.

Chai-Suri Society: the Ecological, Political and Social Setting

The Suri are an East Sudanic (Surmic)-speaking group of agro-pastoralists, somewhat comparable to other East African peoples many of which have been well-studied in anthropology (Nuer, Dinka, Maasai, Turkana, Karimojong). Their historical origins are still unclear, although they have clear linguistic and cultural connections to other agro-pastoral East Sudanic (Para-Nilotic) speaking groups in the region. At present they form a community with a strong sense of group identity, an aversion toward a settled agricultural way of life, a 'warrior ethos' (on which more below), and a cultural focus on cattle. For the most part of their recorded history (in oral tradition) of some 200 years, the Suri were independent cattle-herders in the Ethio-Sudanese borderlands. The Suri region became part of Ethiopia in the early twentieth century, but, being remote from the highlands where the central state was located, it was never well connected or integrated into it. The Suri consist of two sub-groups, the Tirma (about 11,000 people) and Chai (about 16,000). The remainder of this essay will deal with the *Chai*. They live in the area southwest of the small town of Maji, about sixty miles north of Lake Turkana.

Environmental and Economic Factors

The Chai area is an undulating savannah lowland zone south of the Maji highlands in southern Ethiopia, near the border with Sudan. The land is fertile due to the volcanic soil, but rainfall is unreliable, especially in the plains where they keep their cattle-herds. The rain is insufficient for permanent, intensive agriculture and does not guarantee the successful shifting cultivation of staple crops (maize and sorghum). Apart from cattle-herding and cultivation the Suri are engaged in hunting. At the end of the dry season (March–April), there is a problem of water and pasture, with staple-food supplies running very low. They have both agricultural and agro-pastoral groups as neighbours.

The most prized possession of the Suri are their cattle-herds. Cattle do not provide more than about a third of the food supply (milk, blood, occasionally meat) but are a store of wealth which is necessary for establishing social bonds and marriages and which can also be traded for grain in times of need. In a cultural sense, the possession of cattle is also tied up intimately with ideals of Chai social personality, adulthood and individual dignity both for men and women (who also have rights of possession). Young men are expected to be committed to herding the cattle and defending it against raiding outsiders. On this basic level – i.e. that of their mode of subsistence and of 'competition for resources' – the readiness to confront and use violence (repulsing and/or killing the raider-enemies) is an essential requirement of the Suri way of life, and is not seen in any sense as problematic or contested.

Internal Relations

The Chai have no 'chiefs' but there is a ritual leader or figurehead, called *komoru*. The incumbent always comes from the same ancient clan. He is chosen by community consensus and installed by elders in a special ceremony. He has no executive or commanding authority when in function. His main role is to be a focal point of normative unity of all Chai. The British anthropologist D. Turton, in his work on the related Mursi (cf. Turton 1975: 180), has called the priest-like figure of the *komoru* a 'conductor of absolute power' (connected to the sky-god Tumu). The *komoru* is expected to emphasize values of restraint, to be non-violent, and to reconcile the various domestic units, clan groups and local communities if need be.[2]

The Chai also know an age-grade system, with four ritually separated grades of which the third one (called *rórà*) provides the 'reigning' one (age set) and has its own name. The initiated members of this grade provide the main decision-makers and authority figures. Women derive age-grade status from their husbands, and are not separately initiated.

Chai live in compact villages, with members from various clans. A clan identity is only important for the choice of marriage-partners (exogamy). Several villages form a territorial unit (called *b'uran*), which originated as a co-operative herding unit of its male members. Domestic units led by married women are the foci of social life. There is little stratification in terms of possessions and wealth. Social relations outside village or *b'uran*-membership are formed on the basis of ritual bond-friendship (established through cattle-exchange), with other Suri as well as with non-Suri.

Inter-ethnic Relations

Chai society, both internally and in its relations to other ethno-cultural groups, is marked by frequent violence. Ambushes, robberies and killings between members of the different groups occur on a regular basis. These incidents appear to have gained in intensity in the last decade (see Abbink 1993b, 1994). It is likely that external factors, such as the nature of state – local society relations, changes in the regional power balance, as well as the influx of technologically advanced automatic rifles have played a decisive role here. These factors, to which we return below, have partly disturbed the 'ritual control' of violence within Chai society itself. It can be claimed that Chai violence indeed always moved between the two poles of *ritual containment* and *political strategy*. The former element was related to keeping equilibrium in their own society, the latter to safeguarding access to pasture, water holes, fields, and other natural resources *vis-à-vis* other pastoralist groups (Nyangatom, Toposa and Mursi), and agricultural neighbours (Dizi, highlanders). In recent years there were additional political-ecological factors at play, and these brought them in conflict with the Anuak and the agricultural Dizi people as well (see Abbink 1993a). Especially the relations with the latter, now their most immediate neighbours, deserve to be considered.

Historically, the Chai were located near Mt Naita (called in their language Shulugui), a border mountain between Sudan and Ethiopia. According to their oral traditions they were formed there or 'arrived' in this area about two-hundred years ago. However, in the past decade, the Chai gradually filtered into areas formerly used by the Dizi people for cattle-herding, hunting and apiculture. The Dizi were an hierarchical chiefdom society, with elaborate rank distinctions. Since the early twentieth century they were heavily exploited by the northern Ethiopian settlers, and their numbers dwindled. Relations between Dizi and Chai are important for two reasons: a) both Dizi and Suri traditions maintain that their leading families share common descent and cannot intermarry; b) historically, they instituted a kind of ritual alliance in matters of rain-control. While the Chai (and Tirma) leaders (*komoru*s) were recognized as the rain-making powers in the lowlands, the final authority on this was ascribed to the Dizi chiefs in the adjacent mountains (see Haberland 1993: 253). Under this 'rain-pact' itself, the Chai – in times in drought, food shortage, cattle disease or other problems – were permitted to enter the areas claimed by the Dizi. This important cultural agreement was a kind of temporary sealing of a balance between these groups, and might be seen as codifying the exploitation of different but partly overlapping and complementary ecological niches. There was – and still is – economic exchange between them (cattle, pottery, iron products, grain, garden crops), and also frequent inter-marriage, although mostly in the form of Chai men talking Dizi wives: in itself a sign of Chai dominance.[3]

Suri Culture and the 'Ethos of Assertiveness'

It was noted above that on the level of the Chai mode of subsistence and the readiness to confront raider-enemies, violence is emphatically present. Violent action – raiding, ambushing killing enemy raiders and their dependents – is not seen in any sense as problematic or contested. But the Suri attitude towards violence is more than just essential self-defence. An imagery of tension and of violent confrontations, with the use of force and aimed at domination, is woven into many aspects of Chai life: into ideals of manhood or social personality, and in general in a ritually expressed concern with what we might call 'expansive reproduction': the growth of herds and of family and offspring. For outsiders, this attitude is reflected in many cultural metaphors which permeate Chai (Suri) culture (culture we define here as the more or less durable, shared and transmitted patterns of behaviour in which collective ideals and norms of a group are expressed and which form an element of identity formation), and even in the self-name 'Chai', which means: 'We revenge, we pay (them) back'. For the Chai themselves, this imagery or symbolism of 'violence' does not count as problematic either.

We immediately note two things: first that this 'violent imagery' is mainly an aspect of the construction of the male gender. Females, while sharing the values underlying it, are not socialized to perform it except in a verbal manner. Second, we see that this imagery or symbolism is not seen as problematic or as referring to 'violence' by the Chai themselves. This is done only by external observers who are not part of the culture and who are not involved in the system of local group relations focused on cattle-herding and collective self defence.

The various realms of social discourse which serve to construct shared cultural scenarios for the Chai – and which are even shared in outline by their agro-pastoralist Nyangatom neighbours, very similar to them in way of life – might also be said to have psychological aims: first, to force new members of society to overcome the *fear* of violence, of armed attack, of wounding and killing. Interestingly, Chai say that young boys have to learn to suppress a 'natural inhibition' against the spilling of blood and against violently inflicting harm on others. A second aim may be to inculcate the idea of the immanence of violence, i.e. death, or the flowing of blood, in various stages and crucial moments of the life-cycle. When these two aims are achieved, violence is both domesticated, 'embodied', and made instrumentally useful (see following section).

This violent imagery is expressed in at least the following three cultural metaphors/schemas, which tell us about the *indigenous* Chai conceptions about human motivations and relations. These are important to consider if we want to advance theorizing about violence and warfare and their relation to culture (cf. Turton 1994b: 25).

The *sacrificial* metaphor: the equation of the killing and offering of a consecrated (domestic) stock animal with beneficial effects for humans. This is done at certain ceremonial occasions, for instance: marriage, burial, age-group initiation, a rain-ceremony, installation of a *komoru*, and also at a major public debate, or sometimes in case of serious illness. (As in most pastoral societies, cattle meat is hardly eaten outside a ritual context). The core ideas behind putting a consecrated animal to death are perhaps: *substitution* and *vicarious victimization*, because the violence is performed for the benefit of the human sacrificers. Maurice Bloch (1992) has called it 'rebounding violence', whereby the 'vitality' of a live being once killed ritually is deflected towards humans (utilized for human purposes). The effectiveness of the sacrifice is predicated upon the close (social) bond between humans and domestic (livestock) animals. The cattle also provide the bride wealth, and thus the medium for marriage and, ultimately, fertility. The flowing of blood thus is essential, yielding beneficial results. The idea of sacrifice was also relevant in the context of inter-group relations (see below).

The *purification* metaphor: the idea of purification is pervasive in Chai culture. People involved in homicide or in handling corpses at burials but also in adultery are to be temporarily isolated and cleansed. They can only be made 'normal' members of society again by cleansing themselves with the freshly spilt blood of a stock animal. To purify, in this respect, means to kill and to transfer something of the life-force of the animal which was killed. Humans only then are able to re-enter social life. At the same time, to purify with the fresh blood is to redraw a boundary between individuals who were earlier socially separated by their violence, seen as a transgression.

Jon Abbink

The *achievement* metaphor: a Chai's personal history or social career is important. His/her personality and deeds may live on beyond the life-span, and in this awareness, people try to make a name for themselves, as 'warriors', ceremonial duellers, public speakers, important family heads, or ritual experts. Achievements are often reflected in personal favourite-cattle songs (*roga kiyogá bio*) or battle songs (*kirogeñyò*), which every adult male has. They are composed by men in the junior age-grade (*tègay*). Most men keep working on such songs during their whole life, changing and adding text. Such songs can speak of deeds done in raids and war, in other dealings with neighbouring and/or enemy peoples, and of actions carried out during the defence of cattle herds and of their own favourite animals. Violent moments or episodes are an inevitable and desired element of such achievements.

Another moment of achievement is, of course, gaining social adult-hood. This adulthood is not 'just there' when people come of age, but must be achieved by having shown valour and personal strength (demon-strated in ceremonial duelling, see below), by capable herding, and by going through initiation (by retiring elders) into the senior age-grade. For this, they must have demonstrated their being worthy of it. This is a function both of time passing and of appropriate behaviour of the junior grade (see Abbink 1994, 1998). Hence, adulthood cannot just be taken – it is only reluctantly accorded to the newcomers by the outgoing elders. The ritual of the initiation has 'violent' aspects (i.e. physical harm is involved): elders (both men and women) insult the new candidates, give them exacting and humiliating tasks to do, deprive them of food, and lash them with whips until their backs bleed.

These domains reveal underlying values and violent motifs active in the constitution of the Chai social person, especially *vis-à-vis* outsiders. In their turn, these motifs and values inform *cultural scenarios* in Chai society. Linger (1992) has used the concept of 'cultural scenario' to indicate the expected behavioural 'performances' of values in action. For him, the *briga*, the violent street-encounter in Brazilian urban society, follows a known, shared 'scenario', a scripted course of meaningful action in which the participants know what to expect. It is marked by emotional commitment and shared assumptions and values. Even though the actions are violent and can end in death, they are set in a model, which has psychological and cultural components inhibiting direct aggression but communicating its message. The important point is that *briga* violence, although ambivalent because of its two poles of fascination and restraint, is not aimless, chaotic violence which suddenly erupts. A similar point can be made for Chai violence, which also follows cultural scenarios.

The Exercise of Violence

In this section, the practice of violence, i.e. the production and enactment of some frequent 'violent' behavioural patterns ('scenarios') in Chai society is reviewed. Two kinds could be distinguished: the ritually enacted 'domesticated violence', and the external violence, i.e. relating to non-Chai. In the first instance, violence is *transformative*, i.e. fulfils an essential role for individual Chai in becoming full or accepted members of society; in the second instance, it is *constitutive* of their own *group*, a *necessary inversion* of peaceful social relations in certain conditions requiring distance between them and others.

Ritual Enactment of 'Domesticated Violence'

One finds the following forms expressed within the Chai group.

- Duelling (*thagine*).[4] A major event of domesticated violence is male ceremonial duelling. This is done with big poles made of tough wood, of *ca.* 2.10–2.40 metres length. The main contestants are young men of the *tègay* age-grade (unmarried) coming from different territorial settlements and/or clans. They hold several matches and return-matches over a period of a few months every year, supervised by referees (*oddà*). The *thagine*-duel is strictly contained by rules of procedure, and the killing of an opponent, on purpose or accidental, is prohibited. If it occurs, homicide compensation should be negotiated. Social relations are perceived to be disturbed between the family groups of victim and killer as long as a deal is not made.

  Three aspects of these duels stand out. First, the *thagine* ostensibly is a forum for male competition and acquisition of culturally approved status among peers and also vis-à-vis girls. They allow young, ambitious men, eager to start life as independent household-heads, to show their strength and virility. This latter aspect is explicitly recognized by nubile Suri girls: the duelling provides a place of male – female contacts, whereby girls among themselves make a first choice as to whom their partners might be, although there is *no* correlation of being the winner and being the most popular person. Second, it can be interpreted, in psychological terms, as a training ground for youths to explore the fascination and energy of violence in a controlled manner. Thirdly, the duels are forums where competing village communities within Suri society meet (People from the same village can never compete). On these occasions, where thousands of people gather, these communities (called *b'uran*) are in fact *constituted*.

Figure 1. Chai duelling in progress

- The procedure of homicide compensation (*ligin*). When an internal homicide has occurred, the lineages of victim and perpetrator are in a state of conflict, whereby in principle revenge can be taken at any moment. People avoid normal social contacts. After some months, negotiations are started, by neutral members from another lineage or clan group. These must lead to the fixing of a compensation sum and to the agreement to hand over a young girl to the victim's group. The killer and the closest male agnate of the victim must also be purified with the blood of a sheep. Without this ordered procedure to restore the peace, feuding would ensue.
- 'Blessing of the raiders' (*dirám*). This is an essential ritual supervised and carried out by the *komoru*. Before going on a raid for cattle, participants (who virtually all are of the *tègay* age-grade) have to be blessed and ritually protected from death and defeat. This is done in the compound of the *komoru*, and should proceed according to a strict and faultless procedure. The raiders are smeared with a protective black clay and jump across thorn-bush branches, which symbolically stand for the enemy. They also threateningly face the *komoru* as if to attack him – an act to challenge his blessing and divert the power which he has (via the connection with the sky-god).[5] The speeches by elders

Figure 2. Spilling sacrifical blood in a homicide purification ritual: cutting open a live sheep

and the blessings of the *komoru* are full of violent imagery, cursing the enemies, calling upon the raiders to be fearless and dauntless in their attacks. They are expected to make effective use of violence and to come back with glory (They announce their 'successful' mission upon return in their village with a special boasting song). In the knowledge that the opponents do exactly the same, there is here again no controversy on the use of violence.

- The ritual killing of livestock (*nitha*). This is a very common event, violent although not directed at humans. It is done when people have killed some one (on purpose or by accident), at an initiation-ceremony, a divinatory intestine-reading, a marriage, or a burial. The ideas of substitution and of cleansing through blood and death come back here. The manner in which the cattle or sheep are killed has its own meaning, but is seen as cruel by outsiders: it varies from cutting the throat, or slowly bludgeoning an animal to death (cattle), to slitting open the stomach before it is dead (sheep).
- Body culture. One could see certain Chai *body treatments* as violent, though they are again not 'contested' (except by government agents, who discourage it): the piercing of lips and ear-lobes with sticks and inserting big wooden and clay discs; the making of scarifications with

a razor blade on the arms, back and abdomen of women; the kicking out of lower incisors with a stone, and the 'honorific' *rídò*-scarifications (carved in the skin by an age-mate) for people who have killed. In all these cases, blood flows and pain is inflicted, but only in order to enhance *culturally styled personal purposes:* respectively aesthetics, age status, and personal achievement and prestige in the eyes of peers. It is not seen as a contested infliction of harm. This is all part of the self-conscious cultural body aesthetics which Chai emphasize vis-à-vis other groups, and which is, for instance, completely lacking among the Dizi people.

External Violence: Ritual and Political

We have seen that the Chai had social relations of exchange, ritual friendship bonds (*laale*), and of joint exploitation of pasture and water resources with their Mursi, Nyangatom, Dizi and other neighbours. These groups had close social relations with them, which were fully taken for granted. But, with the exception of the Mursi, such groups remained outside the Suri 'moral community'. As the complementary side of these close social bonds, the Chai always knew various forms of violent behaviour and conflict in their dealings with them:

- The stealing of crops and individual cattle without violent assault. These matters, if the culprits could be found, were resolved through talks and compensation on an individual or family level.
- Ambushes, to kill an individual or traveller from another ethnic group either to rob grain, clothes, tools, a gun, or cattle, or just to kill to prove personal 'courage' (by a *tègay,* a junior age-grade member).
- The raiding of enemy cattle camps or compounds, with violent deaths of both defenders and attackers. These were short hit-and-run raids, with a brief and intense attack under a barrage of rifle-fire and a quick retreat.
- Occasionally: destructive one or two-day battles to destroy enemy settlements or wipe out its people. This was battle-warfare (*kaman*), and was the most serious form of violent interaction between two ethnic groups. Chai have had such fights with all their neighbours, except the Mursi. The purpose in such large-scale attacks was not only to steal cattle, but also to capture women and children, who were then incorporated in Chai society. While the violence used was intense and often deadly (hacking with knives and spears, shooting at close range), forms like rape or torture of the adversaries were, however, unknown.

One notes that the context of this external violence may be partly 'resource competition' and partly political strategy: the (re)drawing of group or territorial boundaries between political units. They do not fight because they are 'separate groups', but the reverse: in order to become so. This also holds for the Chai in their dealings with neighbouring groups (compare the same argument on the Mursi by Turton 1994a).

Relations with the agro-pastoralist Nyangatom were based on an implicit and recognized balance between two similar groups. They had a comparable acephalous organization and age-group system, a similar subsistence base, etc. Violence was a 'normal' social activity, not problematized as such. It also had a code of conduct: even in serious things like cattle-raiding, for instance, there was the rule of the preliminary marking (in the neck) of a few cattle from a targeted herd before the actual raid would take place. Conflict between the Chai and Nyangatom was, in sum, a way to express or assert a boundary with the 'significant other'. The killing of a Nyangatom allowed a Suri man to make the prestigious *ridò* scarification on his arm.

With the agricultural Dizi people, who dominate the highlands northeast of the Suri and have a very different economy, culture and political ideology, relations were not based on perceived similarity. The Chai always had a disdain for the Dizi and their sedentary, agricultural way of life. But their obvious group differences – despite the myth of common descent of their chiefly families – were codified in an explicit 'contract' of rain control, based on the metaphor of sacrifice. In times of drought, the Chai would pay homage to the Dizi chief of the highlands, bringing a black ox and a black goat for sacrifice by the Dizi chief. The political tension (between two basically *unequal* groups) was 'appeased' in this agreement, thus keeping inter-group violence at bay through the metaphor of ritual sacrifice (substitutive violence). There were incidents between individuals of the two ethnic groups, but no major violent conflicts or battles. Neither did Suri apply the *ridò*-markings.

The above elements shape the Suri practice of violence and define their *habitus* (in Bourdieu's sense defined as human dispositions acquired in society due to a process of internalization of external 'objective' social conditions). The *habitus* is also incorporated into action, feeling and thinking of individuals in a specific society, often in a quite literal sense, since the emphasis is on the bodily basis of these dispositions. This is also evident among the Suri. A habitus is, however, not static.

Figure 3. Wolekibo and Mesfin: two members of the *tègay* age-grade

Transformations of the Violent *habitus*

Since a decade, the face of violence among the Chai and their neighbours has changed in some important respects. Although the traditional situation of 'normal' relations between the ethnic groups in the area was not so harmonious as oral tradition asserts and therefore should not be glorified, it is apparent that the past years have shown a serious crisis in inter-ethnic relations. This kind of situation of local crisis and increased violence is seen general in many parts of Africa, due to internal and external factors (often in the context of globalization processes), bringing together various spheres of interaction and articulating conflicts of interests. Traditional rituals and customary law usually cannot achieve what they were designed for in bygone days. Local societies are structurally unable to maintain their integrity and moral fibre, due to drought and famine, population pressure, faulty state policies, tourism (see Abbink 1999), modern education and new criminal activities.

As a result of recent political and other changes in the Maji area, both the internal 'ritual' Suri violence as well as the violence towards other groups tend to break the bounds of custom and to turn into the uninhibited use of force (This was also the opinion of the Chai elders, though expressed differently). While this use of force makes new options available for local people, it also tends to endanger the co-existence of groups as well as the peace in Chai society itself. Relevant factors have been population movements in the Ethio-Sudan border area due to the Sudanese civil war, increased local conflicts about pasture and water holes, periodic drought and famine, epizootics, a temporary retreat of central state authority from the local scene (especially in 1991–3), and generational conflict among the Suri.

All this was coupled with the rapid spread of automatic weapons among all groups, which changed the extent and intensity of violent encounters (see below). These factors have contributed to more inter-group conflicts, a decline in market contacts and a virtual halting of shared use of the environment and of mutual social contacts (including intermarriage and ritual friendship bonds). A three-year record that I kept of violent incidents between the Chai Suri and the Dizi (leaving out the conflicts which either group has had with *another* neighbouring population), shows at least sixty incidents with a fatal outcome, the number of people being killed ranging from one to several dozens per case. (With other ethnic groups like the Anuak and the Nyangatom the Suri also have violent conflicts, but due to geographical separation between them, the number of confrontations and of casualties has been less than with Dizi and highland villagers).

One of the problems to explain is why violence 'got out of hand' and led to a break-down of social relations between the Chai and other groups. Is it because their cultural models and their *habitus* were, in a sense, 'violent'? In the course of the conflicts with the Dizi, one can see a *qualitative* difference in the view on, and exercise of, violence, especially among the members of the *tègay* age-grade (see Abbink 1994): violent action — attacking and killing — became an aim in itself, a medium of self-glorification and of personal status which, while based on assumptions and ideals within Chai society, has gone well beyond them.[6]

To understand why this happened, we recall two general factors. First, the Chai subsistence base. They are transhumant herders and shifting cultivators, not sedentary farmers: they have never invested in long-term agricultural adaptation but in mobile cattle-herding. For them, boundaries between 'territories' and 'resources' are not to be strictly observed, it is against the nature of their open economy and flexible 'membership policy'. If such a closure occurs, due to conquest and exclusion policies (e.g. of Nyangatom, due in its turn to population growth and also Kenyan military pressure) or to developments of 'sedentarization' and administrative boundary-making, violent conflict cannot but increase. This is what has happened in the past decade. There is less and less room for Chai to follow traditional strategies of conflict resolution: avoidance, migration, or division and territorial spread of groups.

Second, the process of state expansion in the Maji area. Since the turn of the century, when it was nominally incorporated into Ethiopia, Maji has always been a 'frontier area', incompletely administered and on the margins of the state monopoly on violence. Recent efforts to re-establish the state after the change of regime in 1991 have 'problematized' all expressions of Suri violence. The state is by nature presenting itself as the normative, overarching authority which should have the exclusive use of legitimate force as well as combat 'harmful customs'. Local violence of Chai or of any other group is proscribed, regardless of its context (this was already the case under the previous state-communist regime of Mengistu). The state representatives have also, at various points, tried to prohibit many Chai activities or customs: not only cattle-raiding, ambushing, etc., but also the more innocuous things like animal sacrifice (the killing of cattle for divination or funerals), the customs of ear- and lip-plates, removal of lower incisors, and body scarification (These were called 'harmful customs' in the 1987 constitution of the previous regime, a concept which returns in the policy documents of the post-1991 government). Recently, in 1994 and after, it was also tried to ban the ceremonial duelling contests.

It is obvious that this so-called 'civilizational offensive' represents an assault on the socio-cultural fabric of Chai society. As the Chai are held responsible for most of the violence in the Maji area, state officials think that by reforming the what they see as overall violent character of Chai culture they can halt violent conflicts. It is, however, likely that if this state campaign to 'reform' Chai culture – by banning the customs just mentioned – would be successful (it is not), the violence against non-Chai would notably increase when these domesticated forms of violent expression would cease to exist. In addition, while the state discourages or forbids even Chai self-defence and redressive action against enemy raiders, at the same time it cannot guarantee defending the Chai and their territory against such raiders (e.g., from the south or from Sudan), nor protect them from drought and subsistence crises, factors which necessitate at least some violent action. More immediately important factors stimulating the overall use of violence have been:

1. The wide availability of automatic rifles and ammunition from both Sudanese and Ethiopian sources.
2. Continued ecological pressures: drought, cattle disease, more scarcity of bush land for cultivation and pasture for livestock. There was a major famine in 1984–5 and again one in 1994, and in early 1997. This contributed to theft, ambushes and raiding.
3. The conflict in southern Sudan, which became the source of population movements in the region, pushing the Toposa to the western borders of the Suri territory, thus making their pastures and their old ritual sites, chiefs' burial places and settlements unsafe, and posing a threat to their cultural and also physical existence.

The effect of such changes in the socio-political and physical environment on the Chai, and on their use of violence in their relations with other groups, has been dramatic, although it is not a one-way causal chain – the developments in their own society have combined with such external factors to reinforce crisis and violent conflict.

It could be seen most clearly in the crisis in the age-grade system, which is the core of their political organization and internal order (cf. Abbink 1994; 1998). In the age-grade system, the elder or reigning age-set of *rórà* is to be accorded respect and obedience from the younger one. They occasionally expect to be honoured and, in a metaphorical sense, 'fed' in recognition of that fact, e.g. by being offered sacrificial cattle. Their blessing of the land and the cattle and their authority on the basis of age is seen as a necessary element in the social order. But it was resented by the reigning age-set called Neebi (= 'Buffaloes') that the *tègay* were always taking violent initiatives on their own, not sanctioned by public decisions at meetings. The *tègay*, mostly younger herders who lived in the cattle camps (in an area six hours' walk from the villages), could assert themselves because of the power of their rifles and on their growing economic leverage (as herders and as gold traders: see Abbink 1993a). Also in other domains the respect of the younger generation toward the elders and parents was diminishing, even within families: personal property and heads of cattle were often taken away by youngsters, without the consent of the parents.

The growing violence perpetrated by Chai youths initially convinced Chai elders (who control the date and the proceedings) that the new age-set initiation, which was already due in the early 1980s, should be delayed.

With this, they expressed that the Chai first should formulate an answer to their problems, such as being exiled from their country, recovering from the drought and famine period in the mid-1980s, running into trouble with the Dizi and the Anuak (which endangered normal social relations and trade), and not respecting the elder generation. The *tègay* were blamed for all this, and the elders did not have a clear answer to the problems. The increased violence had brought out internal contradictions in the age-grade system and the authority structure and norms it was supposed to uphold. In fact the metaphor of age organization as a cultural model of ordering social life was fundamentally disputed.

The availability of automatic weapons, now acquired by virtually all men, led also to changes in the concept of violent action and to new violent practices. Above, we have discussed some core elements of the cultural basis of 'violent imagery' and action among the Chai. In the new situation, their values of male achievement and reputation, raiding and hunting exploits and ceremonial duelling provided a fertile basis for the *expansion* of violent performance by means of the new weapons, for instance:

- Compared to the spears, knives and old three or five-shot rifles of a generation ago, the possibilities of the Kalashnikovs, FALs and M-16s seem to have a fascination and momentum of their own. Their availability not only leads to mimetic exercise of violent acts by the *tègay* vainly seeking recognition still structurally denied to them (see above: the delayed age-set ceremony), but also giving the possessors the idea of 'social self-sufficiency': they explicitly de-emphasized the value or even the need of normal social relationships as formerly maintained with the neighbouring groups.

- The weapons also have been put to new use. For example, there have been some unprecedented instances of Chai killing their own cattle to prevent it from being captured and taken away by enemy raiders (This has also been observed among the Tirma, and among other newly armed pastoral groups in Uganda and Kenya, the Pokot, Turkana, Karimojong, etc.). The reason given by the Suri herders of this highly controversial and much debated 'innovation' in violent practice is that the Nyangatom raiders hide between the captured cattle. There has also been the gunning down of Dizi elders and women and the killing of unarmed Dizi girls in ambushes, things not done in the recent past. Through this violence, exercised largely with impunity, the Chai and Tirma became more and more saturated with the feeling of power, and challenged not only the Dizi peasants but also the state army. This built up until October 1993, when a big Ethiopian army attack caused several hundred of Chai and Tirma (men, women and children) to die. Only after this obvious defeat, the elders decided to hold the age-set ceremony, initiating and conferring adulthood on the 'delayed genera- tion' (see Abbink 1998). Since then, Chai Suri violence has decreased. The Tirma sub-group, which has not yet performed the initiation ritual, shows at present a higher level of violence than the Chai. Two other internal changes in Chai society are the following:

- In the past six or seven years, the institution of *thagine*, the ceremonial duelling, has undergone a metamorphosis. First of all, the frequency of the contests has much increased. They are held almost every two to three weeks over a period of three to four months after the main harvest of sorghum (September–November, and after that as well, e.g. in January and in the time of the first rains in April–May. Secondly, the influence of the elders (including the *komoru*) and the referees over the contesting parties has diminished: nowadays, the young men and their friends continue as they like, and after one party has 'lost' one contest, they grab their Kalashnikovs and start shooting (usually, but not always, in the air) to show their irritation. This had led to several accidental killings. One can hear the Suri elders say that the meaning of duelling is being eroded. We see here another cultural scenario in flux, whereby accepted meanings of 'violence' are transformed.

- There has been an increase in feuding: when a homicide is perpetrated, Suri seem to lose the patience to sit out the traditional compensation talks. The kin group of the victim, if strong enough, demands imme- diate damages, or else call for retribution. Such feuding conflicts also affected the family of the *komoru*. Among the Tirma-Suri, for instance, there has been a long line of killings between two lineages since one of their two *komorus* was accidentally shot dead: by a Tirma. This in itself is unprecedented.

The above forms of violent behaviour are now also contested within Chai society: elders, the *komoru*, and women especially talk against wanton violence against Dizi and other travellers, against unprovoked killing and robbery of former Dizi bond friends, and against the shooting at duelling grounds.

The changes in the exercise of violence both within and without Chai society points to major shifts of meaning. In fact, we see a movement from ritually contained violence to political and instrumental violence, the aims and meaning of which are less clear to everybody. There is a phase of deep uncertainty and sometimes fear, of a transition of meanings. There is an awareness that many of the *tègay* generation have abused the cultural norm of status acquisition on account of killing an adversary: this happened only in battle with recognized, long-standing enemies (i.e. not with Dizi and other highlanders except after manifest injustices). The *tègay* do it repeatedly, 'without a reason', and break the rule of restraint in violent behaviour.

Concluding Remarks

The Chai-Suri cultural style is marked by normative ideals of male personhood and peer status which accord value to assertive behaviour, which may translate into violent behaviour when material interests and competitive economic and social relations with other groups are involved. Suri culture can, however, only be called a 'culture of violence' – reproducing violent behaviour as a template, an ideal or a *habitus* – in its relation to, or opposition to, those outside their moral community.

Chai-Suri expressions of violence have shown important modifications in recent years. While ecological and material conditions play a role in explaining this, an anthropological, cross-cultural understanding of the new dialectics of violent action needs to take into account how violent processes actually unfold on the basis of symbolic–cultural representations and how they establish meaning, either instrumental or expressive.

In a way, violence breaks the bounds of normative culture, and of the social system. The ritualization of violence is diminishing, and more unstructured and unpredictable forms emerge. We see here a society pushing against its own structural and cultural limits[6] that where the result of the long process of social evolution. In relations with neighbouring groups (especially Dizi and Nyangatom), this Chai violence can still be seen as a 'language', a communicative act, but mainly one of intimidation. Violence in this sense 'bridges' the communication failures that have emerged, but it grounds group relations in suspicion and fear – in the absence of shared frameworks of control (cf. the breakdown of the rain-agreement with the Dizi and of the fighting code with the Nyangatom).

A more neo-functionalist explanation of violent behaviour, as offered in recent evolutionary approaches, seems of limited value because it tends to assume what has to be demonstrated in each empirical case (cf. Knauft's criticism, 1987/8, 1991). For instance, the interpretation of Chai violence seems to preclude an easy association between successful raiding or violent behaviour on the one hand and reproductive success on the other. Comparing census-material and involvement or prestige in raiding of dozens of Chai men did not give any meaningful correlation. The most important killers were not more popular with women and did not have more wives and children. Neither did they have larger herds. Certain rules make accumulation of this sort difficult: the captured cattle is being divided among all participants of a raid in a time-consuming and laborious procedure. Other facts which refute such a connection include the position of the *komoru*: he usually has a large number of wives and children and the largest herd of cattle, but he is noted for his reconciliatory and mediatory role, and his role-model de-emphasizes aggressive behaviour and aimless violence. We also saw already that in the *thagine* ceremonial duelling the victors are *not* the universally popular guys outshining the losers: all participants regardless of their place on the list of honour are esteemed.

What the examination of the Chai case suggests is that 'violence' is an essential, inherent part of social life, and need not be always be seen as a contested practice, in the sense of unexpected or 'irrational' behaviour towards others. This was true for the Chai and the Nyangatom – both with the same focus on cattle-herding, both with a stratum of 'warrior-herders', and with the underlying idea that violent self-assertion, both in ritual and in collective defence, was inevitable, a part of life. When people were killed it was said to have been 'bad luck' for them, caused by, for instance, failing ritual protection. It was not contested *in itself*. With the Dizi it was different, but we have seen how the latters' perception of illegitimate, excessive Chai violence in recent years was partly generated by the breach of a previous 'historical contract', and by changing regional and state-local society relationships, where different forms of incorporation into overarching political structures and value systems (as expressed in the fight over the monopoly on the means and exercise of violence) of both groups led to regional discrepancies and conflicts. The violence against the Dizi is now also problematic among the Chai and is the issue of many debates (cf. Abbink 1998).

'Violent practices' of the Chai are a traditional concomitant of their evolved survival strategies as cattle-herders in a precarious natural and human environment. Their *commitment* to the herds – to feeding, defending, and expanding them – has led to a close socio-cultural bond between humans and cattle, symbolically elaborated in their cultural style and their values of social personhood and achievement. Violence is, however, not simply a 'selectively advantageous trait' of Chai behaviour. Their ideals and values certainly reflect a complex violent imagery, but at the same time a pervasive sociality within and beyond their society, suggesting that, on this elementary level also, both are inextricably linked. This again shows the ambiguity of violence as a category of social action: it constitutes and it undermines sociality, the latter especially when released form its cultural formulations.

When the Chai mode of existence is becoming more precarious or even undermined, either by long-term disturbances in ecological conditions or in the inter-group and state relations putting them at a disadvantage, a recourse to more 'hard violence' will be likely. Traditional understandings between local groups then lose importance, the regional equilibrium is disturbed, and an overarching accepted state structure is not present. Also, the continued availability of modern weapons and plenty of ammunition has had a seductive effect on Chai young men, prompting them to use violence *beyond* any instrumental necessity. As we saw, this has led to serious internal contradictions within Chai society, and to decisive changes in traditional Chai meanings of violence.

In most of the situations which we presented, violence in Chai society can be seen as a means to symbolically construct a group identity, or 'we-consciousness' – it is not there automatically. This consciousness is based upon ideas of clan descent or affiliation, language, and a cultural aesthetics expressed in decorative customs, but forged into an enduring group identity – or at least into one valid for some purposes – within the network of competitive and exchange relations with other groups in the region. As such, violence is inevitable, a fact of life, and not in any sense problematic or destructive or an irrational regression to evil human nature. When we talk about the violent 'images' in Chai discourse, the usefulness of Riches' definition (see above) is limited: from a Chai point of view, much of their violence is not 'contestably rendering physical hurt', but only uncontested, legitimate self-defence, retaliatory or pre-emptive damaging of enemies, or beneficial sacrifice of animals, with which no one in that context would argue.

Finally, this question of violence being 'contestable' in local Chai terms would perhaps only arise when (a) according to the normative authority figures such as elders and the *komoru* the people, especially the younger generation, defy the rules and obligations and act on their own account, thus changing or undermining the social order; (b) when new forms of aggressively violent and wanton cruel behaviour would appear, such as rape, torture, hired killing, or nihilistic destruction, well-known from (post)modern industrial societies. The possibility that such forms can emerge may not be precluded (as we know from cases elsewhere in Africa). Subjectively perceived economic exploitation, unbalanced state interference, artificially hardened ethnic boundaries, unsolvable problems of resource competition combined with factors like the easy new technology and power of killing (due to the spread of automatic rifles, hand grenades, and other small weapons) may prepare the ground for it. Also more intangible factors connected to the process of globalization, such as the penetration of a new cultural 'language' of visual images or of a fantasized reality evoked by imported Western or Asian violent videos, might enhance this process, as they can lead to internalizing new habituses of violent practice and performance (In the Suri country there is at present one rather unruly 'frontier town' where such videos are now becoming readily available, also seen by visiting Suri). This process may then invalidate – or at least transform – customary codes of restraint and social order,[7] as the Suri are gradually included in the globalized domain of 'displaced signs' and 'commoditized symbols' through the new media, tourism, Christian missionizing and imposed state modernization projects. The transformation of violence has been a multi-faceted historical development in Western (and other) modernizing societies. In recent years such a process has been occurring – though perhaps at a faster pace – in extraordinary situations of disturbance and upheaval in, for instance, Papua New Guinea, Mozambique, Liberia or Sierra Leone. The combined impact of the interference of the state (with its hegemonic project), the availability of automatic weapons, the new 'video culture',[8] and increased antagonism between competing groups (e.g. 'ethnic') might create a new discourse of violence. This would have an impact on traditional understandings of violent performance. What seems likely in any case is that more central state authority in the Suri area will transform cultural notions and patterns of violence but not cause the disappearance of violence itself.

Notes

Fieldwork among the Chai Suri in southern Ethiopia was done in 1991–94 with generous support from the Royal Netherlands Academy of Science (KNAW), the African Studies Centre, Leiden, and the Netherlands Organisation for Scientific Research in the Tropics (WOTRO, WR 52-610), which I gratefully acknowledge. I also thank the Institute of Ethiopian Studies (Addis Ababa University) for institutional support, local officials and inhabitants of the Maji and Adikiaz area, and Mr John Haspels, representative of the EEMCY and LWF in Tulgit, Maji zone. I am most indebted to the Chai people of the Makara settlement. I benefitted a lot from the critical comments on a first draft of this paper from participants in the International Seminar on the 'Ambiguity of Violence' at the Institute for Advanced Studies in Social Anthropology, Göteborg

University (July 1995). This chapter is a revised version of a text earlier published in *Cahiers d'Études Africaines* (1998). I thank the Editorial Committee of CEA for their permission to use that article.

1. Violence is used here as in the definition given in the Preface of this book. Compare also Corbin (1977).
2. More on the authority structure among the Chai in: Abbink (1997).
3. In the course of time, the Dizi — who also kept cattle in the lowlands — came to adopt several customs related to the 'cattle-culture' of the Chai, but they never developed a comparable assertive ethos, emphasizing for example, personal violent performance, militant defence of the cattle herds, or a specific decorative 'body culture'.
4. In this and other sections I draw partly on material first presented in Abbink (1993a; 1994).
5. In the film *The Mursi* (1974, Granada TV, Disappearing World series, UK), the similar ritual among the Mursi, called 'spearing the priest', is shown.
6. In fact to such an extent that the cohesion of Chai society itself was endangered (see Abbink 1998).
7. Professor Bruce Kapferer rightly emphasized this point in discussion.
8. Its emergence and adoption in Africa should be investigated in detail. The negative effects of violent and sadistic videos after their displacement to, and appropriation in, other socio-cultural settings are grossly underestimated.

—5—

Tolerating the Intolerable: Cattle Raiding Among the Kuria of Kenya

Suzette Heald

Introduction

What does it mean to be a warrior? What does it mean to be a thief? Historically, the two are closely linked in the pastoral and agro-pastoral societies of Eastern Africa where political opposition was expressed largely through cattle raiding. The feud, as we learnt from Evans-Pritchard (1940), is a social relationship and a central social institution in such societies. Yet, the fate of these 'raiding societies' has diverged sharply in this century. To simplify, in the northern arid areas, Ethiopia, Sudan, Somalia and the northernmost parts of Kenya and Uganda, pastoral societies have been caught up in the maelstrom of wars. To the south, in the better watered areas, we get a contrasting pattern, of relatively stable state organization and an overall decline of the pastoral sector of the economy as crops have increasingly been produced for the market. Both developments have had a particular effect on the roles of young men. In the first group of societies, the military wing of the pastoral economy has become ever stronger as the weakness of the state and the influx of advanced weaponry has put a premium on defensive potential (Fukui and Markakis 1994). As these societies have become ever more bellicose, we hear of younger and younger men taking up arms to defend their groups or recruited into armies fighting nationalist causes. In the second group of societies, as raiding has lost its political valence, it has increasingly come to be regarded as common theft, a mark not of gallantry but of crime. It is these societies that have seen in the recent past self-help used not as an instrument for inter-group competition but as a means of intra-group control.

In January 1995, while doing fieldwork in Kuria in southwest Kenya, I was given a lift to town by a Luo driver. The conversation turned, as did so many in that month when raids were a nightly occurrence, to cattle theft. Why, the Luo asked the Kuria also travelling with us, didn't they solve the problem once and for all? In his community, some ten years before they had rounded up the cattle thieves, doused them with kerosene and set them on fire. They had had no problems with cattle theft since then. In other circumstances, with other ethnic groups, I would surmise that he would have been joined in a hearty swapping of stories, of how witches had been wiped out in this place, thieves in that place, and so on. His disquisition on the relative merits of lynching and burning as ways of collective murder would have merited intense and knowledgeable comment. The Kuria heard him through but made little comment.

The Problem

Alone of the settled agricultural communities in Kenya, the Kuria, at least to a point, tolerate cattle theft and cattle thieves in their communities. The times that I have been in Kuria, in the mid-1980s and again in the mid-1990s, have coincided with 'security crises', with considerable sections of the population in outcry against stock theft, demanding measures to be taken to deal with the perpetrators. And measures have been taken, ranging from collective cursing by the elders, to putting individual men to the oath to extract guns or confessions and to the entire destruction of the homesteads of suspected thieves and their subsequent, if often only temporary, expulsion. Yet, the extreme measures which have become notorious from other areas of Kenya where lynch law has often become the rule are unknown. One could say, perhaps, as yet unknown. One thing which is unclear is how far these purges are part of a normal cycle, whereby redressive measures are periodically brought to bear when raiding exceeds a certain level of tolerance and how far they signal more far-reaching changes in Kurian attitudes to such theft? Do, for example, the campaigns of recent years signal a divide between a heroic and a civil society, with the heroes of yesteryear being reclassified in the process as thugs and thieves?

In taking up this problem, much of what I say can only be speculation, necessarily tentative on the basis of the *courte durée* of anthropological fieldwork.[1] Its importance lies in that it takes up issues which are only just finding themselves on the anthropological agenda: issues of crime, violence and attitudes to theft. Hobsbawm's writings (1959, 1981) on social banditry have found a ready response in historical work on African societies but, despite the increasing levels of crime plaguing African cities and countryside, anthropological attention (with exceptions, as always) has been elsewhere.[2] We have no ethnography of thieves and thieving in Nairobi or Harare. Who are the thieves? How are the gangs organised? Are they simply the poor and displaced, or do their networks link them also to the affluent elite? As significant, we have little data on changing attitudes in the rural areas. This latter issue takes us directly into the traditional territory of the anthropologist, to the way existing modes of endeavour and attitudes have and are being transformed under the impact of capitalist economic forces in the context of the problems (and weakness) of modern state formation in Africa (Heald 1986a, b).

It is here that I want to make a start by examining the operation of raiding in one particular locale in Kenya, seeing it as an outcome not only of a set of historically determined attitudes but as fully imbricated in the complexities of the present. Yet, in so far, as it deals with an agropastoral system in which political relationships are expressed predominantly through cattle rustling, some of the interest of the study lies in the way the Kuria might also be seen as recapitulating processes which occurred in other Kenyan communities half a century or more ago.

The Kuria

Kuria is very much frontier-land. In the far south-west of the country, it lies literally at the 'end of-the-road', on the border with Tanzania. Travelling there for the first time in 1984, it seemed as if the journey was not only one of space but also of time. Entering Kuria, one was immediately confronted by a distinctive pattern of life in the scatter of heavily fortified homesteads, with their circle of houses protecting the inner cattle coral, and the corresponding lack of the usual signs of modernity. As if to emphasize this divide, one was also warned of the danger of bandits on the roads and advised not to travel after dark. There were large areas of land which appeared deserted, apparent no-man's lands, between the Kuria and their neighbours to the west and north, the Luo and Kisii. To the east lay another war zone, with Maasai and Kipsigis in the Rift Valley.

These wars have historic roots in the territorial push northwards of the Kuria from Tanzania. The Kenyan Kuria represent only the northernmost extensions of the clans, with much of their settlement of fairly recent origin, some as late as the 1950s.[3] Yet, Kurian expansion was not only achieved at the expense of other groups, it was also played out internally. The Kuria are no undivided 'tribe'; the four territorial clan divisions (sing. *ikiaro*, pl. *ibiaro*) of the 110,000 Kuria now in Kenya – Bwirege, Nyabasi, Bukira and Bugumbe – effectively stand in a relationship of permanent hostility to one another.[4] While territorial expansion is still an issue in

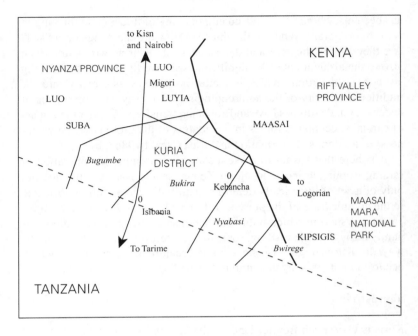

Figure 1. Sketch map of Kuria District in Kenya

some border zones, today the relationship of Kuria clans with each other and with the neighbouring groups is expressed largely through reciprocal cattle raiding. From the modern state one traverses a journey that takes one back to patterns of very local, tribal war.

Yet, what remains is not an unmutated 'tribal system'. The hybridity of forms that we now associate with the periphery is clear. Remote and inaccessible in colonial times, economic development came late to Kuria. It has only been in the last twenty years, with the establishment of tobacco contract farming in the area in 1975, that the basic economic development of the region has been put on the agenda (Heald 1991, 1996, 1999). These years have seen an enormous growth in both agriculture and commerce, and today education has become a priority for many Kurian families. In all this, strategies have largely followed those that have become character-istic of the Kenya small-holder sector, with families seeking to provide for their needs, both current and future, through a combination of farming and off-farm cash-earning activities. In 1993, the area was created a 'district' and Kurian identity was given the recognition that is usual in Kenya: the 'tribe' was literally on the map.[5] For Kuria this was an enormously important symbolic development; a source of pride and potentially also a source of wealth. A district, with its own MP, can exert leverage for development money for road building, the extension of telephone lines and for the provision of electricity to its main market centres. It gives access to the centre. We can thus say that Kuria has thus now joined the 'mainstream' of Kenyan state and culture, but it does so at an enormous disadvantage, literally 'behind', and, as yet, with few educated and elite members to sponsor either development for the district at large or the fortunes of individuals in the competitive employment market that characterizes Kenya today.

The Persistence of Raiding: An Emerging Criminal Economy?

Kuria then stands at the cross-roads, both literally in terms of its geographic position on the border and, more metaphorically, between a tribal agro-pastoralist life-style and a more horticulture-based peasant economy with their different structures of motivation. One way then of tackling the problem of raiding might be to describe it as it appears in the competing discourses of Kurian life: that which for convenience sake we may term the 'traditional' and that associated with modern development. Operating in the interstices between the two, it is legitimated in the first and castigated in the second; deemed unlawful, backwoods, atavistic, disruptive, the harbinger of poverty not progress. These discourses are manifest in different ways. The first is not so much heard as seen; it is centred on the household, lived out in the daily routines of life, whose assumptions can be articulated but rest essentially on the taken-for-granted messages of the *habitus*. Here, raiding, bringing back the cattle of the enemy, draws together the importance of cattle with the glamour of the raider and the lineage of courageous deeds. The second is more truly the realm of articulated public discourse, linked with the district, with the agencies that have come to be associated with change, with 'development'. Yet, while raiding draws its legitimacy only from the former, it cannot in fact be dissociated from the latter.

The Chief of Police, keen to underplay the problem, was quick to describe raiding as the 'sport' of the young men. This gloss, while containing a germ of truth, was clearly inadequate as a description of a situation in which cattle rustling involved not only the 'young warriors' but the elders, headmen, chiefs, police and security forces, and possibly even some teachers and pastors, all in varying degrees of involvement and complicity.[6] It is thus no mere traditional past-time. While possibly still 'sport' for some – a mark of daring, the sign of an age grade – its integration into market commerce makes it big business for others, the shadowy 'remote controls' who are believed to direct and organize much of it. At this level, it is yet another feature of the informal economy and of the widespread corruption of the modern Kenyan state, aided by Kuria's border position with its lucrative smuggling opportunities. At this level too, raiding shades into other forms of theft and banditry.[7]

The object of this raiding is clearly theft and not killing. As it is described, a common practice runs as follows. A small group of men from one clan area raid into the territory of another, bringing the cattle back under the shelter of night into their own territory where they are able to cross over the border into Tanzania. The cattle may then be exchanged with cattle raided by their Tanzanian clansmen, with these Tanzanian cattle then smuggled back into Kenya, on occasion even on the same night. Such cattle are all but untraceable and, despite the paper formalities operating at the daily cattle markets, are easily dispersed through marketing and butchering outlets in Kenya, many probably filling the lorries destined for major towns such as Nakuru and Nairobi. What is clear is that raiding of this kind requires considerable co-ordination and organization. It also requires the complicity of large sections of the population who participate at some level in the 'trade' or who proffer a blind eye, whether paid or unpaid. With the average cow worth around £80 in 1995 prices, the profits are considerable and it is not surprising that suspicions are rife that much of this money finds its way back into the pockets of the administration and security forces.

The New Techniques of Raiding

Another element of the contemporary situation is the use of *guns*. Probably the majority of these are fairly crude home-made blunderbusses. However, since the early 1980s, modern rifles have also entered the system. Initially, this appears to have occurred as a by-product of the disbanding of the Tanzanian army following the war with Uganda. Kuria soldiers in Tanzania finding themselves still with their rifles and uniforms but without pay took to older ways of provisioning themselves.[8] The army and police have also been a source of employment for Kenya Kuria and these days most such guns are believed to enter the area through retired or discharged members of the security forces who, through their contacts, are able to acquire such weaponry.

The possession of guns is held to have had a decisive effect on the nature of raiding. In the old raiding system, with bows and poisoned-tipped arrows the main weapon, the balance is held to be more or less equal between the two sides. The rustlers must come by stealth, vault or burrow under the homestead defences, and remove from inside the corral the barricades which close the single gate. They may then make off with what cattle they may, ideally without rousing the inhabitants. The raiders are vulnerable to attack during this process; particularly when a single raider is alone in the corral dismantling the gate defences, he is surrounded by the circle of house doors, from any of which he may be attacked. With guns, this situation changes. The raiders, less afraid of making a noise, may openly threaten the use of firearms, station men around all of the house doors, and drive off all the cattle with very little fear of pursuit. If they have come in force, they may leave a picket around the home to protect their rear for an hour or more after the main body of raiders has left with the cattle. This, despite the fact that the majority of raids are probably still of the old type, is seen to have changed the nature of the opposition.

Overwhelmingly it seems that the raids are 'slept' through and the depredations of the raiders are not discovered until a family member ventures into the corral in the early hours of the morning. This fact seems strange to both the Kuria and to the observer. Nights are of course never silent – the cicadas and bull-frogs see to that – and, during storms, an army could surround a homestead without notice. But clear nights and dry earth are usually preferred by rustlers who must run their cattle back to safety under cover of the dark and prefer not to leave too obvious a trace.[9] Further, most households keep dogs and their barking often disturbs what peace there is in the night. But, on the night of the raid, one is told that the dogs did not bark. Some people suspect that the raiders arrange to drug the animals though sorcery. However, it would also appear likely that the defenders, not knowing whether the raiders have come armed or not, see the argument for discretion and find that they have unwittingly 'slept' through the raid. Few cattle are ever recovered.

Responses to Raiding

This is not to say that Kuria are passive victims in the face of raiding. During times when it becomes intense and raids are a nightly occurrence, men take to sleeping outside their homestead in the bush. Inside, they argue that they have little chance of defending their cattle; guarding outside, they are both ready for the raiders and have the element of surprise on their side. Their poisoned arrows also come into their own, picking off their targets without betraying the whereabouts of the archer. In some areas as well, during periods of exceptional risk, neighbours may undertake a collective guard. But, these can only be temporary measures. For men who increasingly see their livelihood in terms of agriculture, such night vigils, as well as the nights and days out tracking the raiders, take an unacceptable toll of their energy. Thus, as rustling intensifies, as it does periodically, there is growing pressure to control it. This has both outside and inside implications.

In the first place, increased raiding signals a threat of all-out war between the clans involved. The ever-present cold war changes into a hot one. Passions are inflamed and raiding is coloured more and more by the idea of revenge. Acts of violence tend to flare up at places where the communities mix, for example, at trading centres in border areas. The escalation in raiding patterns in the early 1980s (coinciding with the influx of guns following the Tanzania/Uganda war mentioned above) led to war between Bukira and Nyabasi in 1982, with armed battles between the two sides. This resulted in the virtual abandonment of several up-and-coming trading centres which lay along the border between the two territories, including that at Kehancha, near the administrative centre, which languished for almost ten years. And, despite Government attempts to control the situation by the establishment of a permanent camp of the paramilitary General Service Unit in the border zone at Chinato, the troubles continued, with raiding in all locations increasing during 1984 and 1985. The danger from such raids was said to be so severe that men had to keep vigil at night outside their homesteads for almost an entire year. The situation came to a head in July 1985, when the President announced an amnesty for those holding guns, an amnesty that was later extended until the end of August. The administration, acting in collaboration with the councils of ritual elders in each of the areas, acted vigorously to pursue the culprits.

These elders of the secret council (*abagaaka b'inchaama*) remain important in all the Kuria territories, though probably retain greatest respect and fear in the easternmost territories of Nyabasi and Bwirege which border on the Rift Valley. During the amnesty of 1985, the elders co-operated with the local administration in extracting guns from the suspected thieves, putting the suspects through oathing ordeals (*ekehoore*) which are believed to have an immediate and lethal effect on the guilty and their families. They also have other powers in the ordering expulsions and cursing and all of these were used in 1985.[10] While oathing was prevalent throughout Bwirege, Bukira and Nyabasi, in Bugumbe, on the western boundary of the Kenyan Kuria and generally regarded as the most peaceful area, the elders pursued the different policy of expulsion.

The entire homestead of the men accused at public meetings was razed to the ground, goods looted and the livestock driven away to be eaten on the hoof.[11] Over 100 families were said to have been expelled in such a way. In Bukira, similar action was taken but on only a handful of suspects. In the absence of official confirmation estimates of the number of guns collected varied considerably.[12] However, what is of interest is that traditional mechanisms were brought to bear to control the holding of guns and the influx of firearms of the early 1980s was in some large measure successfully counteracted. Certainly, this action against the thieves had an effect, with raiding at a much lower levels for a while.

Raiding, Agriculture and New Markets

By the late 1980s, however, raiding was again on the increase and the 1990s were to continue this pattern, with raiding tending to intensify in the latter months of the year, from October through to February. Flanked on three sides by other Kuria groups, proud of its roughneck reputation and its nickname of the 'hammer', Bukira is regarded as the source of much of this raiding. Yet there are evident difficulties in dealing with the system as if it only concerned Kuria clans in Kenya. Raiding is part of a wider system, involving other ethnic groups and also, and most importantly, with approximately two thirds of their population over the border in Tanzania, other Kuria. Nevertheless, it is possible that local opinion contains some truth. The only official statistics that I was able to see were reported at a meeting of the security officials from Kuria and Trans Mara districts in January 1995. They listed the number of cattle thefts reported from both districts during the previous months where the tracks led over the district boundaries. With over five times more inter-district raiding parties returning to Kenya Kuria than leaving it, they suggest that the epi-centre for raiding might well be Kuria.[13]

If this does indeed approximate to the real picture, we are confronted with a somewhat paradoxical situation, that is, that the impetus towards raiding is coming not from the pastoral side of the equation, as might be expected, but from the agricultural. This invites speculation on how far changes in patterns of raiding – and specifically its intensity – might be attributable to recent economic changes in Kenya Kuria.

The relationships and causality involved here are complex and can only be skirted over briefly. One thing which is clear is that there is a growing economic divide between the Kuria on the different sides of the international border. The Tanzanian Kuria, without the impetus given by intensive tobacco contract farming, have not developed the horticultural side of their economy to anything like the same extent as the Kuria in Kenya. Indeed, Michael Fleisher (personal communication; 1997) who has recently made a detailed study of raiding among the Tanzanian Kuria, thinks that they may be neglecting it further in favour of the pastoral side, at least in so far as this latter is expressed in raiding. Given that many, even the majority, of these stolen cattle end up in Kenya, the possibility exists that the upsurge in raiding can be attributed to the new markets consequent upon raised demand in Kenya. In the years up to the mid-1980s, probably most of this demand was for cattle to exchange as bridewealth but this is coupled at the present time with the demand for meat, now regarded not just as an item for feast days and holidays but as an everyday commodity. This demand has been swelled by a sharp decline in cattle numbers in Kuria itself. The large herds of even the recent past are no more and herd sizes have in fact decreased by almost 50 per cent in the last ten years alone. Some of this depletion may be due to increasing land pressure on the Kenyan side and the consequent loss of pasture lands. The investment strategies of the first tobacco farmers in Kenya were largely into the existing modes of accumulation, with cash converted to cattle and cattle into wives (Heald 1991). This has resulted in a rapidly increasing population. And, as mean homestead sizes have grown, herd size per homestead has decreased, from 11.3 head of cattle in 1985 to 5.8 in 1995.[14] However, the most immediate reason given for this depletion in stock is not the lack of pastures but rather the danger inherent in keeping cattle. Four head of cattle are said by many today to be the optimum number, just sufficient for both ploughing and milking.

The predatory side of the pastoral economy, as Spencer (1984) refers to it, thus might well carry the seeds of its own destruction, as the dangers of holding cattle increasingly outweigh the benefits.[15] Indeed, there is already some irony in the fact that the Kenyan Kuria keep their identity as cattle raiders even though they can no longer claim renown as cattle-keepers. But the implications of this relationship are more far-reaching. Agricultural prosperity would seem to have put the raiding system into over-drive, with an immediate spin-off effect in the decline of stock-holding in the areas most badly affected. In the long term, this may sound the death-knoll for cattle rustling too. But, short-term, as areas become 'raided out', the system goes on, carrying the war outwards. From this perspective, the existence of pastoral and agro-pastoral economies on the borders of Kenya Kuria (including that of the Tanzanian Kuria) represent for the time being a handy reservoir of lootable cattle.

Political and Social Pressure on Raiding

Whatever the complexities of this wider raiding eco-system, in Kenya it is immediate relationships with neighbouring Kuria clans which are the ones most often seen as the issue. Certainly, at the political level, they are the only ones susceptible to local counter-action. For example, at the beginning of January 1995, following a sharp rise in raiding during the previous month, the Nyabasi made a raid on a very well-known and well-defended homestead in the neighbouring territory of Bukira. They came in numbers, with guns, and openly challenged the warriors to come out and face them. The noise could be heard from a mile away. They drove off with between forty and fifty head of cattle. This was a spectacular raid, a symbolic challenge which struck deeply into community relations. Such action by raiders can, however, decisively backfire. The raiders are seen as pushing their communities into war in an attempt to cloak their actions in its legitimacy. The disadvantages of this situation for the majority of Kuria are only too evident. Revenge may assuage community pride, but it does little to practically help those who are its victims. Speeches are made at the many informal moots and assemblies (*iritongo*) that spring up in Kuria neighbourhoods at such times – against the immiseration caused by theft, for the necessity for the clans to unite against the thieves rather than let the thieves perpetuate the old divisions, and so on. The Kuria have a range of strategies available at such junctures and all might be resorted to. Thus, inquisitional procedures are set in motion in local areas to discover the identity of the thieves and pressure is put on the councils of ritual elders to take action through their control of magic. The same powers as came into play in 1985 were again used in 1995, and again these took different forms in the four territories. For example, in early January, the ritual elders of Bwirege publicly cursed all the age sets of its thieves, a measure which was held, after the death the following nights of two men whilst raiding, to be immediately and patently successful.

Pressure too can be exerted on the administration. Following the raid mentioned above, deputations were made by both the Nyabasi and Bukira to the senior chief and he organized a joint moot between the two hostile clans, a meeting which drew over 500 people. Joint moots of this kind are extremely rare and suggest either peace-making or, as in this case, an attempt to pre-empt war. Speakers stood up in turn, one from Nyabasi followed by one from Bukira. All but one spoke against war. The only man who advocated measures likely to inflame emotion – that the Nyabasi should be forced to return Bukira cattle– was shouted down by the assembled crowd before he had gone a minute into his speech.[16] Men argued instead for the clans to co-operate in tracking the thieves and for them to be publicly denounced. Indeed, the most intent and dramatic moments of the meeting came towards the end, when the chiefs were asked to read out the names of the thieves in their areas – names which had for the most part been furnished anonymously during the proceeding week, on slips of paper left in the road. When the chiefs declined, on the pretext that they had left such papers at home, men from each side stood up and began reeling off the names of the thieves operating in their areas. In this act of public dissociation and shaming, the two clans came together, if only temporarily, in common purpose.

The equivocal role of the local administration is an aspect which requires some comment; not all the criticism was self-criticism. Voices were raised not only against prevailing clan attitudes which automatically give sanctuary to their own thieves but also against the administration and its complicity with the thieving gangs. Accusations were made that the chiefs, sub-chiefs and headmen were all too-ready to be bought off by the gangs and that members of the security forces were also effectively raiding. They demanded a moot in which the District Commissioner was present so that they could name these names as well. This wish was reluctantly acceded to and followed some two weeks later. The administration did then order investigation into a number of chiefs, though no action was ever to be taken against them. More assuaging of public sentiment at the time, was the round-up of about twenty suspect thieves on the eve of the first meeting presided over by the District Commissioner. These men were all arrested for questioning and held in the local jails for many weeks. As was expected, eventually no charges were pressed against them. While the populace generally sees this as further evidence that the police have been bribed, the police have a ready justification in terms of the stringency of evidence required for a prosecution. Word-of-mouth and circumstantial evidence, by itself, would be plainly insufficient to carry such cases in the Kenyan courts. But, this holding operation, with its suspension of the normal procedures of bail, was successful; it proved that some action could be taken by the authorities and it was considered a sufficient deterrence for the thieves. Four or five weeks in a local Kenyan jail is, with reason, considered a fairly stiff punishment.[17] The raiding between the two clans abated.

Cultural and Social Complexities of Raiding

In combating raiding it is clear that the Kuria are fighting a powerful coalition of modern interests as well as against old structures of motivation. And running through all this is the ambivalence attached to the thieves themselves. Are they stock thieves or cattle raiders? Are they motivated by the basely economic or by collective pride tied to the symbolic value of cattle? At one level, one's own thieves are the defenders of the area, staging raids to evidence retaliatory strength, a source of security in so far as this deters the opposition as well as of communal pride. At another, it is they who bring danger upon the community in the form of the predatory raids of others. They hover on the divide, hero/criminal. It is a fine balance and one, which at times of severe raiding, they can be turned upon as the enemies within, bearing responsibility for the communal insecurity. Nor is this all, for it is widely believed that the prime motivating force for theft is purely selfish, and this leads the thieves into alliances which totally vitiate their role as champions of the community. In particular, the widespread nature of raiding, points not only to high levels of organization but to actual alliances between the gangs of different areas. It is not just a matter of Nyabasi men of Kenya collaborating with their own clansmen in Tanzania, it is a question of them also being in league with their traditional enemies in neighbouring Bukira. Thieves are thus depicted as operating in a manner analogous to witches. It is your own raiders who pick the targets and guide the enemy raiders through your territory. Nor are these enemies only other Kuria clans; there are cases where Kuria are suspected of dressing as Maasai for raiding purposes and many claim that the conspiracies stretch over the district boundaries and that there are ethnically mixed gangs operating.[18]

Many African cultures seem to have a fine understanding of the ambivalence of power; Janus-faced it can be used for both good and evil, just as human motivations veer between collective and self-interest, between the cultural ideal and individual expediency. This imaging of the negative underside of the person and of social relationships is particularly apparent in witchcraft beliefs. In contemporary Africa they have been seen to provide alternative discourses of modernity (Comaroff and Comaroff 1993). Giving substantive form to hidden predatory forces they personalize in local idioms sources of evil which derive from the conjunction of local and global. Linked to the polarities of wealth created under the impact of the state and capitalism, current patterns of belief have been interpreted as an indication of the threat these pose to the moral values embedded in rural societies, highlighting areas of moral ambiguity. As Mary Douglas (1970; 1991) would put it, they are implicated in the drawing and redrawing of the group's moral boundaries. In this context, as I have argued earlier and in a different context (Heald 1986a; 1989), ideas about thieves and allegations of theft involve similar definitional issues. In taking up this subject again, I follow the same leads, moving from the structural underpinnings of the system to an examination of it also as a problem of values, of emotional as much as political territory. Just as witchcraft beliefs are inextricably bound to concepts of the person, so too are ideas about theft. Among the Kuria, at one level, the raider represents the cultural ideal of masculinity, the bedrock upon which family and social relations are constituted. At another, the raider represents its deviant or negative potentialities.

The Ambiguities of Masculinity

In age-organized societies such as the Kuria, masculine identity changes in the course of the life cycle, from the valorized militarism of the 'warriors' through to the assumption of their role as household heads, with autocratic powers over their families, and on to the acquisition of magical powers with growing age.[19] All these forms of power are associated with violence, directed out in youth, in the home – in middle age– in the right to beat wives and children, and more ambivalently in old age, when their witching powers may be used in a community context, agents for control as well as for destruction. Yet it is warriorhood which carries most strongly the masculine ideal. Llewelyn-Davies for the Maasai has described the *moran* as 'undifferentiated masculine potential . . . a masculinity that transcends the statuses of boy and elder' (Llewelyn Davies 1981: 347–8). The same is true for the Maasai's neighbours, the Kuria. Men of all ages may address each other as *mora*, 'warrior', a sign of equality, respect, and honour. It is a term conferred by undergoing the rites of circumcision, when the warrior-youths take up the role of defenders of the homestead, and to all extent become independent masters of themselves, with rights to marry and to inherit the land of their fathers. Unlike the Maasai, Kuria youths marry soon after circumcision, bringing their wives to live in their father's homestead. They separate to establish their own homestead, in the ideal-type case, when their own sons are old enough to guard the cattle, that is shortly before they in turn are circumcized in early adolescence.

The emphasis on military valour played out in the circumcision rite – so common in East Africa – leads me to wonder if psychoanalysis had developed in Africa and not Vienna, if the death instinct, the importance of the aggressive impulses, would not have replaced the sexual ones in primacy. The strongest emotion that a Kuria man can experience is held to be *itiindi*. It is an overpowering emotion, manifested often in an uncontrollable shaking which cannot be simply identified with fear, for if it is fear it is only that particular experience of it that precedes battle. The Kuria associate it with three main activities: facing circumcision, fighting, and lastly, self praising. This latter is perhaps the most interesting, as it links the emotion with acts of self assertion, with claims to renown. Men begin self-praising at collective rituals following their circumcision; it is the act in which they introduce themselves to the community; an act of poetic declamation, in which in clever and figurative ways, they will tell of themselves, their deeds and those of their families (see Heald 1997).

Cattle raiding, with its daring and risk of death, combines all three aspects of masculine potential as does no other activity. But also, in being acted out, it shows the limits of the system. The costs are in the constant insecurity, in the threat of war at the community level and, at the personal level, in the oscillation of affect between pride and fear. The men who return home after a successful raid, bellowing in triumph like pawing bulls, on the next find themselves out tracking, uttering the eerie alarm calls of the zebra. They are both hunter and prey. Kuria warriors are not like the Maasai *moran*, cut off from normal society, but 'family men', involved with their neighbourhoods and charged with the defence of their households. They cannot be oblivious to the hardships caused by raiding, of the families left destitute, without the milch cows to feed their children or the oxen they need to plough. In the local community, the booty of the raider translates into his neighbour's loss. The two sides are held together by the *quid pro quo* of raiding, by the dialectics of effect and affect, by a constant testing, we might say, against the reality principle. The tolerable and the intolerable from this vantage point may be taken to be different sides not only of the oscillation between the Kurian experience of relative peace and war but of themselves: social knowledge and self-knowledge go hand in hand.

Thus, despite its calls to a heroic form of masculinity and daring, cattle raiding in practice displays itself as a structure of moderation. If the thieves keep inter-clan hostilities alive, it is they who are offered up almost as sacrificial victims as a brake on such violence. While the situation is always uncertain and wars have occurred even in the recent past, the Kuria have evolved political strategies which are mainly successful in keeping their wars cold rather than hot. And most of these strategies are 'traditional'; modern changes while to an extent destabilizing the system have not as yet brought them into question. Indeed, the existence of these remedies addresses some of the puzzles about feuding societies. How exactly did they maintain their famous 'balances'? Admittedly, such balances were always more of a theoretical construct than an empirical reality, but the answer here lies not in the literal massing of warriors on either side, nor in mediating institutions such as leopard skin chiefs, nor in the impact of cross-cutting ties deriving from marriage, for the Kuria clans do not intermarry.[20] Rather, we see it in the readiness to pre-empt escalating violence by taking action against one's own. Rather than uniting for the purposes of standing against, Kuria clans appear most disunited at such times.[21] Yet, such action as is taken against their own thieves again appears temperate. There is no total dissociation nor, one could add, any change in basic moral attitudes. Indeed, the existence of thieves allows men to still identify with an hegemonic ideal; despite their changing way of life, to continue to maintain that they are *all* thieves.

Concluding Remarks

Let me draw towards a conclusion. In effect, what I have done so far is isolate a sector from Kurian life, whose form and assumptions are subsumed in a certain cultural logic or rather practice, with its contradictory pulls both towards and away from violence. In enacting the violence of raiding, Kuria confront their contradictions and existential insecurities, both social and individual. Indeed, one is inclined to see it in terms of Freud's *fort/da* game, in which loss and recovery, pain and pleasure, vulnerability in the face of circumstance and ability to control it, are constantly played out. One could further add a libidinal element. Cattle, as symbolic objects, are clearly erotic signifiers; the means to wives that you steal from the enemy to exchange within the clan. The sleeky-backed cattle from Maasai, so much healthier than the Kurian stock, are a frequent topic of praise poetry and often said to have formed a necessary component of bridewealth in the past. War thus is linked to marriage and intrinsically implicated in the construction of out-group and in-group identities, collective and personal.

To return at this point to the question with which I began this paper: how might this analysis help us understand the transition in attitudes to the thief that has characterized contemporary Kenya? As I have emphasized throughout, the Kurian experience is not one of stasis. At present, raiding still operates to keep alive not only the divisions between the clans, but the economic and political egalitarianism of the old order, which was – for men only, one has to say – an egalitarianism of opportunity, if not of achievement.

Increasingly, this is challenged by the new economic and moral order, where riches are seen to be hard-won and differentially obtainable. As people turn to 'stealing with the pen' or 'stealing from the soil' – both rhetorical metaphors in common use – thieves appear more and more as 'free-loaders', tempted by high returns rather than by persistent effort. The young men who get sucked into the system are often deprecated as school drop-outs, destined for a short life span for many a raider gets killed in the course of a raid. For them the valour but not the rewards. These would appear to be largely siphoned off by those involved in the organization and marketing rather than in the actual raiding. As one Kurian friend said to me, he had never known a rich thief; he had, however, known many a dead one. It is thus not altogether surprising that the young men who bear the risk often have a more equivocal attitude to cattle raiding than their elders.

As I said at the beginning, it is tempting to see Kuria as on the point of divide between the values of the old heroic and a new civil society. Yet the point of change has not yet been reached. However profound the economic changes, however ultimately threatening to the very nature of this agro-pastoral society, there have been no comparable political ones. As people say, there will be no peace in Kuria as long as the clan territories (*ibiaro*) remain. Despite the potential tightening in Government administrative machinery, in part made possible by the creation of Kuria as a separate district, there are few indications that the administration has the political will to attack the raiding system at this level. Yet, changes in the nature of raiding and the ambivalence in attitudes to the rustlers themselves, do indicate a possible future trajectory if the raider's role was to lose its political valence. Then, I think that there may be little to stop these trickster heroes being turned upon as criminals and lynched as they have been in other Kenyan communities.

To speculate further, such a process may well be accompanied by a new kind of moralizing discourse. I am struck by the differences between the Ugandan Gisu of thirty years ago – who did lynch thieves – and the Kuria in this regard. The Kuria seem reluctant to condemn anything or anybody out-of-hand. They are quick to evoke extenuating circumstances, from being drunk to poverty as the factors lying behind family violence, for example. Gisu conversations, by contrast, were deeply evaluative: good and bad were probably the most frequently used adjectives and carried categorical totalizing implications (Heald 1989/98). It was a much more polarized, Manichean universe. In societies where violence is still taken as a constitutive part, as well as a right of men, it is interesting to ask what this might imply for the inner structures of the self and its motivations? What I think I am moved to suggest is that the hatred which is exhibited by lynch mobs, for example, may well evidence a psychic splitting of a new and different kind. As there is a growing distance and tension between the old – but still held – ideals of manhood and actual lives, the thief might well be seen to represent the 'bad self'; in effect, the prerogatives of the older order of values that can no longer be readily expressed. The attitude it partakes of is that of *ressentiment*, the rage against those who dare to do what one no longer dares, found in Nietzsche's bad conscience, of course, probably rather more than in Freud's moral if punitive one.

Postscript

This chapter was written on the basis of fieldwork done in the years 1984–95. In January 1999, I received a letter from a Catholic priest working in the area who writes that in December 1998 the assemblies called by the elders (with the support of a new District Commissioner) had now 'gone rough on the thieves and suspected ones. They have killed over 20, others remain maimed and many are still in hospital'.

Notes

1. Fieldwork among the Kuria began in 1984, with subsequent visits in 1985, 1986–87 and again in 1995–96, in all a total of around 12 months. It was made possible by two research grants from the Economic and Social Science Research Council of Great Britain and a supplementary grant from Lancaster University. The first version of this paper was prepared for the conference, *Cultures Under Siege: Psychological Anthropology in the Later Twentieth Century*, at Utrecht University in August 1996. I am also grateful to Malcolm Ruel and Michael Fleisher for their comments on an earlier draft of this paper.
2. For examples of such work by historians see particularly Crummey (1986). In the same year, a special issue of *Africa* (vol. 56, pt 4) on Crime and Colonialism also consisted mainly of articles by historians. Little appears to have changed since then, with few articles in anthropological journals taking up the subject. For example, a keyword search through the Anthropological Index for 1965–94 yielded over ninety entries for 'Africa' and 'witchcraft' but only one for 'theft', which dealt with the theft of antiquities in Mali. Though this doesn't evidence the literal lack of any articles on theft and raiding, it does give an insight into anthropological priorities and topic areas, with apparently little coding of any 'crimes' apart from witchcraft.

3. In fact the situation is complex as the Kuria appear to have initially migrated down from Kenya and then recolonized the area during the course of this century (see Kjerland 1995).

4. There is some debate about the use of the term 'clan' to refer to the Kuria *ibiaro*. Ruel refers to these divisions as 'provinces', stressing their territoriality, a territoriality which has been reinforced by the colonial as well as post-colonial administrations. However, current practice in Kuria is to translate the term as 'clan', in recognition of the fact that these groups have a sense of unity which derives also from claims to common genealogical origin and totemic affiliation. Totemic affiliation also plays a part in moderating warfare and clans sharing the same totem should not raid each other. In Kenya, Nyabasi and Bugumbe are both Zebra people but, since their territories are separated by the broad swathe of Bukira, the question of mutual raiding does not really arise.

5. It was previously a division of South Nyanza District, which combined the Bantu speaking Kuria with a largely Luo speaking population.

6. Such involvement has a long history and people could quote cases going well back into the days of colonial rule. However, it was not solely a matter for rumour and speculation for the 1980s saw also a number of cases where elite members of the community were prosecuted, including chiefs and a primary school headmaster.

7. Banditry has become a serious problem in the last ten years or so, with most roads in Kuria deemed unsafe for motor vehicles during the night and some unsafe even during the day. Buses, *matatus*, business vehicles and private cars have all been ambushed; their occupants beaten up and in a few cases shot. Schools, Missions and business premises in Kuria have also suffered from thefts, with generators, water pumps and motor vehicles stolen.

8. It is relevant to note, as it gives some idea of the scale of this problem, that Kuria, though only 0.6 per cent of its population, represented about fifty per cent of the Tanzanian army in 1980 (Fleisher 1997; personal communication).

9. The necessity for the cattle to be able to run was held to make exotic cattle less vulnerable to raids, though there have been recent cases when such animals were taken, often only to be slaughtered along the path and the liver and other valued portions of meat removed.

10. Such curses take a number of different forms and can be collective as well as individual. A common tactic is to curse the age sets of the raiders. Another particularly powerful form of curse is to curse one's own descendants, a curse which follows down the generations. In

1996, the ritual elders of one area of Bukira were considering removing old curses made in this way in the 1930s and again in the 1950s and remaking them. The old curses were now felt to be acting in too arbitrary a manner, afflicting the innocent while the guilty escaped.

11. An interesting sidelight on this is revealed in Ruel (1959). Butende location (now part of Bugumbe) pursued a similar course of action against its thieves in the 1930s, with the age sets, as in 1985, inflicting collective punishment against its renegade members. Then, however, the thieves reported their age sets to the colonial authorities and it was they who were prosecuted and fined. In the post-colonial situation, there was no such division of 'legalities' and the action was questioned neither locally nor through the judicial process.

12. All matters to do with raiding are regarded as a security issue by the Kenyan authorities and no official statistics are available.

13. Unfortunately, these statistics did not include data on cattle transfers over the Kenya/Tanzanian border.

14. This is based on longitudinal survey data collected by myself in 1984/5 and 1994/5. See further Heald 1999.

15. Spencer (1984) considered the predatory aspect of pastoralism to be less effective way of increasing herd size than peaceful husbandry under the control of the elders. Fleisher (1997) examines in some detail how this predatory aspect may have definite adverse effects on herd size, by raising mortality levels in a variety of ways, as well as through the dangers inherent in holding stock, leading to sale or conversion of cattle into wives. There is some direct indication from my survey in Kenya that the fall in cattle numbers correlates directly with raiding intensity. Bukira who had the greatest number of cattle in 1985, but suffered the greatest number of raids, had the least by 1995, the fall being from 15.3 per homestead to 5. Fleisher (1997) tells a similar story for the Tanzanian Kuria, where again herd size has fallen.

16. This was an elder of the secret council of Bukira and underlines the ambivalence with which these elders are often regarded. The opposition of elders and warriors in terms of their propensity towards peace and war respectively (see Baxter 1979; Spencer 1988) cannot be taken as read in the Kuria context. Indeed, at many moots, the opinion is voiced that one should listen to the young who, charged with the nightly tracking of stolen cattle, talk more sense (and more of peace) then their elders.

17. The police do at times act vigorously against theft, especially banditry and especially when this had been directed at prominent members

of the community. This is sometimes marked by extreme brutality, as they lay into people, women as well as men, in an attempt to extract information. Those arrested in such conditions can expect harsh treatment and deaths while in custody are not unknown. However, in other circumstances, the Kuria suspect that the thieves are easily able to buy favourable treatment, including buying their way out.

18. The Kuria are hardly unique in this development. Widespread, inter-ethnic alliances of stock thieves, able to cross boundaries to avoid detection by the authorities and to exploit variables in market prices were a feature of the colonial economy in the Rift Valley from 1920 onwards (see Anderson 1986).

19. See Ruel (1997) for further details on the life cycle and the ritual significance of the eldership ceremonies.

20. This is a tactical rather than a prescriptive endogamy. There is no rule which limits marriage to the clan. Indeed, rather the opposite sentiments are frequently expressed. 'Marriage is free' one is told, 'one can marry from anywhere' but, in practice, the majority of marriages are within the clan, with few going over the boundaries into the neighbouring territories. However, there are marriages with other ethnic groups, and these have a long historical dimension, in some cases going back to times of drought and dispersal when Kuria exchanged their daughters with groups further afield who could offer food or cattle. In the recent past, due to the wealth brought by tobacco, there has also been an influx of wives from the neighbouring Abaluyia and Kisii.

21. For a further discussion of this issue and the opt-out strategies available in systems resting on segmentary loyalty, see particularly Gellner (1969).

–6–

Rethinking 'Violence' in Chinese Culture
Barend J. ter Haar

The place of violence – however defined – in Chinese culture has hardly been studied in a systematic way.[1] I suspect that at least one reason for this lack of attention is a feeling that this is not an interesting question, since we 'know' that violence did not play a large role in Chinese culture anyhow. As I hope to show in this preliminary exploration of the secondary literature, this is by no means self-evident.

The common approach to the study of the use of violence in Chinese culture is in terms of the conceptual pair *wen* ('refinement') and *wu* ('martial violence'). Generally, their use is deemed unproblematical and they are transferred from the primary sources to a scholarly discourse as if they reflect a more general binary pair 'harmonic, peaceful' versus 'violence, military'. Scholarly perceptions of the past are re-framed in these two terms as if they are precise analytical tools (Bodde 1991: 304–6; Kam and Edwards 1995). Full investigations of the two terms as they are actually used in Chinese language discourses itself are largely limited to pre-Han philosophy.[2] In the process all kinds of uninvestigated presuppositions flow into these terms and one may wonder whether it is advisable to study violence in China solely in indigenous terms.[3] A more balanced semantic analysis should also include other terms, such as *luan* (chaos), *bao* (excessive violence), and *bing* (military violence).

In this essay I look at the changing use of violence in Chinese elite culture, defined here somewhat simplistically to mean 'the actual use of or threat with physical force to change a situation, living being or object'. Furthermore, a distinction needs to be made between sanctioned (i.e. socially and culturally approved) and deviant (i.e. not-culturally approved or pathological) violence. We are concerned here only with the first type, although the second type is undoubtedly partly connected to people's perceptions of the first type as well.

The common position on the place of violence in Chinese culture is that already before the founding of the Han dynasty in 202 BC, there was a turning point away from 'martial violence' (*wu*) towards 'refinement' (*wen*). The most sophisticated treatment of this view is by Mark Lewis, who has argued that originally sanctioned violence was an essential element in the self-definition of social elites. For this reason, they also restricted the use of such violence to themselves. From the fifth century BC, the performance of violence was no longer the monopoly of the elite, but extended throughout the general population. Violence was now perceived as something that man originally shared with the beasts, and hence problematic.[4]

An alternative position stresses that the civilian ideal triumphed over the military ideal during the Song (960–1276). Here, the Tang (618–907) is perceived to represent the heyday of military power, symbolized in the provincial governors who had taken over local government in large parts of Tang China. The triumph of the civilian ideal entailed the rise of an elite based predominantly on the examination system and the establishment of civilian institutional control over military power (in contrast to the independency of military power during the latter half of the Tang dynasty).[5] This scholarly position is based on very real changes in the institutional context of military violence, which are then mistakenly generalized to the use of violence in Chinese society as a whole.

In fact, Alastair Johnston (1995) has recently shown that embedding military power in a civilian institutional context did not mean relinquishing violence as a legitimate means for solving perceived conflicts. Even during such 'civilian' (*wen*) dynasties as the Song and the Ming (1368–1644), violence was actively used in dealing with neighbouring states, indigenous local cultures (especially in the south) and rebellions. Even if civilian officials no longer fought themselves, they were not necessarily opposed to violence as such.

What we can see is a very gradual trend away from the use of different forms of violence as part of the creation of an elite identity. This trend was by no means completed before the founding of the Han dynasty in 202 BC and first affected the male educated elite, before spreading to other social and gender groups. Eventually, these changing attitudes towards violence should be placed in a general history of feelings and emotions, but this is a task for future historians.

Violence to Solve Elite Conflicts

Confucius, supposedly the primary source of the social norms of the educated elite of the imperial period, was not at all against violence, albeit within the context of proper behaviour ('ritual'). He taught the skills of archery, chariotteering and moving troops, but disapproved of tactics.

Hence, his disapproval did not refer to violence as such, but to the loss of a chivalrous ethic and the changing nature of war (Seyschab 1990: 119–20, 140–1). Interestingly, Confucius also stated that one ought not to sleep under the same heaven as the murderer of one's parents. Admittedly, this statement is contained in the Book of Rites, but it is confirmed by other statements from the Confucian traditions of the third century B.C (Lewis 1990). This shows that changing attitudes to violence were not necessarily the result of the spread of Confucian values, but had their own cultural dynamics, even if later Confucian ideologues would claim them as their own.

As Mark Lewis has pointed out, during the pre-Han and Han periods blood revenge for close relatives and friends remained prevalent, to the extent that there existed professional avengers. It was still very much an elite (as well as general) social norm, and an intrinsic part of the Confucian moral order.[6] Actual and rhetorical behaviour towards political or personal enemies in the pre-Han period was remarkably gruesome, to the extent that even rulers would (threaten to) eat the flesh and organs of enemies or traitors (Cheong 1990; des Rotours 1963, 1968). The act of consumption was nòt described as socially deviant, whether it actually took place or not.

The ongoing practice of private blood revenge squarely contradicted Qin and Han prohibitions. However, these had been instituted as a corollary of the monopolization of violence by the central state, rather than out of disgust with violence as such. The impact of these prohibitions was therefore largely determined by the strength of the state. During the following period of political disorder, blood revenge therefore continued to be practised among the educated and social elites, despite repeated prohibitions (Ch'ü 1961: 78–87; Lewis 1990: 88). We also continue to find stories in official sources of the consumption of flesh out of revenge. On the whole, these stories might still involve members of the political elite, but no longer members of the educated elite. They served to illustrate the cruelty and inhuman nature of the victim or consumer involved (Cheong 1990: 80–92; des Rotours 1963: 395–403, 409–11, 414–15; 1968: 8–10). Such incidents were now increasingly felt to be abnormal and after the Tang they are no longer reported in the official historical record.

By the Tang, it was finally accepted in elite circles that blood revenge should not be tolerated (Ch'ü 1961: 85–7). However, even then this acceptance was a qualified one. Liu Zongyuan (n.d., *juan* 9: 387–90) has written a famous text against blood revenge inspired by an actual case. A fellow official had sentenced someone to death for practising blood revenge, but at the same time donated a flag to the place where this person had lived in honour of his filial piety. At the end of his text, Liu Zongyuan noted his agreement with an old commentary, traditionally ascribed to Confucius himself, which permitted blood revenge in those cases when someone should not have been executed. Thus, both he and the local official were still ambivalent about the custom. In other social circles, the practice never disappeared at all, although its subsequent history is still relatively unclear.[7]

The logical parallel to the use of violence to settle private conflicts, was its use to settle political disputes. During the Han dynasties and the subsequent Period of Disunion, many officials were executed or forced to commit suicide for their political views, both in northern (supposedly more 'barbarian') and southern (supposedly more 'refined') China (e.g. Beck 1986: 321–2, 343–5; Yen 1968: 85–9). The ideal of 'refinement' was already gaining in appeal, with its focus on literary activities, calligraphy and the like, but this did not exclude the ongoing use of violence by its practitioners.

A good example of the flow of changes is the history of the Xu family, who belonged to the southern elite. They sponsored the revelations by the medium Yang Xi (330–386), which formed the basis for the southern Daoist tradition of Maoshan. Family members had long combined both civilian and military careers, and they had never had any qualms in killing people. Likewise they had suffered themselves from forced suicide, execution, and murder. During the revelations to Yang Xi, the responsibility for this violence was made clear and guilt was assigned to the appropriate persons. It was also revealed that one should relinquish such a violent life. At the same time the demonic beings that plagued the members of the Xu family were still combatted by military means – namely by divine armies under Yang Xi's overall control (Strickmann 1981: 122–4, 145–7, 147–50). Thus, violence remained perfectly acceptable on a religious level.

Especially in the South, there was a long term trend towards relinquishing the military career as a proper elite occupation (Holcombe 1989: 118–20, 133–6), but even then political violence was not easily given up. A case in point is that of the southern politician, historian and poet Shen Yue (441–513), in whose family we can see a shift from military to civilian careers, spanning several generations. When Shen was still small, his entire family was executed for their involvement on the losing side of a coup. He and his mother barely escaped. Much of his subsequent life was concerned with freeing himself from the military tradition by being conspicuously civilian (Mather 1988: 7–14). All the same, he eventually got involved in extremely violent political struggles, and had no qualms in advising Xiao Yan (who became the famous Emperor Wu of Liang, and fervent supporter of Buddhist traditions) to have the deposed Qi boy emperor murdered in 502. The boy was then simply beaten to death, an event which still haunted Shen Yue at the end of this life (pp. 10–11, 123–31, 221). He may not have engaged in violent behaviour himself, but was nonetheless an active participant in the violent political culture of the south.

The attitude of a Yan Zhitui (531–591) shows us something of the differentiated views that someone might have on violence. Yan came from the south, but had lived most of life in the north in the service of northern dynasties. He is considered a representative of the ideal of 'refinement'. He disapproved of violence towards animals and advocated a number of typical literati ideals. At the same time, he felt that his children should master archery for self-defense. He criticized southern Chinese elites for their excessive softness, which went as far as forbidding high officials to ride a horse. In his chapter on study, however, he observed that people of his generation (one suspects he is referring to northerners) knew only horsemanship, the wearing of armour and how to carry a long spear and a strong bow, without having studied strategy, topography, and the signs of heaven.

In his chapter against becoming a warrior, he quoted a list of people of his own surname who had been active as a soldier and had achieved very little. He went on to stress that he himself was weak and unsuitable to become a warrior (implying, of course, that one need not be a warrior to accomplish something politically). At the same time, he disapproved of those contemporaries from the educated elite, who had modest physical strength (unlike Confucius who could supposedly lift a gate) and little knowledge of weapons, but still engaged in military enterprise and rebellion (Yen 1968: 57, 114–17, 128–30, 202–3). Yan Zhitui clearly was not against 'martial violence,' nor against warfare, but felt that one needed to combine experience of actual fighting with strategic understanding. Even scholars should know something about fighting for their own good. Incidentally, this is precisely the attitude towards violence that is advocated in the pre-Han handbooks on military strategy (Johnston 1995: 61–108; cf. Yen 1968: 43, 49–51).

The continuing literati ambivalence towards violence in social practice is confirmed by Denis Twitchett, who concludes his study of Yu Di (d. 818) and his family, by noting how violence and the flaunting of the law were fairly common phenomena among the social and intellectual elites of the late Tang period. The Yu's were not simply uncouth military men, but came from a long-standing elite family and possessed a substantial cultural level. They were implicated in murder and bribery. Yu Di's son was implicated in a murder plot on one of the Chief Ministers of that time, together with the latter's colleague, namely the famous poet Yuan Zhen (779–831). Yuan's good friend Bai Juyi (772–846) was himself on good footing with another, equally morally improbate son of Yu Di's. Both Yuan Zhen and Bai Juyi were great critics of the mores of their times, but at the same time saw no qualms in befriending some of the principal representatives of these mores (Twitchett 1988: 29–63, 50 n 72, 58 n 113; cf. McMullen 1989b: 23–82, Liu 1985: 208–20). Although we cannot speak of the reestablishment of 'martial violence' in creating an elite identity during the Tang period, except on the level of court elites, the ready use of private political violence as such was not yet relinquished.

By and large, the evidence on political disputes after the Tang appears to indicate that private violence for political purposes became less common after the Tang. Instead, the mechanisms of state power were used to the same end, such as banishment to malaria infected regions (common during the Tang and Song), forced retirement and political executions (e.g. Hartman 1986: 56–7, 64, 84–6; Fisher 1990: 94–5). Therefore, relinquishing the direct practice of violence did not mean that it was given up as a political tool in more indirect ways as well.

Still, the Ming custom of having officials beaten up in the imperial court could now be seen as exceptional from the perspective of the educated elite.[8] The custom is traditionally explained as the influence of more violent Mongol (barbarian!) norms, but it could be explained equally well as the repenetration of non-elite values into court circles. The Ming imperial house was of very low descent and their personal environment (both eunuchs, wives and concubines) was always recruited from people with a low class background. This succesfully prevented powerful families from creating privileged connections to the court, but also had implications for the education of imperial children.

Distancing From the Body

Parallel to the changing attitude towards real life violence, we also see a growing rejection of the violation of the body in elite circles. This is quite visible in a number of (attempted) changes in elite liturgical practices. An all-important pre-Han ritual for forming groups at all social levels had been the covenant sealed by the consumption of human or animal blood. By the fourth century AD, it had fallen completely out of use among the educated elite (Lewis 1990: *passim*; ter Haar 1998). In classical Daoist traditions, the ritual was continued, but the blood was now replaced by cinnabar – which was also red and symbolized a similar type of life giving transformation (Mollier 1990: 79–80, 118).

Part of the same trend was the growing rejection of bloody sacrifice (i.e. offerings of bloody meat that involved killing) and spirit possession (i.e. lack of self-control). At the time, many cults were devoted to people who had died a violent death. Their spirits retained an unspent energy that made them linger on and made them into a constant threat, because they needed blood (=life force) to enable them survive. In exchange for bloody meat sacrifices, they could also be of great assistance to their worshippers. Originally, such sacrifices had been a standard part of the sacrificial liturgy and were practised by all layers of society (Kleeman 1994: 185–211). In the oldest scripture of the southern Daoist Lingbao tradition, the adept still had to sacrifice an ox and to sacrifice, as well as eat, a goose (Strickmann 1981: 138). However, the disappearance of bloody sacrifice from Daoist ritual traditions was virtually complete after the fourth century.

An important role in this liturgical change was played by the advent of the Daoist Heavenly Masters tradition, which was introduced to southern China by northern refugee elite families after 317 AD, when the north had been conquered by 'barbarian' peoples. At that time this tradition had fully relinquished bloody sacrifice. The southern Maoshan tradition was an attempt to come to terms with the Heavenly Masters criticism of local culture, whilst retaining essential elements of older southern occult traditions. It formed part of a large scale adoption of elements from the northern ideal of 'refinement'. As I already noted, the southern elites eventually came to see themselves as the foremost keepers of the ideal of 'refinement,' presenting the north as uncivilized 'barbarians'. The resistance against the ritual use of blood and meat would be carried by both Daoist and Buddhist traditions, but always remained an elite enterprise (Strickmann 1981: 136–7; Stein 1979).

Daoist traditions from the fourth century on stressed introspective journeys and communications with the supernatural world. This world was inhabited by stellar essences, who did not need any bloody meat sacrifice. Their worshippers tried to model themselves on these beings, abstaining from actual sexual contact and eating meat, and leading an impeccable moral life (Bokenkamp 1996: 166–79, 188–202; Robinet 1989). The existence of a body was almost literally denied.

We can trace a similar shift in another age-old ritual practice, namely the exposure of the human body to obtain rain (Schafer 1951). At first the king or his representatives performed this ritual. It was called 'exposing (*pu*) the shaman in the sun' or 'burning the shaman with fire'. 'Exposing' meant leaving in the burning sun, and 'burning' literally meant burning on a stake, in imitation of exposure to the sun (Schafer 1951: 169–73). It is interesting that this term did not yet have any pejorative meaning, and only came to mean 'excessive violence (*bao*)' later on. It was a custom with high status, modelled on the mythical kings Yu (of the Xia) and Tang (of the Shang) (Schafer 1951: 136–7, 141, 161; Gernet 1959: 555). History records examples of Tang, Song and Ming emperors who offered to practice ritual exposure or really did so. It is also frequently mentioned of Han officials that they performed ritual exposure or burning (in the latter case, the rain always came before the actual burning could take place). Later, at least one Tang and two Ming officials also practised it (Schafer 1951: 134, 136–40). Apparently, the need to inflict violence on oneself had became too problematic for members of the elite. It was commonly practised by religious specialists, especially shamans and Buddhist priests – incidentally, the Ming emperor in question had been a Buddhist monk and one of the two Ming officials was a lay Buddhist (Schafer 1951: 135, 137, 139–40; Gernet 1959: 554–5).

The main Buddhist scriptural antecedent for ritual suicide came from the Lotus Sutra, according to which the King of Medicine had once sacrificed himself by impregnating his body with fragrant oil and then setting it alight in honour of the Buddha. Erik Zürcher has noted that self-mutilation was not practised in Indian Buddhism, despite numerous scriptural antecedents. This suggests that the use of the King of Medicine as a model served to legitimate the incorporation of existing indigenous practices. In China suicide by burning and a range of minor forms of self-mutilation, became common practices, which continued into the present century, both by fully ordained Buddhist monks and lay believers – men and women (Zürcher 1959: 281–2; Gernet 1959; Welch 1967: 298–300, 325–8; T'ien 1988: 152–3). From a Buddhist perspective, this underlined the seriousness of one's resolve and demonstrated the worthlessness of their bodies. Furthermore, ritually speaking they were already dead anyhow, having left the family formally behind. I suspect that most people will have seen this type of self-inflicted ritual violence first of all as a forceful demonstration of religious power, in the same way as different forms of bloody self-mutilation by local mediums.

Devout Buddhist believers used their own blood to copy a sutra or to write solemn vows (Faure 1991: 138–9; Welch 1967: 323). This strongly resembles the traditional use of blood to empower oral promises by drinking it (in the blood covenant ritual), or on amulets and statues by applying it to their surface. The reason for using blood in all of these contexts was the same as the considerations behind the bloody sacrifice, namely that it represented a life force. Consuming or applying blood therefore meant the concrete transferal of this force to one's mouth (making it into a powerful organ of speech) or object (increasing the power of that object).

When we speak of Buddhist monks and nuns, we should not overlook that during the pre-Song period these still often included members of elite society. At first, these forms of self-inflicted violence were not considered problematic and until the early Song they could still be performed in the presence of local elites and officials (Stevenson 1996: 10–14, 18–19, 21, 23). Thereafter, these practices were increasingly perceived as problematic.

In the same way, obviously violent forms of suicide such as killing by the sword were replaced by less bloody practices. During the late imperial period, it seems that suicide was usually performed by hanging, poisoning or drowning. Sufficient gory aspects still accompanied a suicide (viz. failed suicides leading to disfigurement, discolouring, the tongue hanging out of the body in the case of hanging, swollen bodies in the case of drowning etc.), but these were also ignored in the written record.[9]

At the same time that self-mutilation and suicide became problematical for the educated elite, even when performed by Buddhist believers, they became ever more common among women and non-elite men. Cutting off a piece of one's own flesh to prepare a healing broth for a sick relative was considered to be the culmination of filial piety. On an elite level, suicide became the prerogative of women in the so-called female chastity cult. It was deemed better to commit suicide than to remarry. When violence was performed in the proper moral context, it was very difficult to avoid tolerating it, even for outspoken Confucian figures. Opposition tended to come from the side of the bureaucracy, who were concerned about the private nature of this violence (Elvin 1984; T'ien 1988; Cheong 1990: 93–103, 116–23).

The persistence of violence as a form of cultural expression of power and moral values shows that the long-term trend away from violence was a highly modified one. Not only was it largely an affair of the educated male elite, but this same elite continued to admire the Buddhist practitioners and women who carried out such violence. Especially when carried out in the name of filial piety and female chastity, many Confucians (= male educated elite) were forced to approve of it.

Not surprisingly, the rejection of violence also influenced healing practice. During the Han, the demonological paradigm of illness still dominated society as a whole. This paradigm defined illnesses as violent attacks by concrete demonic beings and prescribed the use of counter-violence to deal with them (Unschuld 1985: 34–50, 67–73, 215–23). Whereas the Han imperial court still practised the exorcist Nuo ritual in its full form, it was continued as a court ritual until the Tang dynasty only in watered down form and eventually replaced by the more civilized *mulian* plays.[10]

Under the educated elite, the demonological paradigm of healing gradually lost in influence after the Han dynasty, but remained important among other social groups until most recently. It was replaced by ethical medicine (in which moral faults were blamed for diseases) and by correspondence medicine (whose theories were based on the notions of Yin and Yang, the Five Phases, and analogies derived from the political organization of the nation) (Unschuld 1985: 73–100; Sivin 1995). Demonological medical concepts were now given a different, non-violent meaning (Unschuld 1985: 67–73). It is no coincidence that the proponents of correspondence medicine from the Song and later periods usually had an educated elite background.

Already early on, traditional Chinese medicine did not advocate the internal examination of the body and concentrated on the tongue, the pulse and outward aspects of the body in order to set a diagnosis. In texts that were compiled somewhere in the first century BC or AD there are indications that postmortem examinations had once been made. The only recorded pre-Song dissection dates from AD 16. Otherwise most anatomical knowledge will have been based on analogies derived from dissections of animals intended for human consumption and autopsies of criminals. It did not lead to the systematic expansion of and interest in medical (rather than criminological) knowledge of the inside of the body.[11] In very early days, surgery was not entirely unknown in China, but even when cataract surgery was introduced by Indian monks, it did not take hold (Unschuld 1985: 144–53). Close involvement with the physical body became every more problematic, until this side of the body was rediscovered during the nineteeth century (Unschuld 1985: 212–15).

The Cultural Expression of 'Martial Violence'

As long as the 'martial violence' ideal was still alive, people wanted to carry weapons in public. At first, it was therefore quite acceptable for officials and men of standing to carry real or symbolic weapons, such as the famous poet Pan Yue (231–300 AD) who proudly wore his crossbow in the streets. He also had a habit of whipping one of his minor officers, who later took revenge and accused him of attempting rebellion. As a result, Pan and his close and distant relatives were executed.[12] Pan's behaviour suggests that 'martial violence' and literary activities could still be publicly combined. His case also underlines the violent nature of third century political life.

Already during the Han dynasty, the possession and carrying of weapons was a topic of debate. As Hans van Ess has pointed out in an unpublished paper (van Ess, n.d.), much the same arguments were used then as they still are today. The legal possession of arms was seen as a personal right that signified freedom and was advocated by members of the old elite in favour of a weaker state (and more independence for them), whereas restricting possession was depicted as a means for enhancing public security and advocated by officials who supported a stronger state – in which they were making a career (van Ess 1994; cf. Ban 1962: *juan* 64: 2795–7; *juan* 40: 2056).

During the Han, everybody could still carry weapons, even in the imperial court, but eventually carrying weapons came to be limited to visits to the court. In the Jin court, officials wore adorned ritual swords made of wood, jade or horn, which was continued during the Tang dynasty. Higher Sui and Tang mofficials had ornamental lances above their doors. The fact that real weapons were replaced by ritual versions suggests that the reason for their removal was first of all maintaining of safety (given the frequency of political murders, a reasonable consideration). The social norm prescribed that one carried weapons in court, and therefore they were replaced by symbolic weapons. Only after the Tang, this custom was discontinued and even the symbolic representation of violence in court became inappropriate (Harada 1937: 142–8; Zhou 1984: 160, 240).

Part of the ideal of 'martial violence' was its regular practice outside a combat situation, such as hunting, archery, or polo. Someone's accomplishments in these activities contributed to one's public identity, whether in the form of a demonstration of martial vigour or an actual competition of martial agility (Bodde 1991: 292–300). With the decline of the ideal of 'martial violence', these forms of martial action all went out of fashion among the educated elite. The precise dating of this process is difficult due to the lack of sources (Bodde 1991: 295–6).

Archery had been an important elite ability for centuries, advocated for instance by Confucius himself. It had become a partly ceremonial activity by the Eastern Han, when students at the national academy would shoot arrows at targets, on which their questions were written. All the same, we have seen that Pan Yue carried his crossbow around in public. Ge Hong (283–343), the scion of an important southern family, proudly wrote that while he was in the army he had shot down two cavalerists and one horse with his arrows, in order to save his life.[13] Two-and-a-half centuries later, Yan Zhitui noted that in his time people south of the Yangzi River considered archery to be military archery, not to be practised by the well-dressed scholars. However, they continued to practise ceremonial archery until the early Sui. In the north, scholars were still well-versed in military archery and received prizes for their ability. Yan approved that children learn this useful skill, as long as they did not 'bring down small birds or cut down animals by archery' (Yen 1968: 202–3). Clearly, the shift away from archery was very gradual and took place faster in the south, though even there ceremonial archery continued to be practised.

An interesting case is that of polo, which also illustrates the need to differentiate between court and general elite circles. The social history of the game has been analyzed by James Liu, who proposes to see it as an indicator of cultural change in Chinese court circles. Polo differs from the indigenous example of archery, because it was probably introduced through the foreign cultures that conquered the north before the Tang. It became especially popular from the seventh century onwards, and attained a large following in court circles, but never among the social and educated elites. It is the subject of exquisite paintings and many written texts until the late Tang. Already by the Northern Song, the game was played by professional players and court entertainers. It had apparently become a ritualized court activity. After 1125, polo and other martial activities in court circles gradually disappeared, under the ongoing critique by members of the educated elite (Liu 1985; Bower 1991). In a sense, the history of polo was always closely linked to the martial nature of the Tang and – to a lesser degree – Song imperial courts. Its lack of success in broader circles partly reflects the expense of the game (such as the costs of maintaining sufficient suitable horses) and partly the extent to which the shift away from 'martial violence' had already progressed by the Tang period. Its disappearance was an indicator of cultural change in court circles, but also of the increasing impact of the educated elite on the imperial court.

Thus we can conclude that the various martial pursuits all went out of fashion among the educated elite after the Han dynasty, even though at different paces. By the Song, we can speak of a general lack of interest in athletic games among elite circles (especially those who were or aspired to be members of the literati status group). Another example is that of cockfighting, which was a popular literati pastime and frequently the topic of literary treatment until the Tang period, after which it rapidly fell out of literati favour. It did persist in society in general, although here too there seems to have been a gradual decline in interest. Although the violence is enjoyed only vicariously, the descriptions show that people enjoyed it in a very personal way. (Cutter 1989, esp. 131–3).

Athletic and violent games were replaced by aesthetic pursuits and various board games, such as the literati game *par excellence* Encirclement Chess (=Go) or also Elephant Chess (=Chinese Chess) (Yasunaga 1981). By the late imperial period, violent playing by children was strongly disapproved of in literati educational ideals and practice (Saari 1990: 80–3, 151–2, 168–9), and it would be interesting to document the socialization of 'refined' attitudes further back in time.

The bracketing out of physical processes and outward emotions towards ever more introspection and self-control was paralleled by a similar shift in the visual arts. Alexander Soper (1967: 51–2, 65–8; cf. Bower 1991: 32–3) already noted that until the Han, battles were frequently depicted and in very observant detail. These depictions were produced for elite consumption, indicating that the first rise of the 'refinement' ideal before the Han did not entail an immediate and complete rejection of martial violence in all elite circles. Soper also suggested on the basis of literary evidence, that battles were still being depicted during the Period of Disunion, but then in a fairly bloodless manner and without the indication of actual combat. By the Song, even such depictions had become rare, at least in elite painting. Soper sees the decreased depiction of explicit battle as the result of a larger trend in which emotions could no longer be expressed explicitly.

James Cahill (1994: 114–23) has recently elaborated Soper's sugges-tion by pointing out the general disappearance of precise depictions of reality, of which emotions and violence formed a part. For instance, until the early Song, the demon queller Zhong Kui was still depicted killing off demons in his usual violent and cruel way. Thereafter, he is still depicted as frequently as before, but now rarely in such an explicit manner. This is remarkable, since the killing of demons has always been a very bloody and violent affair. In the same way, a nature painting from 1321 is an absolute exception in its depiction of insects actually devouring each other. Otherwise, the norm was since long the purely aesthetic and isolated depiction of insects and larger animals (Whitfield 1993: 15–21, 51). Fierce emotions and violence were banned from painting, regardless whether springing from the so-called amateur-literati or professional schools.[14]

Ironically, the rise of cultural practices to create a softer, more harmless type of female took place at the same time that the male elite rejected violence as a part of their own identity. One of these practices was the binding of female feet, which was an often painful violation of the natural form of the foot (Ebrey 1993: 37–43). It accompanied (as well as symbolized) the gradual loss in independence of women during the Song and Yuan, at least from a legal perspective and in public life (Ebrey 1993). Equally ironic, the use of violence by women remained unproblematic, as in the common practice of self-mutilation out of filial piety and suicide out of the wish (= pressure) to preserve female chastity.

Controlling Others

Violence in controlling and subduing others was not a problem, as long as the elite could pretend not to be directly and personally involved. A good example of the enforcement of order and social hierarchy by means of violence is the use of penal violence (which, quite unsurprisingly, is never called 'martial violence [*wu*]'). Here we see that maiming punishments (such as tattooing and the amputation of bodily parts, such as ears, nose, hands and feet, and sexual organs) were used increasingly seldom from the Western Han onwards and discontinued formally in the Sui code. However, despite the rationalization of this change by arguments about the moral nature of rulership, the decisive reason was the use of convict labour from the Qin dynasty, which cannot be performed by mutilated people (McKnight 1992: 328–34, 385–92; Hulsewé 1955: 102–28). Tattooing remained in use much of the time (McKnight 1992: 348–51; Bodde and Morris 1967: 96–7) and violence as such was not rejected.

The standard penalties of the imperial period would be beating with a stick, penal servitude (i.e. forced labour), exile and death – increasing in severity from strangling to beheading and finally slicing up (McKnight 1992: 334–6; Bodde and Morris 1967: 76–102). Significantly, destroying the integrity of the body counted as a more severe punishment. Frequent use was made of all kinds of torture in order to enforce confessions, causing terrible pain and lasting mutilation, when not even death. Punishment and torture were carried out by menials, but under the personal supervision of officials who belonged to the educated elite (Huang 1984: 273–9; Kuhn 1990: 15–25, 142–3, 162, 170–83).

The way in which penal violence was applied further contributed to the reproduction of social hierarchy, since members of the governing elite were exempt from torture and could expect less severe corporeal punishments (MacCormack 1990: 142–57). This shows that it was not the rejection of violence in general, but its application to the educated elite that was the real issue. Once more we can distinguish a transitional period, during which this social distinction in physical punishment was established. The *Book of Rites* stated that corporeal punishments should not be extended to officials, but Han period New Text scholars argued that, since officials possess the faculty of ascertaining guilt, they were morally obliged to take their fates in their own hands and commit suicide. The alternative was that a trial took place, which could result in the public execution of an official, but also in his subsequent release (van Ess 1993: 258–64). The use of violence was not an issue at all, for these commentators even advocated suicide (unthinkable in later times) and had no qualms with the execution of fellow members of the elite either.

Eventually the interpretation of the crucial *Book of Rites* statement changed and only then did it become a general prohibition that exempted officials from physical punishment, extending this immunity to their direct relatives as well. It became the most lasting privilege of all legal privileges enjoyed by the elite.[15] During the Qing, this exemption was expanded to all those who had obtained an examination degree, including even the lowest licentiates (Ch'ü 1961: 182–3). Given the common use of torture and violent punishments, these were highly significant privileges and powerful status indicators.

Violence continued to be liberally used in the controlling of others, but the dominance of the myth of the shift from *wu* ('martial violence') to *wen* ('refinement') has been quite succesful in preventing any scholarly investigations of this topic. Violence was used against servants, farmers, children and wives, and subjects in general. Physical force and terror were used liberally towards people suspected of transgressing the law, already during the preliminary interrogations and again as a means of punishment. When one was convicted, one was given a number of beatings or various other forms of corporeal and shame punishment. Prison was not a corrective institution, but served to keep people until trial or final punishment (McKnight 1992: 385–506; Bodde and Morris 1967: 76–112). The use of physical force in controlling tenants (to extract rents and other services) and maintaining local social hierarchy still need to be investigated. China's pre-modern (and modern) harmonious society was and is one based on force and terror for those who transgressed the norms that were (and are) set and maintained by those higher up the social hierarchy.

The trend away from the ideal of 'martial violence' towards the ideal of 'refinement' was embedded in a larger trend towards controlling emotions, a trend which has not gone unnoticed, but still needs to be studied in a systematic way. The original moving force in the shift towards the ideal of 'refinement' was its expediency to political elites who lacked a monopoly on military power. It was a very effective alternative means of claiming political superiority, based on educational and cultural norms that were hard to acquire outside the elite and could be defined by them at will. This ideal had its own cultural dynamics, for the need to prevent too many outsiders from taking part in the ideal, necessitated constant changes in the collective definition of 'refinement'. Instead of a Confucian elite, we should probably speak of an elite of refinement that ruled premodern China. The underlying ideals were furthered by members of the educated elite(s) irrespective of their Buddhist, Confucian or Daoist backgrounds. The move away from violence was a general socio-cultural trend that cannot be tied in directly to the the writings of Confucius and Mencius, or the spread of Buddhist strictures against killing. Confucius was not against violence as such, Mencius did not oppose animal sacrifice.[16] The overall trend started before the introduction of Buddhist teachings and practices, and its evolution cannot be directly related to the history of Buddhism or any other philosophical and religious teachings.

It is no coincidence that imperial houses, who first established themselves on the basis of military power, struggled to maintain something of their original martial identity despite ongoing criticism by the educated elite. Even that supposedly most civilian of imperial houses, the Zhao family of the Song dynasty, tried to maintain a martial look in court, whether by taking part in martial sports or, at the very least, by organizing such sports as a court spectacle (Liu 1985: 211, 215–24). Two of the most successful Ming rulers came to power after extensive warfare (namely the founding Hongwu emperor and his *de facto* successor the Yongle emperor). A third Ming emperor regained power by a palace coup, after he had lost power as the result of his capture in battle by the Mongols. Several later Ming emperors also tried desperately to maintain this martial identity (Twitchett and Grimm 1988: 322–5, 339–40; Geiss 1988: 404–5, 415–39). When they were unsuccesful, the Ming emperors turned away from government altogether.

It is commonly assumed that China was a culture which condemned violence and awarded great prestige to the literary (e.g. Harrell 1990: 1). This view is based on a construction of 'reality' as the educated elite want(ed) to see it, not on the actual direct or – as importantly – indirect use of violence by this same elite. It is solely an ideological construct, for educated and social elites had no compunctions in using violence to maintain control. It is imperative that we distinguish between the gradually decreasing use of violence to create an elite identity, and the use of violence per se.

Notes

I wish to thank Göran Aijmer, Hans van Ess, Valerie Hansen and Jens Tappe for their comments upon earlier versions.

1. Important exceptions are the studies in Lipman and Harrell (1990) and especially Johnston (1995). I have been unable to incorporate Joseph Needham and Robin D. S. Yates, *Science and Civilisation in China,* with the collaboration of Krzystof Gawlikoski, Edward McEwen, and Wang Ling, vol. 5 *Chemistry and Chemical Technology,* part VII *Military Technology: Missiles and Sieges,* Cambridge: Cambridge University Press (1994). A detailed bibliography on this topic can be found at http://sun.sino.uni-heidelberg.de/staff/bth/violence.htm
2. Rand (1979–80) and Turner (1993). An exception is McKnight (1992: 191–8).
3. Stephen Harrell (1990) wisely ignores the two terms altogether.
4. Lewis (1990). Also Waldron (1991: 1074–5), based on philosophical discussions of violence.
5. For an authoritative statement see Fairbank (1974). For the Tang, see Pulleyblank (1976: 33–4) and McMullen (1989a). For the Song, see Haeger (1975). All Chinese history textbooks reiterate similar points of view.
6. Lewis (1990: 80–94). Also see the remarks by van Ess (1993; 1994: 162–4.)
7. Unlike McKnight (1992: 969) – based on a study by Sôgabe Shizuo – I do not think that Song feuding was a new phenomenon. On Qing feuding in southern China, see Ownby (1990) and Lamley (1990).
8. Geiss (1988b: 449–50); Fisher (1990 93–4). On the violence of the two founding Ming emperors, see Dreyer (1982: 100–4, 140–8, 214–17).
9. This a relatively underinvestigated topic, see Hsieh and Spence (1981: 46) and T'ien (1988: 15).
10. Bodde (1975: 75–127) and Harper (1987: 239–83). Personal communication by Wilt Idema on the *mulian* plays.
11. Unschuld (1985: 78–9) and Sivin (1995: 12–13). On Song anatomical knowledge in a criminological context, see Brian McKnight's (1981b: *passim*) translation in *The Washing Away of Wrongs*.
12. Liu (1976: 310). On Pan Yue as poet, see Lai (1994: 409–25).
13. Bodde (1991: 292–3); Yen (1968: 203 n 1). Compare the case in Tanigawa (1985: 118–19).

14. This move is paralelled by the move from 'outward' to 'inner' alchemy during this same period, which we cannot investigate here for reasons of space.
15. Ch'ü (1961: 177–85). The dating of this change still needs to be investigated.
16. We saw the example of Confucius above. As Cutter (1989: 142) points out, Confucians did not necessarily oppose animal sacrifice and Mencius decries the niggardness of a ruler in substituting a smaller animal for a larger one to be sacrificed.

7

Butchering Fish and Executing Criminals: Public Executions and the Meanings of Violence in Late Imperial and Modern China
Virgil Kit-yiu Ho

Violence is generally taken as a phenomenon which is universally shared. We all seem to know intuitively but with unreserved certainty what violence means or what constitutes an act of violence, both with regard to the past and in the present. If one accepts the notion that 'any act that threatens a person's physical or psychological integrity is a form of violence' (Salmi 1993: 16), then one is bound to be alarmed by the prevalence of violence in diverse facets of life. However, such a simple and too generalized definition tends to turn the phenomenon into an ever present negative potential in social life. Such a notion of violence is devoid of any contextualization and severed from other possible implications of social significance. The simplified view may perhaps serve us to recognize violence more easily 'by definition', but it will not help to bring out the complex and ambivalent cultural force of violence as a symbolic device in contextual social discourse. Nor will it help to clarify the layers of possible socio-cultural meanings which are embedded in an act that we intuitively recognize as 'violent'. This essay sets out to explore tentatively the possible meanings of public violence in the context of executions in China from the 1840s onwards. It questions the validity of a universal concept of violence and hopes to open up alternative ways to view violence as a cultural idiom.

The Anatomy of Violence in the Chinese Context

David Riches and many other anthropologists draw our attention to the danger of imposing an Anglo-Saxon view of 'violence' on other cultures which may appear as 'violent' in the eyes of the alien English-speaking person (Riches 1986: 13). Even so, many contemporary Chinese men and women have adopted Anglo-Saxon views of 'violence' in their daily discourse. In present-day China and Hong Kong, the term 'violence' is commonly used under a strong Anglo-Saxon influence; it connotes an excessive, illegitimate or immoral use of force intended to inflict harm – physical or psychological – on another person. Today, diverse forms of individual and social action such as the butchering of animals, the act of killing, the practice of martial art, the playing of ball games which involve bodily contact, children playing with toy guns and so on, are seen as manifestations of 'violence'. Since an endless number of instances of personal behaviour and social activities tally in one way or another with the broadly conceived Anglo-Saxon notion of 'violence', Chinese society is becoming increasingly and alarmingly 'violent' in the eyes of the increasingly 'Westernised' Chinese.

Despite a strong impact of the West, many Hong Kong and mainland Chinese still continue to conceive violence in a distinctively Chinese manner. Facets of life viewed as 'violent' in most Western European and North American societies, do not arouse similar concern in Hong Kong and China. For instance, Cantonese martial art movies lure their fans with highly explicit scenes of blood-splattering fighting. Many Cantonese are fascinated by watching the public slaughtering of animals, especially big fish. In big fishmonger shops in Hong Kong, it is common to find photographs of slaughtering scenes of exotic fish posed at the front of the shop as a means to attract the attention of passer-bys. In one such incident, which took place on a Sunday afternoon in mid-October 1995, the butchering of a seven feet long fish captured the attention of the mass media in Hong Kong. Local newspapers and television networks helped to popularize this event through their sensational reportages – before, during and after the butchery. On the day of the 'big event', hundreds of people flocked to the seafood restaurant in Saikung to witness the occasion. The spectators, both old and young and from all walks of life, were tremendously excited, exhilarated and very amused by the scene of the butchery. Some hectically captured this moment of bloodshed for posterity, using their sophisticated video equipments. No one present at the scene would have described the event as violent, cruel or revolting. The occasion was enjoyed more as a happy family outing (infants and children with their parents formed a large part of the audience), than an exposition of public violence or a lesson in cruelty. The butchering of exotic – though less large – fish has become a regular and popular weekend event in the seafood restaurants along the waterfront in this part of Hong Kong.

The English word 'violence' is commonly translated into modern Chinese as *baoli* which in its daily usage in contemporary Cantonese not only means 'the exercise of physical force so as to inflict injury on or damage to persons or property' *(Shorter Oxford Dictionary* 1984), but also connotes an excessive and brutal use of force. However, the term *baoli,* seemingly, does not exist in classical Chinese. If a writer in traditional China described violent conduct, he would very likely use the word *bao* – the closest correspondent of the English word 'violence' in classical Chinese – instead of *baoli.*[1]

The idea of *bao,* however, connotes rather different meanings from the modern-day term *baoli.* In classical Chinese, according to the authoritative dictionary *'Zihai'* ('Ocean of Characters'), *bao* is used to describe a 'forceful action', 'ruthlessness', 'ferocity', or 'fighting with bare hands' and other similar meanings. *Bao* also carries the meaning of 'when a master (or monarch) disregards or ignores the well being of his servants (or subjects); or when a socially inferior person rebels against his superior or his senior'. In this latter sense, *bao* has little to do with excessive use of force to hurt another person, because this is not the crucial idea involved in the concept of *bao.* Rather, what semantically constitutes a violent act is when the action is a forceful violation of established social and political orders, or against ethical norms. In other words, *bao is* never used as a term describing, in a general way, an act of application of immoral force. It has been, and remains so, a highly positively morally loaded word which connotes very specific socio-cultural meanings. If a person was convicted of a serious crime, his coming execution was not necessarily conceived as an act of violence and the force to be deployed might not be construed by officials and commoners as something excessive or against the socio-politico-religious order.

Our present-day concept of 'violence' is seemingly inadequate to explain China's past experience in public executions. The present-day Chinese notion corresponding to 'violence' is not without ambiguity, as the cases of butchering of fish and animals, and *kungfu* movies seem to indicate.

Another example can be seen in the strikingly different manner that the State broadcasting network of the People's Republic of China (hereafter PRC) employs when portraying crime and punishment on television. In Guangdong Province in the south, one of the hit television programmes is a kind of 'Crime Watch'. In many episodes, police videos are shown, documenting the bloodstained scenes of crime. As a rule, the badly mutilated and bloody corpses of the victims are depicted in meticulous detail and often in close-ups, several minutes long. The message to the watchers is straightforward: these are the results of serious crime and unforgivable acts of violence – violence in the sense of an excessive use of force implying an immoral disruption of the social order.

As an interesting contrast in the same programme, footages of 'mass meetings for the announcement of sentences' are also shown. In these, soon-to-be-executed criminals with their hands tied and sometimes their feet chained, are made to line up to stand motionlessly in front of the camera, by heavily armed public security officers. Their heads are shown with face down, expressing shame, guilt and regret. Once the sentence has been passed, the name, crime and sentence are written on a long bamboo stick which is placed at the back of each convict (sometimes, as an alternative, written on a long strip of white paper which is glued to the chest). After this they are taken for a public parade on police trucks. Everything that goes on takes place in good order and is under full social control. The message to the public is an unambiguous one: the execution of these criminals by the State is not an instance of violence but a graceful act of defending the socio-ethical order. In both official rhetoric and common daily discourse, State executions are rarely understood or described as *bao* or *baoli*. Nor is the force used construed as 'excessive' as the modern discourse on 'violence' would imply. Hence, the notion of violence (*bao*) should be re-examined in relation to public executions, and especially so with reference to traditional China. It can possibly be understood in the following ways:

1. An execution involves the use of physical force that inflicts harm on the object for the action.
2. An execution may be perceived as an *excessive* use of force which transgresses basic cultural ideals such as the importance of compromise and forgivefulness.
3. Public executions are construed as brutal shows of force that eventually kills without disrupting the established social, cultural and ethical orders.

The ways a person perceives and draws meaning from an act of execution, will depend on a web of complex factors, ranging from his social and occupational backgrounds to his beliefs and personality. A criminal will understand the event very differently from an executioner, whose perception may again be very distinct from that of the procuratorial official, whose ideas may, once again, be completely different from the various comprehensions of the spectators. Attitudes and interpretations are diverse.

Views from the Umpire Box

The pragmatic political functions of public execution in China and in many other societies, are reasonably well known as a result of the many outstanding works on the topic.[2] Public executions, in terms of being a means to manifest in full the power of the State, broadcast an unambiguous message. However, in his overseeing the public execution of a convicted criminal, a magistrate in late Imperial China performed a function more complex than being a mere representative of the absolutist power of the State. He also fulfilled a moral-religious duty, ensuring the rule of law and the triumph of justice.

In the context of nineteenth-century China, a procuratorial official at an execution was a representative of the Imperial government, which in theory monopolized the power of taking a person's life after having conducted a 'fair' trial. All public executions, therefore, had to be inspected by a magistrate. Before the event the magistrate announced to the crowd what crime had been committed by the convict and the punishment he had been found to deserve. This part of the public drama helped legitimize the execution as an act of repair rather than a haphazard misuse of force. In the eyes of those officiating, the act of execution was not necessarily connected with violence in the sense of *bao* or *baoli;* immorality was not a relevant semantic component in construing the event. The force used was seen neither as excessive, nor as ethically improper, as the term 'violence' would suggest; hence, an execution was not perceived as an act of destructive immorality.

In this public drama of execution, various symbolic idioms were employed to assure that the act should not be wrongly understood as an immoral manifestation of *bao,* but be given the lustre of a graceful act of justice and of moral triumph. One of these idioms was to subject a convict to a process of dehumanization, so effective that by the time he was taken to the public execution ground, he would neither be pitied, nor recognized as an ordinary man, but regarded as a kind of beast or, even worse, a demon. This was accomplished in a number of ways. First, a convict was usually locked up in a *yamen's* (magistracy's) prison in which he was deliberately underfed and denied even minimal hygienic care. Though conditions in most *yamen* prisons were never appropriate, some of them, according to contemporary accounts, were absolutely appalling.[3] As a result of such confinement, by the time of his execution a convict would already have become so emaciated that he looked more like a demon than a human being — his brail loosened and hair in disarray, and his physique so weakened that he could hardly stand; his body was filthy and stinking. They were consciously made to look detestable and horrible. As a contemporary missionary recorded:

> Their deathlike countenances, emaciated forms, and long coarse black hair, which, according to prison rules, they are not allowed to shave, impart to them the appearance of demons, and fail not to convey to the mind of the beholder, feelings of horror, which are not, indeed, easily dispelled or forgotten (Gray 1875: 301).

Second, on the day of their execution all prisoners, after being summoned to the local magistracy for the public announcement of their fate, were carried by coolies in rattan baskets to the execution ground, instead of marching on their feet. When the procession arrived at the place, the convicts were mercilessly 'tumbled out of the baskets as if they were mere dirt' (Gray 1875: 485–6). The scene reminisced that of some sort of domestic animals being brought to the abattoir. Although the act of carrying a prisoner in a basket might have been due to such practicalities as weakened and frightened convicts being too frail to walk, it might also convey the impression of a captured demonized creature being taken to the execution ground where 'it' would be beheaded, just like an animal at a marketplace or an evil spirit being killed in an exorcism.

Third, after that a convicted criminal had been decapitated or mutilated in public, his body would be exposed in the open, ranging usually from overnight to three or more days. After that, his corpse would be dumped into a mass grave. In nineteenth-century Canton, such a grave was located in the eastern suburb of the city. In Peking it was in the western outskirt. Moreover, in Canton before the 1860s, a malefactor's head would be piled up in a receptacle for criminals' heads as a public warning to any potential lawbreakers. In later years such heads were kept individually in coarse earthen tubs containing quicklime and so displayed at the execution ground. It is also recorded that the heads of decapitated pirates and burglars were commonly exposed in the immediate vicinity of the scenes of their crimes. These heads were either exposed in cages or attached to the tops of long poles (Gray 1972: 67–8; Tao 1972: 67). In addition to its admonitory function, the display of heads may also have had something to do with the severity of the punishment: an incomplete corpse, or a mutilated carcass, would 'render a body unfit to receive the soul again' (de Groot 1989: vol. 1: 342–3). Thus the act was intended to be totally destructive so that its impact on a criminal would be felt even in his afterlife. The soul of a decapitated person, due to the incompleteness of his corpse, would be degraded forever into a malevolent hungry ghost.

The dehumanizing process of his punishment, starting with imprisonment, was effectively ensured to extend far into his afterlife.[4]

John H. Gray, a perceptive nineteenth-century observer,[5] witnessed and later wrote a detailed account of one public execution in mid-nineteenth-century Canton. This vivid record, which deserves to be quoted in length here, indicates the religious-moral role of both the procuratorial officials and the executioners:

When the time has arrived for making the condemned men ready for execution, an officer in full costume, carrying in his hand a board on which is pasted a list of the names of the prisoners who are that day to atone for their crimes, enters the prison, and, in the hearing of all the prisoners in the ward assembled, reads aloud the list of the condemned. Each prisoner whose name is called at once answers to it, and he is then made to sit in a basket to be carried once more into the presence of a judge . . . The process of pinioning the malefactors having been accomplished they are conveyed through the right or eastern arch of the three-arched gateway, into the presence of the magistrate whose judgement-seat has been removed from the court and placed in the porch of the inner approach to his official residence. His last duty to these men consists in summoning each into his presence, in order that a strip of bamboo, on which a piece of paper bearing the criminal's name has been previously pasted, may be bound to his head. This is done that when they are conveyed through the streets of the city to the execution-ground, the citizens may note what criminals have been led forth to execution. In March, 1860, I witnessed an execution of the second class at Canton. There were only three criminals . . . [they] were carried to the common execution-ground, which is beyond the city walls, in the open baskets which are ordinarily used for this purpose at Canton . . . The procession was headed by a company of spearmen . . . and behind the prisoners, marched another company of soldiers armed, some with spears, some with swords, and others with matchlocks. They were followed by three equerries who proceeded a large sedan chair of state, in which was seated the . . . deputy ruler of the county of Namhoi, in whose presence, as sheriff, the execution was to take place. After three equerries who rode behind this chair, was carried another sedan chair of state, in which was seated an official whose duty was to pay adoration to the Five Genii on the occasion. In close proximity to the place of execution, there is a small temple in honour of these gods, and they are regarded as having the power of preventing the spirits of decapitated criminals being hurried by revengeful feelings into inflicting injuries on the judge, magistrates, and others who have administered the law. In the rear of these state chairs a herald on horseback carries in his right hand a small yellow banner bearing two Chinese characters implying 'By Imperial decree'. Without this banner the Wye-Yune or sheriff dare not authorize the executioner to strike that fatal blow. On arriving at the ground, where the executioner was conspicuous by the bright blade he carried, the spearmen filed off and arranged themselves on each side of a table covered with red cloth. The Wye-Yune took his seat in a chair, also covered with red cloth, in front of the table. The pirates were unceremoniously ejected from their baskets upon the mud . . .When an assistant executioner had placed the prisoners in a kneeling position, with their heads bent forward . . . the Wye-Yune . . . ordered the executioner, through a herald, to deal the fatal strokes. In less than twelve seconds the unhappy men were standing in the presence of that God of whose might, majesty, holiness, justice, and mercy, they had lived and died in a state of ignorance . . . (Gray 1972: 63–5).[6]

Through this eyewitness' account we may now try to explore the symbolic drama constructed in this series of acts, paying attention both to the ways these acts were construed and the various religio-political symbolic idioms which were used. First, it was through the use of the various sets of Imperial symbolism in the course of the proceedings that a strong political message was communicated. Only the State and the Imperial Court possessed the absolute and final power of taking the life of a condemned criminal. The procession of the Imperial forces and subsequently the execution in front of a small yellow Imperial banner and a congregation of government officials and soldiers, were all clearly staged as a political celebration in which the power of the State was intentionally made manifest to the public.

Second, the fact that the last summon of the prisoners took place in the open courtyard and the porch instead of inside the *yamen* is another indication of the process of dehumanization. The condemned had now been further degraded into polluted objects whose entry into the magistrate's office was denied lest that their presence would defile the place. In official view, a magistrate's *yamen* was a solemn place that demanded absolute respect from everyone (Tao 1972: 4–5). A convicted criminal in his demon-like shape was considered no longer fit for this place of decency and Imperial authority.

It should be recalled that the prisoners, after the process of pinioning had been accomplished, were taken through the right or eastern door into the open courtyard, where the magistrate would verify their identities. In another description of the event, Gray tells us that once this process had been completed, the prisoners were carried away in baskets through the left, or western door, to the execution ground – convicted criminals were considered to be unfit for leaving the *yamen* through the respectable main central gate. The west, represented by the mythical animal White Tiger in Chinese geomancy, also symbolizes death, destruction, danger and a season that sees the ascendance of the cosmic force of *yin* (Feuchtwang 1982: 151–4). Exiting through the western door in this context, therefore, further disgraced the prisoners, pronouncing the beginning of their fatal journey to the underworld. Once they were taken to the site – Gray seems to have forgotten to put this into his notes – the prisoners were stripped half naked to their waists, regardless of sex. In this action the last and remaining bit of the symbolic traits of civilization retained by the criminals – their clothes – were stripped off at the order of the authorities (Jin 1991: 22–3).

Third, Gray's account also reveals that the red colour was given unusual attention by the attending Imperial personnel. At the execution ground the soldiers filed off on each side of a table covered with a red table-cloth; the magistrate's chair was also overlaid with a red cover. In the reminiscences of a scholar – who being the son of a local magistrate had spent a large part of his childhood at different *yamen* in Henan and Hubei Provinces – the magistrate and the procuratorial officials were all dressed in red overcoats and red hats throughout the procession and the execution (Tao 1972: 78–9). Red is commonly regarded as a life-giving colour, as much as the colour of wealth and of good fortune. It is also taken as a marker of divinity and hence a colour with exorcistic power (Eberhard 1988: 248–9). Through utilizing the symbolism of the red colour, the authorities tried to convey a moral and political message to those who were present at the execution: this was an auspicious and happy occasion in which the forces of righteousness and justice won another exorcistic battle against the forces of demonic evil and darkness.

It must be added here in passing that the timing for a public execution in the Imperial period was also symbolic, carrying particular meanings. In official rhetoric, neither the granting of amnesty,[7] nor the execution of convicted prisoners was allowed to take place between the Spring and Autumnal equinoxes lest the natural power and the moral order of this season – of life-giving growth – would be disrupted by the act of taking a human life (Chen Guofu and Qin Peihao 1947: 44; Wang 1994: 18). But the results of academic research tell us that out 'of crimes punishable by death in Qing China, over 40 per cent called for immediate execution. Those guilty of such acts could never benefit from the Autumn or Court Assizes. They ordinarily faced only a local trial, the regular review, and a quick death' (McKnight 1981a: 109). These conflicting reports provide us with yet another example of a discrepancy between what was ideal and actual practice in Chinese institutional history. The reports also show that in terms of the Imperial ideology, the timing of an execution should not be *ad hoc*. However, it is in the choice of the exact hour for most executions that the symbolical importance of time becomes transparent. Most executions were carried out either at the third *ke* of the *yin* hour, which is about four o'clock in the morning, or at the third *ke* of the *wu* hour, which is just about midday. In the former case, it is known that an execution could be implemented only after the dark nightly sky was brightened by the first rays of sunlight. In other words, no execution was allowed to take place in the dark hours. They were part of an Imperial world of brightness, separated from demonic darkness. It is perhaps due to a strategic awareness of this symbolism of timing that most executions were by preference to be carried out at the *wu* hour.

The act of paying homage to the deities in a temple nearby the execution ground, was understood by Gray as a means to ask for spiritual protection from the deities against possible vengeance by the decapitated criminals. This ritual might also be an act of thanksgiving to these supernatural beings whose blessing had contributed to the arrest and the execution of those demonic criminals. In this way, the act of execution was constructed not as an example of violence implying a disruption of the established order, but, on the contrary, as a divinely gracious act which reaffirmed and safeguarded the socio-cultural-political order that had been threatened by these criminals' truly violent acts.

Fourth, the procession of the execution team bore a close resemblance to the procession that took place during the local Cheng Wang Festival – Cheng Wang is a god generally worshipped as the magistrate of Hell. No record of this festival as celebrated in Canton is available to me. As a convenient alternative, a vivid description of a similar festival in Shanghai in the 1930s may be consulted – though this is not to suggest that the festivities in Canton were conducted in exactly the same way. This recollection is drawn from the autobiography of a local herbalist doctor, who grew up in Shanghai during the Republican period.

In his reminiscences, the procession of Cheng Wang in the Chinese City of Shanghai was held three times a year, namely during the third, the seventh, and the tenth moons. On each of these occasions, the statue of Cheng Wang was placed on a gold-plated sedan chair which was carried by eight participants of the procession in the city, together with statues of deities of other local temple cults. The procession was led by four outriders. They were followed by a team of 'police runners' who were dressed in uniforms – blue gown, red belt, black or red hat – as that of *yamen* runners in the Imperial days. They carried with them a pair of 'tiger head boards' on which were written 'Be quiet' and 'Give way', official sign-boards with inscriptions of the various official titles of Cheng Wang, a variety of instruments for judicial torture and lacquered weapons such as spears, swords, knives, sticks and so on. A Chinese marching band played loudly on their gongs, Chinese shawms and drums, amidst the noise of burning firecrackers. Immediately followed a large group of over one hundred citizens/worshippers who all wore yellow shirts (hence calling themselves *huangyi huishou*).

Another group of women were dressed in red shirts and trousers, with a white skirt tied around their waist; they paraded in front of yet another group of worshippers who dressed mainly in blue short-sleeves. These groups of participants took up the guise of would-be-executed prisoners of the 'old days' – some were fettered or chained, some put up a strip of bamboo stick at the back of their heads and they believed that by dressing up this way and taking part on this occasion like this, their temporal sins could be alleviated. Following closely this band of 'prisoners' was a small group of men who dressed as executioners with fearsome big knives in hands. Behind them were tens of young boys and girls all clad in spectacular traditional gowns of legendary deities and fairies. This was followed by yet a group of men in black clothes and purple belts, with warrants and torture devices in hands, taking up the guise of *yamen* runners from hell. At the end of the procession came the luxuriously decorated sedan chair on which was placed a statue of Cheng Wang. The procession had to pass through the city and its suburbs, before the participants eventually congregated at the mass grave of unclaimed bodies (*wanren zhong*) at the southern suburb where the worshippers offered incense sticks and food to the homeless ghosts, while the representations of the deities were lined up before this site, apparently as a means to pacify the locality (Chen Cunren 1973: 182–5).

One of the major points of interest about this procession is that it closely resembled the procession of condemned criminals, led by the concerned officials, before a public execution. The Cheng Wang procession was an imaginary enactment of a mundane reality. The only major difference was the parade of 'deities' and the carnival-like atmosphere in the festival. The close resemblance in form and content of the two processions leads us to conjecture that the magistrate in charge of a public execution might actually be a temporal representation of Cheng Wang whose duty was to ensure the accomplishment of divine justice on earth. The magistrate did not only oversee a gruesome display of State violence in a public execution but, furthermore, he supervised a cosmic act of punishment, which was fair, just, moral, and divinely sanctioned.

This inter-changeability between the role of a mundane, temporal magistrate and his transcendental counterpart in the underworld, is brought to the fore in the short story 'New and Old' ('Xin yu jiu'), written by Shen Congwen in the 1930s.[8] In the story, the male protagonist is a soldier in the late-Imperial forces who is very skilful at beheading condemned prisoners. Each time, after he has decapitated a prisoner, he rushes immediately to the Cheng Wang temple not far from the execution ground, and hides behind the main altar. Meanwhile, the procuratorial magistrate and his entourage will march from the execution spot to the same shrine at a slower pace. As soon as the officials arrive at the temple, the procuratorial officer presents a bunch of incense sticks to the deities. Then a *yamen*-runner, who pretends to have just found a decapitated corpse in the execution ground, 'rushes' to have this reported to the magistrate. An *ad hoc* court of justice is then formed inside the temple. At this point, the executioner surrenders himself to the magistrate, while at the same time begging him for mercy by knocking his forehead against the floor. The magistrate, as a rule, orders him to be flogged. When the mock flogging is finished, a red packet of lucky money is handed over to the executioner by the magistrate as a reward for his 'excellent' job (Shen Congwen 1977: 123–7).

This literary (but not fictitious) account of the practice of public executions provides us with more interesting clues to the expressive force of capital punishment. First, the event was not only a political celebration, but also a dramatized ritual. Seemingly the magistrate regarded himself as a temporal counterpart of Cheng Wang and the executioner as a Hell's spirit-soldier whose job was to enforce judicial torture and executions. The boundaries between reality and theatrical performance, what was real and transcendental, political and religious, collapsed and all distinctions blurred to converge into one single whole or entity, which in many respects had the same narrational structure as traditional Cantonese opera (Ho 1994). The act of execution became a blend of the enforcement of penal justice, the buttressing of imperial and moral ideologies, and the presence of transcendental support and cosmic justification.

In spite of all its ideological justification and symbolic load, the act of execution, paradoxically, remains ambiguous in its moral implications. In Shen Congwen's literary reconstruction, as mentioned above, the executioner, despite having done a good job, had to beg for the magistrate's pardon for taking a man's life. His moral responsibility for killing could only be washed off by the symbolic means of mock flogging. In the context of nineteenth-century Guangdong, it came to the notice of Wells Williams that an official executioner was not always the person to perform; sometimes it was another criminal taken out of his prison (Williams 1882, I: 514). The ideologically moral and commendable act of decapitating a condemned culprit was seemingly not moral enough to offset the risk of pollution incurred by any incident of unnatural death. This tallies well with the behaviour of present-day executioners in the

PRC. An eyewitness tells that they always put on a pair of white gloves before they shoot a convicted criminal through the back of his or her neck. As soon as their 'job' is done, they must dispose of the gloves at the site of the execution.[9] A local informant in Zhongshan also reports that once the executioners have performed their 'duty', they all immediately take off their uniforms and have them incinerated. Therefore, despite all rhetoric about the necessity of exterminating non-human criminals, the executioners seem uneasy about the implementations of the punishment. They are involved in the act, and yet, also made detached from it.

Views from the Spectator Terrace

The ambiguity of some executioners brings out an important and related dimension of the spectacle of capital punishment: the response of the public. Southern Chinese, especially Cantonese, consider an event of violent death as both menacing and polluting (Aijmer and Ho 1999). Execution – because of its consequential outcome of unnatural, brutal death – is highly inauspicious and therefore to be avoided. Paradoxically, occasions of public execution were – and still are – never short of eager on-lookers. The occurrence of the pollution of violent death does not seem to be feared by the spectators; they do not necessarily view the occasion as a one of contamination.

Chinese theatre audiences could be very serious about a scene of execution. The theatrical staging of beheading a criminal, usually at the end of a play, serves important religious-cum-moral functions in the drama. It punishes the bad elements, and reinstates and appraises what is good. To many theatre audiences, this was, and still is, something absolutely necessary. There have been incidents in which audiences refused to leave the theatre (which they were asked because of an approaching storm) until the final act, including the public execution of the bad character, had been performed (Su 1984: 101–2). The ending of a play had to be morally impeccable. Dramaturgical narration might be a reflection of common attitudes. Theatre might also help its audiences to make 'better' sense of the events of execution in real life. The spectators of such occasions might be guided by their theatrical experiences to intuit that they were actually witnessing the carriage of divine justice – much as they comprehend what they usually watch on the stage.

An interesting contemporary case in Shanghai was the public execution of a murderer named Yan Ruisheng who had killed a prostitute for her money to sustain his addictive habit of gambling. The case was heavily publicized by Shanghai mass media. On the day of his execution, which was carried out in a suburb of Shanghai, at least 5,000 people jammed the local trains to the area in order to attend and witness the event. Among them were many prostitutes who came to see that justice was finally done to the murderer of their 'sister' (Chen Cunren 1973: 176). This case of homicide became a nation-wide topic for gossip and the story was adopted into Shanghaiese and Cantonese opera repertoires, producing big hits (Chen Dingshan 1971: 69). The two worlds of theatre and reality coalesce and help to make sense of one another – the criminal is ritually executed both on stage and in real life.

Feelings of the spectators towards the event of public execution were and are, of course, mixed. In contemporary cases, some informants state that they do not dare to watch the shooting; it is too cruel and revolting to see a man being killed. Friends and relatives of a criminal naturally view his execution as a horror and their emotional reactions are predictable. But most people crowding at an execution ground, rarely refuse to watch. On the contrary, they are all eagerly waiting for the moment of decapitation or shooting. In late Qing dynasty Canton, public executions were always well attended, drawing great numbers of spectators:[10]

> [N]o sooner was this bloody act brought to a close, than the sheriff with sword and mace-bearers, and a lot of ragged attendants left the scene. At this moment, a number of populace came upon the ground, and gazed on the headless bodies of their countrymen with the most perfect apathy and indifference (Gray 1972: 67).

According to Shen Congwen's memoirs, public executions in western Hunan in the 1920s, provided the bored encamped soldiers and the residents of the townships with moments of excitement and entertainment. In his childhood, Shen recalls, whenever the news of an imminent execution reached his ears, he would rush to join the other spectators to watch the whole process. Sometimes, on his way to school he passed the execution ground in which decapitated corpses were still lying around. He would then throw small stones at the severed heads, or hit them with a stick to test if they were still 'alive'. Public execution, for young Shen, was a form of amusement, rather than something gruesome or brutal. Likewise, Lu Yan, another writer in the 1920s and 1930s, wrote with slight exaggeration that some of his contemporaries in Hunan watched the decapitation of criminals with great joy and enthusiasm. In his 1924 short story entitled 'You zi' ('Pomelo'), the two protagonists from the countryside regard themselves exceedingly lucky to be able to come upon an execution while they are in town. One of them is so exhilarated by the experience that he describes it as something glorious and something which he will be proud of for the rest of his life; he attributes this to his good luck. He is, however, not alone. In this story, which may be a reflection of reality, we are told that as soon as the news of an imminent execution breaks, a large number of people in the streets rush feverishly to the execution ground in order to occupy a place providing a good view of the coming event. Afterwards, the beheaded corpse, which is now covered by blood, is closely encircled by an excited crowd of people who eagerly inspect the headless body (Lu 1987: 13–20).

In Canton in the same period, execution was commoditized. In 1928, an official daily in Canton published a Public Security Office order introducing a ban on the posting of photographs in the show-windows of the city's photo shops of executed Communist leaders and the naked bodies of women, executed for being members of the Communist Party (GZMGRB 29 February 1928).[11] The report tells us that a display of this sort of pictures was denounced as improper.[12] However, it does not mention whether these photographs also irritated the citizens for the same reason; the fact that they were on display indicates the contrary. This Cantonese fascination apparently survived the ban. When a travel guide writer rambled around the city of Canton in the early 1930s, he encountered a surprise:

[s]earching one day in a Chinese photographer's shop, I came upon a collection of the most horrible pictures it is possible to imagine. One of these showed a local bandit tied to a post and suffering death by that old Chinese method, *the thousand cuts*. Others showed the bodies of men and women killed in a variety of revolting ways during a recent uprising. There was quite a large collection of photographs of prisoners being beheaded . . . (Domville-Fife, n.d.: 88–9).

Although death, especially when resulting from an unnatural cause was – and still is – popularly considered as polluting, it has never deterred people from watching public executions. On the contrary, crowds gather whenever they take place. Hence, it remains unclear whether death incurred from execution is construed as polluting, or not. It is interesting to find that in late-Imperial China there were people who rented from executioners their swords, or borrowed from collectors of this sort of sword. Such weapons were tied to the beds of the ill as they were commonly believed to possess an efficacious power of healing, or to drive away the bad influence of evil spirits (Gray 1972: 31). In present-day Hong Kong, some people are anxiously looking for Japanese swords which were used for decapitating 'enemies' during the Pacific War. These swords are commonly believed to possess the transcendental power of protecting their owners from being harmed by evil spirits. To let a whole family benefit from this source of symbolic expulsion, these swords are generally displayed at some conspicuous place in the living room.

In the contemporary context, as a kind of replacement, local seekers of protection are reported to be collecting empty shells of bullets ejected from the automatic weapons used for executing criminals. A recent report of a public execution in the Municipality of Shenzhen – across the border of Hong Kong – reveals that, as soon as it was over and the corpses removed, 'villagers' living near the execution site rushed to the spot and

> scrambled for the used bullets' metal jackets which they then dipped into the cascades of running blood emerging from the executed prisoners. They believed that these shells are powerful amulets that will scare away all sorts of evil spirits from their owners' premises; therefore, they are placed respectably beside the family altar *(Apple Daily* 16 December 1995).[13]

The important issue here is this belief in the beneficial power of an executed prisoner's blood, which brings up at least two conjectures. First, that death resulting from execution may not be intuited as polluting as are other forms of death – the blood of a decapitated, being the life fluid of a ferocious and demonized criminal, may even be considered a source of protection, because of its menacing 'property'. The long history in China of the anthropophagous practice of eating one's enemies' flesh, is another expression of such an alternative view of death: death is ambiguous, not *always* taken as polluting.[14] A demon's blood, the same with its flesh, is supposedly powerful enough to scare away other demons. In the act of executing a prisoner, some sort of life force is released, which will be embodied in the weapon used in the event. With these life forces lingering in the instrument of execution, a weapon itself will become a true 'knife [that cuts] demon heads' (*guitou dao*) – a weapon which has been 'actually' used by a transcendental agent to perform the virtuous duty.[15] Therefore, the event may be intuited as a highly auspicious one. Red, the colour symbolizing life, goodness, and happiness, was very much in notice at the execution ground in the late Qing context: the magistrate's tablecloth, his chair's cover, the prisoners' clothes, and perhaps also the blood of the decapitated person. Viewed from this angle, a public execution may be seen, paradoxically, as an occasion of both life and death – the finishing of a life as much as the release of life force. Through this potent act of bodily destruction, a flow of life force would spread out to be absorbed by other living persons.[16]

Another and powerful symbolic means employed by the State in legitimizing its position in the public drama of execution, is that the family of an executed criminal is required to pay for the cost of the bullet. It is through this calculated symbolic thrift that the audience of the theatre of death is reminded that in taking the life of a so deserving 'sub-human', the State is actually carrying out a morally justified task which should not burden society. Also, the criminal's family are indirectly blamed for their failure to bring up a child properly. The whole drama is loaded with messages, all pointing to the procedure as an occasion of justified destruction. It is the obligation of the State to punish all evil characters; guilt on the part of the criminal and his family is not only verbalized but intensified into visualized exhibition; the implicative destructive essence of violence no longer matters against its backdrop of moralized human drama.

The interpretations and ideas raised in the pages above are by no means conclusive and there is much scope for further empirical research. This exploratory excursion into the discursive use and understandings of the symbolic architecture of public executions in late Imperial and modern China, is not intended to 'aestheticize' or 'euphemisticize' a violence that no sensible persons would endorse. Nor is this an attempt to generalize the apparently complex attitudes of men towards death imposed.

This essay attempts not only to highlight the ambiguities in the notion of violence in Chinese culture. It has the further ambition to demonstrate an alternative to universalistic legalism in an approach which advocates a search for several layers of possible symbolic meanings that may be embedded in a public execution in China in this period. Objective 'violence' is undoubtedly one of the several dimensions of experience which people draw from when construing and perceiving executions that were – and to a lesser extent still are – performed in public. However, 'violence', in the Anglo-Saxon sense of the word, is not necessarily the only, nor necessarily the dominant, impression that the scene of capital punishment may convey to the spectators, to the executioners, to the procurators and, indirectly, to those 'informed' citizens who have never been to an execution ground. The violent display of official killing is full of connotative significance which cannot be reduced away when we take stock of the social practice of violence on a comparative basis. 'Violence', as a universalistic concept, is apparently inadequate to explain in full the complex and culturally constructed meanings and attitudes that were, and still are, making their multifarious expressions in the context of China.

This chapter has also tried to unveil how different political and cultural symbols have been used discursively by late Imperial and modern Chinese regimes in their attempts at constructing and moralizing the public drama of executions. Today, the modern technology of mass media provides additional and effective means of presenting electronically the officially moralized version of the drama to a much larger audience embracing many millions of people. Executions are today no longer, strictly speaking, conducted publicly. However, dramaturgical elements and political symbolisms are still heavily employed in pre-execution trials and parades as well as in the still prevalent practice of letting the victim's family pay for the bullet. After all, at least in the case of Shenzhen, most public trials of criminals are conducted in a big annex to the Department of Justice, a building which is, interestingly, used every evening as a public cinema showing the latest Cantonese language movies imported from Hong Kong. Drama, spectacle, entertainment, trial and execution are so strangely mixed that categories become fuzzy, roles are confused and the total experience one of violence in a multi-vocal surrealistic display.

Notes

1. I owe this point to my colleague Dr Charles Chan who is a specialist of Confucianism.
2. Foucault (1982); Jin (1991); Lofland (1977); Spierenburg (1984) and Wang (1994).
3. Gray (1875: 298–301; 1972: 50); Jin Liangnian 1991: 77–9; Williams (1883: 1: 514–15).
4. It should be noted that sometimes a decapitated head was allowed to be collected by the family of the convict so that his body could be buried properly together with his head. Relatives of convicted officials or of common prisoners who could afford to bribe the executioner, were usually allowed to collect the head and the body for a proper burial. Most of the decapitated bodies and heads otherwise were simply dumped unburied into the 'Trench of the Bones of Ten Thousand Men' – *wanren keng* (Gray 1875: 679–80).
5. In a comment on a earlier version, Anita Jacobsson Widding (1996) has advised me that John H. Gray's material is not trustworthy. On what authority or special insight she has come to this conclusion is not clear; it remains my conviction that Gray's accounts are indispensable for an understanding of this period in the city of Canton and a

most valuable document complementing various local Chinese sources, especially given the fact that Gray resided in Canton and Hong Kong for no less than twenty six years (Boase 1965: 1217).

6. A slightly different account of this procession and execution by the same author can be read in his account from 'Walks in the City of Canton' (1875: 475–83). This latter version contains a few more details which are not found in the description quoted here.

7. A detailed discussion of the various forms of amnesty in late-imperial China can be read in McKnight (1981: ch. 5).

8. Shen Congwen grew up in a small market-town in western Hunan. In his childhood and adolescent days, Shen witnessed numerous occasions of public execution. The story 'New and Old' is very likely drawn from his personal experiences as a curious observer of executions. For more details about his childhood and adolescence, see his autobiography *Shen Congwen zizhuan* (1977). Kinkley (1987) also provides interesting information on the proliferation of soldiery violence in Hunanese society (for example, ch. 2).

9. I am indebted to Dr Mak Hung-fai for sharing with me his field experiences in the Canton delta region.

10. Public executions were always well attended in all periods in China. The early Ming epic novel 'Suihu zhuan' ('Water Margins') by Lo Guanzhong (1988) contains vivid scenes of execution (for example, chs. 27 and 40). Crowds of anxious and curious spectators are said to have thronged the sites. The execution by slicing of Zheng Men, a well-known scholar-official in the late-Ming period, was eagerly watched by a huge crowd of spectators, some of whom climbed up onto the roofs of nearby houses in order to gain a better view of the punishment. Since the crowd was so big and in order not to let down those attending, the executioners had to set up a long pole on which different body parts and internal organs of the condemned were hoisted as a way to announce to the audiences the progress of the slicing process. Wang Yongkuan, *Zhongguo gudai kuxing* (1994: 7–8). For some of these gruesome photographs of public execution, see Worswick and Spence (1978), *La Cina* (1994) and Spence and Chin (1996). One of the photographs collected by Worswick and Spence shows the presence of well-dressed young children among the spectators at the execution ground who were probably led by their parents to attend to witness this moral drama.

11. To a certain extent, this resembles to the exhibition of pictures of fish butchering in present-day Hong Kong fishmongers' stores. Although the subject matter of these pictures are different, both kinds

point to the idea that Cantonese, and indeed all Chinese, may perceive violent death incurred by execution in a way which is markedly different from that of present-day 'westerners'.

12. Niida's meticulous research into the history of legal practices in Imperial China that the Qing authorities, in the hope of reminding the subjects of the importance of abiding to law, produced horrific drawings of variegated scenes of judicial tortures and capital punishment which were distributed and posted in public areas. Moreover, from the official Ming history we learn that the public execution of Liu Jin, a much-hated mischievous court official, was not only recorded in drawings, but these were also printed and distributed to most parts of the empire to appease his former enemies, some of whom even are reported to have purchased a slice of Liu Jin's flesh to eat it raw (Niida 1980: 164, 169 n 26).

13. A similar expression of this cult of death was vividly reconstructed by Lu Xun in his short stories 'Yao' ('Medicine') and 'Shizhong' ('Exposed in Public'). See Lu Xun (1991).

14. Donald S. Sutton's (1995: 162–5) article on the subject of cannibalism and revenge in historical and contemporary China raises the interesting idea that anthropophagy can be understood as a form of rite of passage, and that 'these cruel and hideous rites, in the eyes of their organizers and participants, represented and produced order . . . [in which] [t]hose labelled class enemies, symbols of local order, were reincorporated in a community ceremony of re-aggregation by physical consumption'.

15. In late-Qing Beijing, executioners were commonly known as *guitou shou*, literally meaning 'the hands [that take] demon heads', and their weapons as *guitou dao* – 'the knives that cut demon heads'. See Niida (1980: 161).

16. This is by no means an exclusively Chinese phenomenon In historic London, we are told that 'there were sometimes people with physical blemishes and wounds who came to be touched by the hand of the hanged man in the belief they would be cured' (Lofland 1977: 296).

8

The 'Tradition of Violence' in Colombia: Material and Symbolic Aspects
Gerard Martin

'Those who call a crime a crime, *are already on the road of sense and salvation.*'

Paul Ricoeur (1967: 93)

Violence as Polysemic

Nieburg (1969) stated that 'violence is ... deeply ambiguous in all its aspects, containing both functional and dysfunctional tendencies, capable of both positive and negative outcomes'. Such a general statement, however, suffers from banality and should be qualified by saying that the ambiguity of 'violence' stems in part from the fact that it is in itself *polysemic*: it can be individual or collective, organized or spontaneous, ritualized or routinized, legal or illegal, intentional or non-intentional, instrumental, non-instrumental or irrational. It may be societal, state-directed, subversive, para-military; it can spring from different motives, sentiments or ideologies. Its use and signification is always anchored in a particular historical and cultural environment, as the other studies in this book amply demonstrate. The fact that violence is studied by different disciplines and from different points of view (functionalist, utilitarianist, culturalist, etc.) also shows that not only general statements on violence, but, even more so, a general theory of violence, will probably always be an illusion.[1] To be valuable, theorizing on violence should preferably indicate clearly what definition of violence is used or what acts or phenomena are supposed to be covered by the concept. A maximalist definition, that states that everything done to a person without being explicitly wanted by this person constitutes an act of violence, actually transforms it into a container-concept. A first distinction is therefore generally introduced between symbolic and physical violence. The concept of physical violence being the more restrictive one, especially if it is reserved, as I will do here, for acts or events where (a tentative) homicide is involved, while the concept of symbolic violence remains a very extensive one, being used for a broad range of phenomena (insignia of power, language discrimination of minorities, inequality between men and women, bullfighting, rituals of birth, initiation or death). This doesn't mean that physical violence itself is not a very broad 'concept': among others, it covers psycho-pathological, criminal, political, state and social violence. However, its application depends less strongly on perceptions and social representations than the concept of symbolic violence (e.g. Northern Europeans considering Spanish bull-fighting an act of violence, while local aficionados name it a sport or a traditional spectacle).

Classifying acts of physical violence as political or non-political, organized or disorganized, criminal or social is often a first step to its understanding. However, in certain situations this first classification may already prove to be very complex if not impossible. This is illustrated by present-day Colombia, where a conjuncture of *generalized violence* has emerged in a context of extreme violence (25,000 to 30,000 homicide victims per year since 1984 and a homicide rate of 70 per 100,000 make it one of the most violent countries in the world). Such a conjuncture may be described as a situation where, under conditions of impunity, organized and disorganized violence proliferate and enter into circular relations, so that very heterogeneous phenomena of violence start to interfere and to penetrate the whole fabric of political, social and inter-individual relations (Pécaut 1996). For those caught up in a situation of generalized violence, the possibility to distinguish between political, non-political, social or criminal violence fades away. Violence presents itself less as a direct consequence of some clearly identifiable phenomena (e.g. a drug economy, political fragmentation, civil war) or as provoked by some clearly identified actors (guerrillas, police, army, paramilitary), than as the context in which society is reproduced. This process of the 'autonomization' of violence in relation to its original contexts is expressed in both the very prosaic character of violence and in phenomena of routinization and banalization of violence.[2]

The fact that in Colombia violence translates itself at the same time in acts of terror (massacres) and cruelty (torture) adds to its complexity. A statement on the ambiguity of violence, such as Nieburg's, hence even becomes more problematic: what can be the 'functional', 'meaningful' aspect of a nightly massacre of thirty-five civilians on a banana plantation or on a village square by a group of guerrillas or paramilitary? Functional or positive violence for whom? Certainly not for the victims, the relatives, the bystanders and others concerned, who seem to use always the same words to describe the violence: senseless, meaningless, barbarian, absurd.

For the protagonists then? Not even this seems to be sure. Because even one would examine whether the way in which the killings, the torture and the humiliations are carried out can be understood as part of a calculated strategy of intimidation and terror (cf. Anton Blok, this volume, Chapter 1), in Colombia, loss of control over violence, processes of decomposition of armed groups, and the entanglement of organized and disorganized as well as political and non-political violence make that 'meaningful' aspects of violence appear to erode while 'functional' dimensions seem harder to discern (even for the protagonists).

The questions of 'meaning' (or lack of it) that the Colombian case evoke in this respect are in part similar to those that emerge regarding other situations of extreme violence, such as the conflicts, wars or genocides in the former Soviet Union, in ex-Yugoslavia, in East Africa or in Algeria. The unforeseen scale and brutality of the violence involved has also been met with utter astonishment, expressing itself in the use of notions such as 'chaos', 'irrationality' and 'barbarism'.[3] Other interpretations spoke of 'tribalism', but it rapidly became clear that no comparison was to be assumed between the new wars and 'tribal' types of war. After all, for traditional Amazonian societies or African 'tribes', violence or war could be understood as being buttressed or reinforced by cultural dimensions such as magic, kinship relations, or myth. Cycles of vengeance, the status of the 'warrior' and the prominence of the military group were understood as being related to culturally specific symbolic and organizational aspects of these societies.[4] The new wars then have a different character, even if they partly involve 'traditional' societies. Violent ethnic, political or religious 'cleansing' prove to be less of a ritual than directly related to modern political problems posed by, e.g., the strategic national and international power-play, demagogy, censorship, manipulation, incitements to hate, propaganda, one-party regimes, or corruption. This also means that while violence or warfare may have played a constitutive role in the development of 'early' states, few analysts understand the new wars as contributing to the stability of new states or as being at the basis of the construction of a new society.

In Colombia the situation is, to a certain extent, even more complex. There is no national war going on, but a juxtaposition of local wars with a multiplicity of political and non-political protagonists. These wars are about down-to-earth interests and not ethnic, religious or major political conflicts. More than 'vertical', revolutionary upward or state-directed downward violence, we see a proliferation of 'horizontal' violence in the form of inter- and intra-group conflicts and local wars between all kind of armed private gangs (guerrilla, mafia, paramilitary, etc.). At the same time, disorganized forms of violence seem to affect the entire society. At present, state institutions are less able than ever to neutralize the emergence and use of violence by non-state actors.This situation is less a consequence of the collapse of state power than of a general 'degradation' of society under the destructive influence of a drug economy in the historical context of a weak state (despite a long democratic tradition).

Since classical sociological interpretations in terms of vertical, collective or political violence hardly apply to the Colombian case, it seems preferable to reason in terms of a *tradition of violence,* that is, in terms of a particular historically shaped relation between order and violence that may take different expressions in the context of a specific political and institutional configuration. To reason in terms of a *tradition of violence* is *not* the same as to reason in terms of a *culture of violence.* In the latter, violence might appear as 'historically inevitable' and imply a certain degree of reification, while the protagonists' freedom of decision to turn to violence or, on the contrary, to abstain from its use, disappears. Neither does a tradition of violence mean that in Colombia expressions of violence have always been identical. It has taken regionally and historically diverse forms and I will insist, in this chapter, on the fact that a period of generalized violence, and especially the element of terror, implies a break with the 'normal' Colombian situation of chronic but moderate violence. Even so, although *La Violencia* (1948–63) and the current crisis both represent a situation of generalized violence, they cannot be understood in identical material or symbolical terms either.

To demonstrate this argument, a thick description of violence as a 'total social fact' for both these situations of generalized and normal violence, would be the most appropriate methodological choice.[5] However, my goal here is less ambitious. Using the Colombian case, the aim is to underline some of the possibilities and limits of a cultural and symbolic analysis of violence in extreme situations of extreme violence. To do so, I will first insist on the background of Colombian violence as a historical problem of order. I will then insist on the fundamental difference between, on one side, the massive, ruthless violence and terror that circulates in a situation of generalized violence, and, on the other side, the more or less controlled, residual, eventual violence that appears as co-extensive to Colombian society in 'normal' times. This change of *Gestalt* between 'normal' and generalized violence expresses itself not only by a change in the intensity of violence and by the new forms under which the violence appears (organized violence, group-killings, terror) but also by the difficulty people experience to represent this extreme violence, to make sense of it. The arguments will be illustrated with reference to events in the Urabá area, one of the regions in Colombia where violence and terror have been particularly intense during the last fifteen years.[6]

A Historical Problem of Order

Colombia has a historical problem of order (see Pécaut 1987b).[7] The current crisis (at least 250,000 homicide victims since 1985) is not Colombia's first major internal conflict. Between 1948 and 1963, a civil war between Liberals and Conservatives (political parties, see below), generally known as *La Violencia,* created a comparable situation of generalized violence, claiming some 200,000 victims. Before that, *La Guerra de Mil Dias* (1899–1902), the last and most dramatic of the nineteenth-century civil wars, had brought terror and disaster to the country. The intermediate periods are generally conceived of as relatively peaceful, but recent studies have shown that phenomena of political and non-political violence were never absent during these years (see Pécaut 1987b; Guerrero 1991; Cruz 1996).

There is thus no doubt that Colombian society generates violent relations and that the violence takes part of its meaning from being anchored in a very particular socio-political history. Chronic political and non-political violence has been a constant element of the social-political process, although with varying intensity. The interesting paradox is that Colombia has – in contrast to other Latin American countries – at the same time a long-standing tradition of institutional stability and democracy, hardly ever interrupted by military regimes or periods of dictatorship.[8] The current conjuncture of generalized violence again occurs in the context of a civil government that claims to respect the principles of a democratic state and the rule of law.

Historical and cultural background factors of the problems of violence in Colombia can best be understood in terms of the chronic weakness of the state and its lack of a monopoly on violence.

(a) As in other Latin American countries, politics in Colombia have traditionally taken the form of a continuous process of manipulation and negotiation between regional and local power contenders, whereby the use of violence is one of the resources the actors dispose of (Anderson 1967). Territorially-based negotiation capacity has survived until today as a central strategy of politics, in spite of the nominal existence of democratic procedures and discourse.[9] Collective electoral control was first created in the prolongation of neo-feudal forms of labour-control, notably around the *hacienda*. To legitimize their territorially-based negotiation capital, *caciques* (local strongmen) learned to speak in ambiguous terms about their control of *pueblos*, that is without clearly differentiating the double significance of people (as a democratic principle), and of village (as a territorial status).[10] More recently, with the rapid modernization and urbanization of Colombian society *gamonales* (local political party bosses) have renewed this tradition by taking to political clientelism to satisfy the demands of fast-growing urban and rural middle classes.[11] The clientelist distribution of public resources thus became a central element of the political game, whereby abuse of public resources, fraud and corruption were chronic.[12] After *La Violencia*, especially since the coalition governments of the so-called National Front (1958–74),[13] politics continued to present itself in terms of (sometimes violent) competition between local or regional political chiefs for monopolization of bureaucratic resources and electoral control. That is: the National Front put an end to the open political violence of the civil war, but the idea that politics has a direct link with violence persisted. At the same time, proliferation of clientelistic practices resulted in the fragmentation of traditional political networks of control, and facilitated, by weakness and opportunistic collusion, the violent penetration of guerrilla groups and mafia-type organizations. These new protagonists, especially the guerrilla but lately also paramilitary organizations, recognize collective control based on distribution of plots of land and other resources, and use openly violent pressure and constraint as efficient ways to create politically and military controlled territories and to enter the political arena.

(b) Political identifications have historically taken an absolute and sectarian character. In the context of a strict two-party system formed by the century-old Liberal Party and Conservative Party, citizenship could not be conceived independently from one of the two political sub-cultures or political communities (*comunidades*). Until the 1950s, when the country had still a 70 per cent rural population, every Colombian was born in a blue (Conservative) or a red (Liberal) village or neighbourhood.

The sectarianism has its own political roots. First, elections were very frequent in Colombia during the second half of the nineteenth and the first half of the twentieth century, provoking a quasi-continuous *polarization* of the political field, especially at the local level.[14] Second, civil wars between political factions and chronic electoral violence – especially during the period of hegemonic Conservative (1902–28) and Liberal (1928–46) reign – reinforced the idea that *politics is war*. Third, the Catholic Church has historically participated in the cultivation of hateful and intolerant political representations and has not played a unifying role in the field of state development: joined up by the Conservative party since the second half of the nineteenth century, the Catholic Church called liberalism a sin and identified it with Protestantism, later with Communism. These sectarian representations manifested themselves during *La Violencia*[15] but also, although transformed and displaced, in the deadly sectarianism of guerrilla groups and more in general in a climate of intolerance that has never disappeared from political life in Colombia.

In spite of the sectarianism they provoked, the Liberal and the Conservative Parties have for a long time been, in a geographically and culturally fragmented country, two political collectivities with which nearly the whole population was able to identify in some sense. They were, for better or for worse, strong elements of national unification.

(c) What sets Colombia apart from other Latin American countries is that it has hardly developed autonomous state institutions. In Brazil and Argentina, for example, a set of regulations meant to institutionalize social conflict and a horizon of social rights came into being during the first half of the twentieth century, in answer to a period of rapid capitalist development. In Colombia, on the contrary, political networks, and not the state, continued to monopolize the mediation with civil society, in spite of a significant personal and financial expansion of the public sector. Moreover, whatever came into being as autonomous state institutions would again be partly destroyed during periods of intense violence.

Without an autonomous, institutional state, there was no place for independent mediation and symbolic representation of social conflicts. Social regulation being imposed more by Liberal or Conservative clientelist networks than by autonomous state-institutions, the strength and historical legitimacy of instruments of justice and public force have always been particularly weak; they lacked professionalism and numerical force and had to operate with precarious materials and under insufficient salary conditions (see Pizzaro 1996). Especially in rural and isolated areas, police and army have often depended for their operation costs (gasoline, lodging, etc.) on private actors (national or foreign enterprises, farmers, planters, etc.). The latter have logically taken advantage of the situation by using the public force as a private security instrument. Hence, private and party-political influences within the justice administration and illegal entanglements of interest and corruption are chronic. Control and decision over the use of violence stayed in the hands of private or clientelist networks, especially on the local level. As Pécaut writes (1986: 10), elites, opposition parties and political avant-garde all share the idea that violence is every now and then a necessary resource to advance their interests. Social relations are thus commonly experienced not only in terms of power or force, but in a lot of cases with the effective use of violence.

(d) The Colombian 'tradition of violence' is at the same time a 'tradition of impunity'. Colombian citizens have never had much confidence in the capacity of the justice administration to live up to the social expectations in this field. This goes together with a strong tendency to private justice, especially in the field of delinquency and crime, even more so since the Colombian legislation traditionally accepts the creation of organized groups for self-defence. There is a long-standing tradition of vigilante groups and para-military organizations. In practice, these groups have had a tendency to slip into typical death-squad activities, commonly referred to as practices of social cleansing (*limpieza social*): execution of beggars, thieves, prostitutes, homosexuals, *gamines,* etc.

Recently the inability of the public force and of the justice administration to prevent a new spiral of violence and terror has once again reinforced the call for private forms of law and order, with the apparent paradox that those who incorporate the new safeguards of society are in part the same as those responsible for the initial proliferation of big violence. Ex-mafiosi and ex-guerrilleros together form, since 1994, the most important paramilitary organization ACCU, that now pretends to eradicate guerrilla groups and other violent (drug) gangs, to give back to the state a 'cleaned-up' country). All this creates a highly unstable situation where the state accepts that new protagonists continue to present themselves in the name of law and order. These phenomena are not merely a symptom of the insufficient monopoly of the state on the means of violence, but also of the lack of a political capacity and will to define and apply a coherent policy of law and order and fight crime.

(e) The chronic weakness of the Colombian state can finally be understood in relation to the fact that constant economic growth was realized during the twentieth century in the context of an extremely liberal development model. Two elements can be emphasized. First, during the largest part of the twentieth century, Colombian development could depend on coffee as the motor of the national economy without the need for major state intervention. Until the 1980s, a strict *free rider* policy has been applied, because Brazil, being the biggest coffee producer, imposed a price policy by impressive state interventions, especially massive, subsidized crop destruction in case of over-supply on the world market. Merchants in coffee, represented by the *Federacion Nacional de Cafeteros*, together with other industrial or agricultural lobbies, were able to impose their interests, and deprive the state from its symbolic role in the regulating of economic relations, as already was the case in the field of socio-political relations.[16] Second, under conditions of permanent availability of *baldios* (virgin public lands), the free access to these has always formed an escape valve, offering possibilities for individual colonization. While for exploitation and colonization of their *frontiers,* Brazil turned to distribution and selling of land on her *frontier* (Théry 1995)[17] and Mexico made use of relatively reliable survey companies (see Holden 1994), Colombia has maintained, until today, the colonial tradition of more or less free access to land, using attribution for cultivation procedures. For reasons of slight demographic pressure[18] and elite interests in land speculation, the social pressure and the political will for state intervention in this field has always been particularly meagre. Infrastructural works to open up the regions and to stimulate their economic development were often promised but seldom realized, except in the centre of the country, on the coffee-frontier. Thus, to a certain extent, not even the minimum conceptualization of a liberal policy (infrastructural works) has been realized in Colombia. At the same time, under conditions of an extremely liberal state, the permanence of open *frontiers* has gone together with continuous conflicts around uncertain land titles and phenomena of usurpation, while it created a place for middlemen and for fraudulent and violent practices of privatization of land and power.[19] The colonization of Urabá since 1960 has again taken the form of a rush of all kind of private interests on the zone, everybody trying to get hold of a part of the available resources.

Experiences of 'Normal' and 'Extreme' Violence

For historical reasons, in Colombia people have thus come to believe, to some extent, that violence is an inherent part of social-political development, and that societal conflicts are 'normally' regulated by violence. This does not mean, however, that all forms of violence are in the same way considered as 'normal' or non-problematic. It is therefore important to analyse at what moment what forms of violence have come to be considered as socially acceptable. To understand the *meaning* people give to individual and collective experiences of violence, we should take into account its historical and cultural backgrounds, but also the *violent experiences themselves.* I will do this by comparing the violent experiences of the 1960s and 1970s, that has generally been understood in Colombia as a period of chronic but moderate violence, with phenomena of extreme violence during, both, *La Violencia* (1948–63) and the current crisis. I will show that the forms and logic of the 'normal' violence of the 1960s and 1970s, and the meaning those directly concerned gave to it, were fundamentally different from those experienced during periods of extreme violence, characterized by a transgression of norms as to socially acceptable forms of violence, revealed by the (re)appearance of massacres, torture, cruelty, and this on a massive scale.

Gerard Martin

La Violencia (1946–63)

Urabá was, like other frontier areas, during *La Violencia*, at once a refuge area for rural people fleeing the epicentres of the civil war and a base for Liberal guerrilla groups.[20] In the northern part of Urabá, traditionally under control of Liberal political chiefs from the adjacent department of Córdoba, violence was limited, as on the Atlantic Coast in general. But in the centre and the south of Urabá, political tensions expressed themselves in open (political) violence. Some Liberal chiefs operating from the interior of Antioquia (partly from Medellín), put their cattle farms and other resources at the disposition of opponents organising forms of violent resistance against the Conservative government. These Liberal guerrillas took the form of a handful of *cuadrillas* (gangs), each integrated by ten to thirty individuals, armed with *machetes* and some carbines, typically organized around family networks and led by former military officers, policemen or other Liberal functionaries who had lost their jobs in 1946, when the Conservatives came to power. *Commisiones de orden publica,* formed by army and police, made incursions to 'clean up' (*limpiar*) the region.[21] Both sides avoided direct military confrontation and took to brutal and violent operations against the Liberal or Conservative civil population. Both sides also expressed more disorganized forms of violence, especially seemingly 'spontaneous' lynch-mobs, that were organized or covered by political chiefs. The latter would also intervene with money or influence to free persons accused of participation in violence and massacres from prison.

Hobsbawm (1981) characterized *La Violencia* as a mass revolution that degenerated to an anarchistic and disoriented civil war. He also spoke of *La Violencia* as one of the biggest peasant mobilizations of the twentieth century, only comparable with the most intensive moments of the Mexican Revolution. However, recent regional studies have shown that in Colombia the peasants essentially remained divided in Liberals and Conservatives; armed Liberal or Conservative peasant groups operated under the direction of political chiefs from one or the other party, and the violence clearly had more to do with the interests of these *caciques* than with the interests of the peasants that formed the armed bands. In contrast to the Mexican insurgents, the Colombians missed not only political autonomy but also organizational unity and a common objective: they never formed more than groups of locally organized *cuadrillas* operating from an extremely limited political point of view.[22] The violence was linked to private interests and to long-standing social conflicts (for example, about land-titles), but also to phenomena of delinquency and non-political banditism.

Paradoxically, what gave a certain unity to *La Violencia*, in spite of its composite character, was the Liberal — Conservative conflict, even more so since it coincided with sedimented collective identities.

During the first years (1948–53), *La Violencia* was dominated by strategies of political, social and territorial control. Later, violence became progressively subject to phenomena of depolitization and banalization, although the official homicide statistics went on classifying the victims according to their political colour, indicated on *la cedula* (identity cards), as if it concerned a physical trait. In reality, an upcoming middle-class of merchants, administrators, cattle farmers, political middlemen and all kind of 'adventurers' made efficient use of the opportunities offered by the confused situation and by the flight of thousands of terrorized people from the countryside. Land speculation, extortion and traffic of stolen cattle proliferated in the shadow of war, political hate being regularly exploited for strictly material goals, greed, and rapine. Anonymous, handwritten threats became a plague: 'They are going to kill you; you better sell your plot of land' *('A vos le van a matar, mejor que vende su parcela';* see Ortiz 1985).

The most remarkable and disturbing aspect of *La Violencia* was that both sides gave in progressively to apparently aimless cruelties, atrocities and sadism. Rape, castration, killing of foetuses, profanation of corpses became frequent.[23] Victims were not only killed but tortured and disfigured, their corpses cut into pieces by a series of special *cortes* (see below). The civil war transformed itself, especially in the countryside, into political extermination by way of local genocide. The massacres imposed themselves especially in the third period of the civil war.[24]

How to understand this *mise en scène de l'horreur*? Where did it come from? Some have represented it as a repetition, a reactualization of comparable acts of cruelty during the civil wars of the nineteenth century, and especially during the *War of the Thousand Days* (in spite of the fact that forty-five years and two generations separate these events). The Colombian anthropologist Maria V. Uribe tried to understand how the massacres inscribed themselves not only in the particular national historical circumstances, but also in a particular symbolic and cultural environment, that is in the Colombian rural world, and more in particular in Tolima. Like other authors who have used a thick description to reveal something of the meaning of the events (see Sanchez and Meertens 1983; Ortiz 1985; Roldan 1992), Uribe insists on aspects such as the use of nick-names by the gang-members, the vocabulary, and the images these gangs adopt.[25] She puts them in relation with a rich, regionally based folk language and local expressions of what we already described as a national 'tradition of violence'. Like other authors, Uribe underlines the important role played by the representation of politics as a *polarization* of society in two opposite and irreconcilable forces, cultivated by sectarian discourse in the media, especially on the radio (Uribe 1990).[26]

Studying the different kinds of gangs that perpetrated the massacres and the individual trajectory of their members, she underlines the progressive degradation of the situation and the brutalization of violence as a *consequence* of individual and social discomposure, in itself provoked by the generalization of violence and terror: the extermination of families put thousands of traumatized people on the road of internal immigration, some of them, mostly men, joined more and more unstructured, roaming gangs that operated now for reasons of vengeance, greed or survival, thus creating an atmosphere of extreme insecurity.

Uribe also shows that the massacres of up to eighty civilians in Tolima, one of the most violent regions of the time, were carried out in ritual fashion: at night, on the patio of the houses (never inside); after a ritual accusation: 'we know that you're a *godo*' (a Conservative), a *chusmero* (a Liberal), an 'informer'; implying dehumanization of the victim (torture, rape). The victims were typically killed (*matar*) by bullet, then decapitated (*rematar*) and then mutilated by some ritual cuts and other brutal acts (*contramatar*).[27] This ritualized structure of the massacres testifies of a strong *symbolic universe* that all parties seem to share, because all protagonists engaged in more or less the same acts of cruelty.[28]

These transgressions have profoundly shaped the social memory of *La Violencia*. But the fixation of attention on the massacres and the excesses of violence has also facilitated interpretations in terms of 'barbarism' (Pécaut 1997). So, while their is no doubt that the violence was strongly linked to political (and later also economic) objectives, *La Violencia* was easily identified with the eruption of the populace on the political theatre, blocking at once the possibility to constitute an interpretation in terms of elite responsibilities. In relation to this, Pécaut has spoken of the 'double humiliation' of the popular classes: first, because they came to realize that they had involved themselves in a war for interests that were not their own, and second, because they were accused of 'barbarism', of having derailed the political violence and brought it to its cataclysm. Under these conditions, the experiences of violence came thus essentially to be thought of in the form of individual tales of catastrophe and disaster.

'Normal' Violence (1960s and 1970s)

The coalition government of the National Front (1958–74) put an end to the open political violence between Liberals and Conservatives that had brought civil war to the country (The intensity of homicide indeed strongly decreased). However, the large two-party coalition did not root out violence as a more or less accepted element of the regulation of social and political relations. Forms of political violence instead of disappearing turned inward, opposing different factions of the *same* party competing for the 50 per cent of public functions and resources that the National Front reserved for each of the two parties. Intra-Liberal and intra-Conservative sectarianism led to violent settlements in different regional arenas, but tended to be covered and silenced by national politicians and the mass-media they controlled.[29] Second, the National Front did not imply a break with the Colombian tradition of weak state institutions: there was no increment of state autonomy, no strengthening of the administration of justice, no reorganization of the public force.

Under conditions of continued weak societal regulation, violence thus remained an implicit norm and practice. This has been particularly evident in frontier areas such as Urabá, where, in the context of an economic and demographic boom, the extreme weakness of state regulation went together with spectacular forms of social disorganization typical of such a recently opened frontier area. Colombian society in general passed through a period of rapid modernization and secularization that expressed itself in a weakening of traditional forms of societal control. I will briefly insist now on the highly composite disposition of the violence of these years, since this has implications for the difficulty people had in making sense of it, and thus for the apparently 'non-problematic' or 'normal' character of the violence of this period.

Every-day violence was particularly visible in relation to quarrels, provocations and fights in the cafés and brothels of the boom-towns, especially in the week-ends, and often associated with heavy drinking (usually knives, sometimes guns were wielded). The atmosphere of the particular boom-town, where larger forms of social integration remained precarious, always attracted people who wanted to spend money after hard work (often made in fourteen days of work and then easily 'burnt' in one night of *aguardiente* drinking). Of course, even more than for the banana workers (for whom Urabá often represented their first salaried job), money burnt in the hands of the planters. Stories circulate about those who lost cattle or a farm during a poker-play with colleagues. Every-day violence being more or less coincidental – often related to sentiments of easily insulted honour – bystanders were less afraid to publicly comment on the facts and to give evidence. Every-day violence has been the domain where we can see the most frequent intervention of police and law.

Little is known about *violent settlements* that may have existed in relation to *business transactions*, and more particularly to more or less illegal affairs. The traffic of stolen cattle, contraband (luxury goods from Panama, the USA, and the Antilles) and the marihuana boom of the 1970s (which affected the whole northern part of Colombia) went together with internal settlements and other violence, mostly by intervention of a contract-killer. Rivalries of a political, personal or business character, might always lead to planned eliminations. Such eliminations were typically preceded by ritualized menaces (anonymous letters in the form of a message or a meaningful image like a cross or a coffin), that left the victim a certain time to settle the conflict or to run from it. The form this execution took (in an ambush) distinguished it from a homicide resulting from social or every-day violence, that typically took place in a face-to-face situation. Also, contract killings were mostly done by gun, they went without public comment, and relatives or friends kept silent, as did bystanders who happened to witness the execution.

Delinquency and crime formed a domain where the operation of justice and police was already very inefficient during the 1960s and the 1970s. It has always been a public secret that the badly and irregularly paid police, customs officials, local sheriffs and judges were more or less regularly taking bribes themselves. It has also been a general belief that delinquents who lost their life caught in the act or on a flight probably had refused to share their business with those who asked for it, or in whose 'territory' they had autonomously operated. Local prisons and police cells were filled with people arrested with relatively small amounts of marihuana, while violent delinquency and crime proliferated and went largely unpunished.

Different *small groups of bandits* and Communist or Maoist *guerrilla groups* added their own share of violence during these years. Their way of operating appears more as an adaptation to the particular conditions of Urabá as a peripheral frontier rather than as a form of resistance or social protest. Contrary to cases in classic banditry studies, in Colombia we are not at all in the context of rural insurgency, and the violence can hardly be understood as a peasant affair.[30] Bandits operated more in terms of the violent defence of their economic interests, realising alliances and bargains with local elite factions, undercutting social solidarity and leaving little space for symbolic interpretations of their acts of violence.[31] At least until the middle of the 1970s, the guerrilla stayed a peripheral and relatively marginal actor in the region. Peripheral because it operated in strategically and economically less important parts of Urabá and hardly affected the centre of the region. The guerrilla imposed 'revolutionary taxes' to planters and landlords, to 'protect' them from cattle-raiding, hostage-taking and extortion. Marginal because they did not dispose of more than twenty to forty members, few arms and few financial resources. Recruitment strategies were ad-hoc and the political-military control concerned relatively isolated colonists. For these small farmers, the guerrilla represented less a kind of new middle-man than an inevitability, once such a group had decided to install themselves in this particular area. Guerrilla groups would organize (popular) executions of supposed thieves and other 'a-socials' in order to convince the local population of their sincere interest to bring back law and order. However, they seem to have been preoccupied chiefly with internal executions.

Public force intervened in labour conflicts on the plantations, but incurred occasionally also in disappearances and other human rights violations. But state violence was at the same time limited. For example, the Communist Party, the most important opposition party, was never declared illegal, in spite of her direct relations with the guerrilla group FARC.[32] During the National Front period, the Communist Party participated in all elections. In Urabá, strong competition between different Liberal party bosses made that there was always a crucial role to play for the PCC, which always had various councilmen in the City Council in Urabá. These participated in all aspects of the clientelistic game, as Liberal and Conservative councilmen did: they might propose their own judges, professors, municipal clerks, etc.; they disposed of certain quota of land to distribute among their clientele; they controlled a small labour union and other basic organizations. The Communists characterized the regime of the National Front as 'closed' and 'undemocratic', and as such they always implicitly justified their support of armed struggle. Paradoxically, the guerrilla thus contributed to the fact that attention for problems of violence, for politics of order and for the fight on crime were essentially conceived by state institutions, but also by most students of Colombian violence, as a problem of purely political violence (upward revolutionary or downward state-directed), while the other forms of violence that freely circulated were apparently understood as non-problematic.

Confronted with chronic problems of violence in Urabá, authorities first proposed an interpretation in terms of the aftermath of *La Violencia,* typically describing all violent actors as outlaws (*bandoleros, bandits, asociales,* etc.). They then turned to an interpretation in terms of typical *frontier* violence, that is, in relation to the chaotic social-economic development of the region since the 1960s. Finally in relation to the rise of guerrilla groups, they called it every now and then a *zona roja* ('red zone'). To come to terms with the acute problems of social violence (essentially related to land and labour conflicts), every-day crime, upcoming drug-trafficking (marihuana), banditism and incursions of guerrilla groups, the authorities proposed *ad hoc* 'solutions', such as the appointment of military as mayors, the institution of a curfew, and regular announcements (but less frequent execution) of military operations. A systematic policy to confront the violence in Urabá or a systematic analysis of the situation was never undertaken during these years. Much in this field also depended on the capacities of one or the other mayor or police commander.

Forms of *collective* violence were rare. Collective actors and conflicts had difficulty to develop in such an unstable, chaotic and heterogeneous environment as the Urabá *frontier*. For example, labour conflicts in the banana sector every now and then took a collective form on certain plantations (especially in the case of arbitrary dismissal), but never in the branch as a whole (12,000 salaried workers on 300 plantations). Given the highly unstable labour market, workers preferred to improve their conditions by individual strategies of constant moving from plantation to plantation instead of developing risky collective strategies. Labour contracts were mostly individual and oral, except for the 10 per cent of the plantations that had collective labour contracts. The application of the law regarding labour rights was arbitrary.

More in general, collective organization or protest that escaped political control would be thwarted or repressed. The strictly local 24-hour civil strikes that would take place every now and then in one of the boom-towns or in one of the hundreds of new colonist villages, mostly in support of a specific public demand (a new school, installation of an electricity plant, construction of sewers, etc.), were generally supported (or initiated) by local authorities and political party bosses, who would thus claim for more resources from national or regional state institutions. Only when such a civil strike would be related to tensions between competing local power contenders, they could lead to riots or confrontations with the local police or military forces. Violent death has been exceptional during such events.

In this context, a labour-conflict rapidly tended to take on a strong personal aspect. There were cases of a worker defeating, attacking, blessing or even killing an administrator, a *capataz* (under-boss) or even the owner of the plantation. The opposite also occurred. The planters – a heterogeneous group themselves, made up of small, middle and big owners – would try to find a solution on their own, if necessary by calling in the police or the army. Some of these events led to criminal investigations, but things seem to have been mostly arranged by money – sometimes after the opportune intervention of local lawyers, who made their business buying out affairs. At the same time, not all the plantation-related violence can be interpreted in terms of labour conflicts: in the overcrowded and precarious encampments that existed on all the plantations, 'horizontal' every-day violence in relation to theft, passion, jealousy, etc. was frequent also.[33]

This kind of *social violence* represents the domain where interpretations in terms of Scott's 'hidden transcripts of resistance' may very well be applied. (The panorama of social violence in Urabá was of course far too large to reduce it to labour conflicts on the plantations: disputes over land, housing, credits, etc., could also turn violent.) Some, however, have tried to interpret *all* the violence of those years in terms of 'hidden transcripts of resistance'. I defend the hypothesis that very diverse and diffuse forms of violence co-existed, as I have tried to show, and that this was also understood as such by those directly concerned. No reductionist analysis to social inequality (and resulting protest or rebellion) can be applied in the face of the highly composite character of the forms of violence during this period. The question to be asked then is how did the people make sense of this 'normal' violence? To what extent was this kind of violence understood as a *modus vivendi*, or even a *habitus*?

Studying homicide in Jamiltepec, a village on the Costa Chica, a frontier area on the Mexican Pacific Coast, Flanet (1982) describes violence as being part of the social game and conflicts of every-day life. She argues that in this particular Mexican setting violence is understood at once as a destiny and as a tragedy. Homicidal violence appeared as mixture of burlesque and anxiety, as something the local people can be proud of, while they laugh about *'la petitesse de notre peur de mourir'*.[34] She shows that violence in Jamiltepec depends on the local conception of the world that is always re-imposed on the victims and perpetrators. But at the same time she tries to make clear what the killer or victim resents *individually*, at the moment of being confronted with death, more or less independently of the social structure and culture in which they live. As Flanet explains, in Jamiltepec killing is also an act of a solitary man, an act that partly escapes reason and meaning.

It is true that in Urabá as well, during the 1960s and the 1970s, the meaning people give to certain acts of violence refer back, to some extent, to the symbolic violence of toughness and aggressiveness of every-day life. In Urabá as well there was a certain cultural character to the violence which does not seem to leave traces other than individual mourning, that does not seem to interrogate the political community or society as such. Fatal accidents on the work-place, traffic victims (bicycles under trucks) and a relatively high child mortality represent the brutality of every-day life in a country where basic institutions of a welfare state hardly came into being. Part of the typical rural setting are things like a pig being killed next door, not by cutting its throat with a knife but by hitting a pole on it's head, with passers-by laughing about the screams of the pig.

Nevertheless, homicide in Urabá cannot be reduced to an exclusively cultural interpretation, as Flanet has proposed for Mexico. In Urabá society is far more fragmented than on the Costa Chica, and the possibility to presuppose a homogeneous, regional (ethnic) culture to which the violence can be related is far less obvious.[35] In addition, as we have shown, violence takes too many forms, too many expressions in the Colombian context. Flanet does not pretend that homicide in Jamiltepec is not linked to conflicts, or that it is not most intensive and problematic when linked to forms of organized violence (guerrilla, bandits, death-squads) that do exist in Mexico, but apparently this is not what characterizes violence on the Costa Chica.

Instead of relating homicide in 'normal' Colombian times to a 'culture of violence', I propose here to see it in relation to what I called above a 'tradition of violence'. A tradition of violence which is at the same time also a 'tradition of *impunity*'. Impunity is expressed not only in the statistics but also in the way people conceive justice and act in case of conflict. People will only turn to the local police chief when it concerns a minor problem (somebody accusing his neighbour of not taking care of his garbage), or when he or she tries (mostly in vain) to neutralize a threat that has become unmanageable. In Urabá, during the 1960s and 1970s, homicide, crime, banditism and the presence of guerrilla foci essentially expressed the weakness of the repressive instruments of the state in its task of providing security and protecting individual property. In conditions of a strong state, the judicial system is the place of sacrifice and rite, because it organizes, limits and dissimulates vengeance, and replaces it by a supposed rational and impartial way of operating (cf. Michaud 1986: 117). In conditions of a weak state there is always the risk of an endless chain of vengeance, because to vengeance there is no end.

Finally, as noted before, in Colombia the heritage of violence, the social memory of very strong experiences with violence and terror, especially those from *La Violencia*, has left deep traces in society. This fact should be taken into account when trying to understand how people make sense of the experiences of violence in the 1960s and 1970s. It also sets the Colombian case apart from the Mexican one studied by Flanet (1982).

Current Generalized Violence and Terror (1980s to the Present)

The current situation of generalized violence in Colombia has come into being since the early 1980s. Organized violence and terror[36] have again come to dominate the scene, displacing the more disorganized and moderate violence of the 1960s and 1970s. The region of Urabá has been particularly affected: since 1985 some 12,000 persons have been killed (on a regional population of 300,000–400,000).[37] A series of local wars between guerrilla-groups, mafia syndicates and paramilitary organizations has dictated the rhythm of violence, producing massacres (up to thirty-five victims per incident) and other acts of terror and cruelty that call to mind La Violencia. In the shadow of this 'organized violence', more 'disorganized' forms of violence and cycles of vengeance have proliferated, while the state's public force has progressively lost control of the situation, engaging in all kinds of informal negotiations with the armed groups on the spot, so as to avoid open war and be able to maintain itself in the region.[38] We see the involvement in paramilitary operations, human rights violations and reiterated accusations between criminal or mafia circles and the forces of law and order. The administration of justice, although significantly modernized and reinforced since the new Constitution (1991), has not been able to combat impunity: in Urabá, 95 per cent of the 12,000 homicides since 1985 are unresolved. After fifteen years, it seems that the availability of diverse private armed groups has become a permanent aspect of the local society (and of Colombia more in general). That impression is strengthened by the fact that the different Colombian governments have engaged, since the early 1980s, in all kinds of ad hoc 'peace negotiations' with all kind of actors (drug baron Pablo Escobar included), as if there is always a card to play for a violent actor, however big his crimes may have been (see Pécaut 1987a). In Urabá, the complex juxtaposition of all kind of wars (war on drugs, dirty war, guerrilla war, war of the cartels, militia wars, banana wars, etc.), and all kind of peace initiatives (with different guerrilla factions, drug barons, paramilitary organizations, urban militias, etc.) have created a situation where nobody believes anymore that anybody is able to control anything as far as violence is concerned.

For the local population, the violence thus presents itself as a multiplicity of deadly facts without any apparent link between them. We find confusion, rumours, fear and a generalization of the law of silence. Every armed faction tries to impose its own interpretation of 'the facts', but nobody seems to believe them, often not even their own members who switch between opposite groups for all but ideological reasons. At the same time, since Urabá is only one of the different theatres (urban and rural) that make up the current crisis in Colombia, people are not able to inscribe the violence they confront in a larger narrative that would give a certain national unity and 'readability' to the situation. Violence, again, appears as extremely fragmented, scattered, decentralized and composite.[39] The absence of a strong political dimension contributes to this impression. *La Violencia*, in spite of the multiplicity and regional diversity of its expressions, received a certain legibility from the conflict between Liberals and Conservatives. But what larger (political) signification can be attributed to the current violence? True: guerrilla-groups, mafia-cartels and paramilitary groups hit state institutions, notably the justice administration and the public forces, and a political dimension thus seems to be present. Guerrilla groups, paramilitary organizations and certain drug barons, such as Pablo Escobar or the Castano brothers, have never ceased to legitimize themselves by political arguments. But the abyss between their words and the every-day reality of massacres, terror and other acts of violence they commit on the civil population in fact delegitimizes their political pretentions and reinforces the impression that violence is for these groups either a lucrative business and/or a way of living. A global interpretation in terms of subversive violence is thus as weak as an interpretation in terms of oppressive violence, the Colombian state in fact missing every control on the situation. Even so, an interpretation of current violence in terms of the restricted democratic character of the regime[40] has limited explanatory force, since the crisis runs parallel to the end of the National Front coalition and to a process of opening up of the Colombian political system (without giving way, however, to a redefinition of the role of the state as a secure agent in the evolution of societal construction). The intensity of unorganized violence and the fact that violence hardly presents itself in the prolongation of collective conflicts make that an interpretation in terms of collective violence has not much explanatory force either: armed groups having first instrumentalized existing land, labour and housing conflicts, before giving them a violent turn, one can hardly speak of collective violence. The violence is neither rationalized by appeals to ethnic, religious, cultural or other conflicts that claim a community or an identity nor by a focus on class conflict or specific social problems. Here is neither a 'clash of civilizations', as Huntington would understand it, nor a communautarian war that aims to impose a kind of lost unity or a new homogeneity (Le Bot 1996).

The fragile society that came in existence in Urabá since the early 1960s was not prepared for the threats of organized crime and hardening guerrilla groups. As a typical frontier, with run-away demographic growth, weak institutions and a serious problem of domestic violence, drug cartels and guerrilla groups, both interested in Urabá given its geo-strategic importance and wealth, found fertile ground here.[41] The multiplicity of armed contenders for power partly explains the intensity of the crisis in the region. Even so, the traditional economic and political interests have never accepted to give up Urabá, as they had sometimes done with less strategic areas. In Urabá, all parties have tended to impose and maintain themselves, while new protagonists never cease to appear.

The civilian population is the main victim of the violence. During the eighties, it still seemed possible to keep away from it and to 'deny' the problem. Most people would strategically negotiate their passive adhesion to the particular armed group that controlled the territory they lived in, but they would often try to avoid more open or active forms of adherence. The local population would make themselves believe that the hundreds of victims of the banana wars between the guerrilla groups FARC and EPL (1985–87) and of the first para-military offensive (1986–88), were mostly persons that were actively involved with one or the other gang, and had thus asked for trouble ... Typical comments in case of an execution were *'Algo debia'* (He had something on his slate) or *'Es que se habia polarisado'* (He had himself polarized). In the case of more 'disorganized' forms of violence, killings would be banalized by designing the victim as a *desintegrado,* a *descompuesto,* a *ladron* (thief), a *falton* (someone who hadn't kept his word), a *hablon* (someone who talks to much) or a *desechable* (a throw-away). To a certain extent, being killed came to be considered as a hazard of every-day life, giving way to a representation not in terms Flanet found on the Costa Chica, but in terms of society as pure survival where violence is no longer something that might or should be controlled. Apparently, only extremely brutal or arbitrary acts of violence (tossing hand-grenades in open-air cafés, the execution of a generally respected person, a massacre) were met with a collective shock and provoking a spontaneous (but often short-lived) refugee movement out of the conflict zone.

One thus observed a certain 'banality' and normality of the violence that seems to contrast with the gravity of the situation. Pécaut (1997) has underlined particular aspects of the Colombian situation that contribute to this impression of banality: the absence of relations between violence and pre-existing collective identities; the opportunities violence offers as a business and a career; the heterogeneous dimensions of the violence;

the patchwork of local networks of control the new protagonists are able to create; the way the private use violence can co-exist with the formal maintenance of a 'state of law'; the satisfactory economic performance and political stability (even in Urabá) in spite of the crisis. For the local population, the new armed groups also seemed to continue, at least at first sight, the modalities of clientelistic control that *gamonales* (electoral barons) maintained traditionally on their local fiefs. It is thus, at once, the complexity of a situation of generalized violence and the Colombian tradition of violence – that is, the apparent adaptability of the use of violence to Colombian society – which seems to contribute to its banality.

Since the 1990s however, with the violence giving more and more way to outright terror, the possibilities for subtle individual strategies of passive adhesion are rapidly restricted. During the regional wars between EPL and FARC (1991–94) and between paramilitaries and guerrilla (since 1995), the local population is forced to choose between two camps (or to flee from Urabá). Decapitations, public exposure of victims, heads stabbed on sticks along the road, and prohibitions to recover the bodies of persons executed and left behind are now used to create new boundaries and to establish total territorial control.

One of the authors of *La Violencia en Colombia,* the classic account of the civil war (see above), recently indicated that identical forms of cruelty as during *La Violencia,* especially the famous *cortes* (see above), seem to reappear.[42] However, one has to ask if these cruelties still inscribe themselves in a particular symbolic universe, as was the case during *La Violencia,* in particular with the ritualized *cortes.* Only in a limited way, I would say. They appear now as largely arbitrary and disjointed. It is true that to a certain extent they represent actualizations of past gestures and actions, but only in so far as these actualizations come to be quasi-mechanistic forms of *mimetism,* undone from its original cultural and symbolic universe, not linked to it. The brutalities as they present themselves in the 1990s are less symbolic, more instrumental, and they represent, more then anything else, typical practices of *dirty wars.* They retake typically forms of torture and dehumanization, as we find them elsewhere in other contexts where terror reigns (torture, rape, cutting off heads, disappearing bodies), the possibilities of innovation being relatively restricted in this field. Such practices can hardly be understood as a way to reintroduce meaning, and much more as a way to induce extreme anxiety and make people flee. They again also appear strongly related to the processes of 'desocialization' inherent in the exercise of violence itself.

Under these new conditions of terror and autonomization of violence, the already fragile frontier society assists at a process of individual desocialization and social degeneration. Extreme distrust and fear take the place of sentiments of social adherence and of forms of solidarity as they could be present in a neighbourhood or on a plantation. Symptoms of escapism testify of the same process: the daily funeral processions of homicide victims seems to pass unnoticed through the crowded streets of the boom-town. Such forms of apparently apathetic behaviour directly result from the difficulty to show emotion in a context of extreme social anxiety and suspicion. The boom of Protestant sects in Urabá and other violent-prone areas has sometimes been explained as an escape mechanism in a situation where all public bonds of solidarity have come under extreme pressure. Singing together for hours and calling each other brother and sister should then be interpreted as a way to reconstruct, on a completely neutral non-combat territory, social bonds.

Some Final Remarks

1. The current violence is experienced as an irruption of the past but at the same time as a 'violence without history'. As an irruption of the past, since individual and collective experiences of violence are understood by a certain reification or myth of violence, as if they do not arise from particular causes and concrete acts. Even more so, since there has not been a verbalization of the experiences of *La Violencia*, collective memory has, for various reasons partly invoked above, never been able to take a socially recognized form. A terror without history, as Pécaut (1997) has shown, since it proceeds in the political context of a fragmented political field and in the institutional context of a state that has more than ever lost control over the situation, while the violence does not inscribe itself anymore in an all-embracing friend–foe relationship, as during the *Violencia*. This time, the massacres are related to conflicts between local power contenders as guerrilla and mafia-type organizations, without references to a general cause, while no other points of anchorage are available: collective identities, civil rights and political citizenship are already historically weak and have suffered and were partially destroyed by the new violence. If we want to understand material and symbolic aspects of current Colombian violence in terms of a 'tradition of violence', such a tradition then should never be conceived of as fixed for once and for ever, because this would give way to an interpretation in terms of a 'culture of violence', that I have contested here.

2. Conflicts are inherent to the construction of society; they participate in reformulating its goals and in redefining collective identities. But it would obviously be a mistake to suppose that every conflict is necessarily

useful or meaningful in explicit political or social terms. In a region such as Urabá, the population has been confronted during more then fifteen years with a lot of 'senseless' conflicts and violence that have essentially provoked the destruction of social order. It is true that from the perspective of the protagonists, the use of violence and terror has in part a strictly instrumental side: their goal is 'political' cleansing and territorial control (see Walter 1969; Merkl 1986; Wickam-Crowley 1990), and, from their own point of view, they may succeed, at least in the short term. But to legitimize their acts, the protagonists pretend at the same time that their objectives coincide with the interests of pre-existing groups in these territories. (As such, the plantation workers have terribly suffered from the instrumentalization of violence by guerrilla and para-military groups.) Those directly concerned could understand the new violence, at least in the beginning, as a variation of traditional forms of control, convinced that force and open violence had always been inherent to the reproduction of Colombian society. But it became rapidly clear that the new forms of control and 'protection' were simply *imposed* (they could not be refused) and this for strictly prosaic reasons, while they were maintained by terror, that is by sowing extreme anxiety among the target groups. To a certain extent one can even say that the protagonists *chose* to use arbitrary violence and terror because they understood it as the only way to impose a control that didn't coincide with pre-existing forms of identity or with a larger socio-political project, as was still the case during *La Violencia*, when political cleansing inscribed itself in an effort to recreate homogeneous red or blue communities.

3. Feldman, in his book on IRA-related violence, introduces a distinction between the 'hardman' and the 'gunman' (Feldman 1991). The violence of the hardman is narrative, performative, visible, individual and related to face-to-face conflicts that concern the actor in person. His violence is related to the cultural and symbolic environment, marked by well defined principles of honour and respect. A challenge or a provocation can put the hardman in a situation where his fists are supposed to do the talking. The bystanders will understand (although not necessarily approve). Although Urabá was never a strongly integrated community such as Feldman's Irish world was, the model of the hardman recalls to a certain extent the relatively moderate violence of the 1960s and 1970s in Urabá, at least as far as social violence and every-day violence is concerned.[43] This is why, to a certain extent, it can also be successfully compared to some forms of classic American frontier violence.

The gunman, on the contrary is described by Feldman as a far more anonymous actor for whom violence is a practical, mechanical, instrumental and organized way of acting. The gunman is masked and an automatic gun has replaced the fists. The violence of the gunman may be instrumental in relation to determined strategico-political goals, but no longer meaningful in relation to a cultural and symbolic universe. This conceptual distinction between the hardman and the gunman, refers us back to the transformation of violence in Urabá during the early 1980s, especially the appearance of organized violence and terror, and the difficulty to make sense of it other then in purely instrumental terms. In a highly strategic context where brute force dominates power relations and leads to societal destruction, the possibilities for an analysis in terms of symbolic or cultural violence seem to be reduced. In a certain way however, Feldman nevertheless investigates the possibilities left for symbolic analysis of the anonymous violence of the gunmen. He describes how the IRA members, by opting for their collective hunger strike (1981), realized an inversion of the (gun) violence by turning it against their own bodies, getting blind before they effectively die. But one may wonder if such kinds of schemes of interpretation could be applied to some of the Colombian phenomena. For example, the regular and sometimes massive inside executions that have affected Colombian armed groups, have often remained hidden and had thus a far less public character then the mortal IRA hunger strikes.

This is not to say that there is no interest or relevance in trying to understand to which extent the current experiences of violence may take a symbolic turn. Alonso Salazar (1990), studying youth-gang violence in the 1980s in Medellín, has clearly described the subculture of death as it is cultivated by the *sicarios* (young contract killers), for whom violence has become a way of living and a first cause of death. For these youngsters, a violent death is 'normal', while a natural death is something quite inconceivable. Salazar shows how they have grown up in a world where the progressive degradation of societal norms and values has lead them not to commit suicide but to commit homicides, a way out of a situation of anomy already foreseen by Durkheim. Salazar convincingly shows that their death-culture is more in particular characterized by the systematic use of inversion of religious symbols, and that the influence of the Catholic Church, which so strongly dominated all social life in Medellín, has not completely disappeared but rather reappears under quite unexpected forms. (Example: a *sicario* wearing a Maria image in his underpants while carrying out a contract murder on Colombia's Minister of Justice Lara Bonilla in 1984).

The limits of these kind of interpretations mostly come from the fact that they concern a symbolic interpretation of violence as produced by those *exercising* the violence and not as produced by those *victimized* by it, be they bystanders, direct victims, displaced persons or refugees. The gunmen, that is the *sicarios*, *guerilleros* or para-military men, may live in a sub-culture of death. Those victimized by them live in shock, anxiety, and permanent terror. They are often unable, unwilling and afraid to publicly speak out about their experiences. Nevertheless, to understand current Colombian violence, and to see if their is still any ambiguity left in it, nothing is more crucial than to listen to their testimonies.

Notes

1. For reflections on the polysemic character of violence, cf. *Violence, Brutalité, Barbarie*, Special Issue of *Ethnologie Française* no. 3 (1991); Jamin (1984) and Riches (1986).
2. An analysis in terms of generalized violence of the Colombian situation has been worked out by Pécaut (1987a; 1994; 1996). The Colombian situation of generalized violence may be understood as a particular case of the State of War, as conceived by Locke. Locke introduced a clear distinction between (a) a societal regression to a State of War, while staying in the context of a State-society, and (b) Hobbes' idea of a State of War as a State of Nature, that is a pre-political, a-historical situation; see J. Locke, *Two Treatises of Government*, Cambridge: Cambridge University Press, 1991 [1960], especially Book II, ch. III, and Peter Laslett's *Introduction*, pp. 98–101.
3. V. Nahoum-Grappe (1995) insists on the stupor of victims and witnesses, in relation to the scale and the outbidding character of cruelty during the war in ex-Yugoslavia.
4. For violence and war in pre-modern societies and tribes, see Foster and Rubinstein (1986); Turner and Pitt (1989); Vincent (1989) and Haas (1990).
5. Two inspiring examples: Geffray (1990) and Ortiz Sarmiento (1985).
6. Urabá is a frontier area of tropical forest, situated on the extreme north-western part of Colombia beyond the last Andean counterforts on the border with Panama. Located around the attractive and highly strategic Gulf of Urabá but separated from its hinterland by high mountains and bad road communications, the region (18,000 km^2) is a kind of *cul de sac*, because a road between Colombia and Panama has never

existed. Since the early 1960s, the eastern side of the Gulf has known rapid economic and demographic development around a prosperous banana-export industry (27,000 hectares) and its boom-towns (Turbo, 40,000 people; Apartado, 40,000; Chigorodo 25,000), extensive cattle-farming and various pioneer frontiers. Urabá is, with the Magdalena Medio, one of the most densely populated frontier areas of the country (20 inhabitants/km²). Violence in Urabá is exceptionally intense since the 1980s and the situation cannot be generalized for Colombia as a whole. However, since the most important elements of the national crisis are present in Urabá, a regional analysis can contribute towards a more general understanding of violence in Colombia.

7. This part of my article is largely inspired by Pécaut's reflections. For the problematic relation between order and violence since the 1950s, see especially Pécaut (1987b; 1989; 1995). For a synthesis of modern Colombian history, see Palacios (1995).

8. The only twentieth-century military governments in Colombia were the ones led by general Gustavo Rojas Pinilla (1953–57) – put in place by Liberal and Conservative party-leaders to make an end to the civil war – and the following Junta (1957–58), that came to power when the same party-leaders obliged Rojas Pinilla, who had become too authoritarian, to quit his job. In the nineteenth century, only the short-lived regimes of Rafael Urdaneta (1830–31) and of José Maria Melo (1854) are generally considered as military governments.

9. General suffrage was introduced for men in 1853, and for women in 1957, but, as in most other Latin American countries, anonymous voting, that is the introduction of a polling booth, only exists since the recent changes in election procedures (1988). In Western Europe, the polling booth was introduced during the nineteenth century (France being the last one in the 1910s). For reflections on this point, cf. Rosanvallon (1992).

10. On the construction of the political field in the Andean countries during the nineteenth century, see Demélas (1992).

11. A growing middle-class affirms itself notably by an important demand for education: between 1951 and 1993, analfabetism diminished from 39 per cent to 12 per cent, and the number of university students was multiplied by thirty. Student scholarships have been a crucial resource in clientelist strategies, cf. Palacios (1995: 296–8).

12. Small wonder that all Colombian political factions, without exception, have stimulated the constant (and uncontrolled) growth of the public sector (some 4,500 functionaries in 1875, against 43,000 in 1916, some 100,000 in 1950 and more than a million in 1990).

13. Colombia has known long periods of Liberal hegemony (1863–86, 1930–46) as well as of Conservative hegemony (1886–30, 1946–53). But there is at the same time a strong tradition of *pactos de caballeros* between both camps to prevent (or to end) violent confrontations, especially during the first half of the twentieth century, after the *Guerra de los Mil Dias*. As a *pacto the caballeros*, the National Front distinguished itself by its institutional character and longevity.

14. This point has been stressed by Bushnell (1996). Presidential, parliamentarian, departmental and municipal elections were held every two years, with only the two last of them on the same day.

15. In some regions, during *La Violencia*, Protestants were victims of systematic Conservative violence, cf. Henderson (1984).

16. The weakness of the public sector has in part its explanation in the tax structure: in 1989, Colombian taxes represented 10 per cent of the GNP, against 24 per cent for Brazil. Important new exports (coal, natural gas, oil) have again delayed the urgency of tax reforms.

17. For the Colombian frontier, see LeGrand (1980). For recent Colombian frontier-areas, see Martin (1996). For the Latin American Frontier in general, see Hennesy (1978).

18. Average demographic density (30 persons/km^2) is low in Colombia in comparison to other Latin American countries.

19. However, the free availability of land in Colombia also contains a 'democratic' dimension, while the selling of land, as in Brazil, in advance excludes an important part of the population from the possibility of social mobility.

20. Three sub-periods are generally distinguished for *La Violencia*: the civil war (1947–53), with some 160,000 victims on a population of 15 million people; the military regime (1953–57); and a period of violent pacification (1957–63), with an additional 40,000 deaths. Once it spread from urban centres to the countryside, *La Violencia* notably affected economically important areas, such as the coffee regions and other central Andean zones. Some 400,000 peasants are supposed to have lost their land. Many took to the cities while others migrated to frontier regions such as Urabá.

21. During *La Violencia*, the police was under the Ministry of the Interior. Its being completely staffed with Conservatives and its participation in massacres on the Liberal population during *La Violencia* led, under the military regime of general Rojas Pinilla (1953–57), to its incorporation into the Ministry of Defence (1954), supposed to be politically neutral. Fear for repolitization of the police has been one of the

reasons why the new Constitution of 1991 has left the police with the Ministry of Defence, in spite of strong societal pressure for its 'demilitarization'. There are propositions to transform the police in an independent institution (cf. Guizado 1993).

22. Hirschman wrote that violence, during *La Violencia*, was 'scattered, local en decentralized' and not 'revolutionary': 'To qualify as revolutionary, violence must be centralized; it must attack and conquer the central seats of political and administrative power' (Hirschmann 1978: 257).

23. Guzman *et al.* (1963: 225–37) describe the case of a woman imploring her torturers to allow her to speak for a last time to her husband. The cut-off head of the husband is then brought in and the torturers oblige the woman 'to speak to him'. She was then raped and left alive.

24. Among the 235 massacres cited by Uribe (1990) for the Tolima region, thirty were perpetrated between 1949–55, the rest between 1955–64.

25. In Tolima, the Liberal gangs were typically called *chusmeros, cachiporros, chapasangres,* or *vampiros,* while the Conservatives were called *godos, chulavitos, chulos,* etc. (Uribe 1990: 92).

26. A massacre being defined as the simultaneous killing of at least four victims by at least three culprits.

27. These ritualized forms of cutting up the corpses of the victims were commonly known as *corte de franela, corte de corbata, corte de mica, corte frances, corte de oreja, corte de florero,* etc. For details on the cuts and their particular significance, see Uribe (1990: 167–89). Guzman *et al.* (1963) make a comparison with scenes of the Greek civil war as described by Nikos Kazantzakis.

28. For a brilliant analysis of the communal horizon of significance in which Catholics and Protestants inscribed themselves during the religious wars in France, and the way this expressed itself in the particular forms of cruelty and violence with both communities exterminated each other, see Crouzet (1990).

29. For a clear description of lasting inter- and intra-Liberal and Conservative political violence since the National Front, a seldomly studied subject, cf. Cruz (1996).

30. More in general, 'close ties of class and camaderie that theoretically bind social bandits and peasants together do not surface in the Latin American context' (Slatta 1987: 192). See on this point also Joseph (1990).

31. Cf. Blok (1988). See also, for a classic debate with Hobsbawm, Blok (1972).

32. The Communist Party (PCC) obtained, during the first non-National Front elections, less then 5 per cent of the vote.

33. Some 90 per cent of the banana-workers are men. In the beginning they are mostly *macho-solos*, but progressively women and children install themselves in the encampments, where the worker has the right on free housing for himself and his family (married or not), while housing in the boom-towns is expensive and difficult to obtain.

34. They say in Jamiltepec, that to be a man 'one has to be able to support alcohol, to have been in prison, and to have received a bullet' (Flanet 1982: 81).

35. In Urabá, there is no evidence of inter-ethnic violence. We may even suppose that every-day violence is partly turned inside, that is intra-ethnic, as in the USA, where 86 per cent of the African-Americans killed are killed by other African-Americans, 75 per cent of Latinos killed are killed by Latinos, and 55 per cent of Whites are killed by Whites (cf. Body Gendrot 1992). In Urabá, 'black' people distinguish themselves in *negros, mulatos, morenos* and *chocoanos*, and cultivate group identities in relation to their original village. The people from the interior, that is from the Andean highlands, are mostly considered as 'whites', but distinguish between themselves for regional origins; Indian communities (Cuna, Zenu, Embera) represent 1 or 2 per cent of the regional population. As in Colombia in general, most of the population can be considered mestizo. Symbolic interpretations of violence and terror on Black and Indian cultures have been proposed by Taussig (1988). But his interpretation is about a very particular setting of a foreign-owned rubber-plantations in the Amazon area at the beginning of the twentieth century.

36. This terror can be distinguished in: (1) the mafia-terror against the state; (2) a politically oriented terror, such as the extermination campaigns organized by paramilitary groups against members of guerrilla-linked political parties, labour-union members, etc.; (3) territorially-based terror as executed by the armed groups to impose and maintain their control within their own organization or on the local population. For the local population in Urabá, the last form has been particularly visible and fearful, see Pécaut (1997).

37. In 1996 alone, 1383 persons were killed in Urabá, including 114 victims of fifteen massacres (IPC, Medellín).

38. For relations between organized and disorganized violence, Martin (1997).

39. This in contrast, for example, to the civil war in Guatemala, where insurrectional and counter-insurrectional violence were always

understood as the two axes that accounted for the crisis and its (political) interpretation, cf. Le Bot (1992).

40. The strict two party-system of the National Front came formally to an end in 1974. Third parties, in particular the Communist Party, could now again directly participate at the elections instead of indirectly, by way of coalitions.

41. It is now generally recognized that the drug economy has been an important catalyst of the degradation to a situation of generalized violence. However, well into the 1980s the drug-economy was rather seen as a useful lubricator for all kinds of business. The presence of various guerrilla groups has inspired interpretations of current violence in purely political terms.

42. Eduardo Umana Luna, in the weekly *Cambio* 16 (28 June 1997), p. 26. A doctor, member of the technical research team of the public prosecutor in Urabá, reported: 'To various victims they put their penis in their mouth and it seems that at least by one of them, they opened the abdomen with *machetazos* (machete cuts), the victim being in full state of consciousness' (Giraldo, Colorade and Perez 1997, p. 21). The weekly *El Colombiano* (25 September 1995) reports: '[In Currulao, in Urabá], six people were massacred. One of them was decapitated, and they then played football with his head. The wife of another, who was also decapitated, was forced to kiss the head of her husband'.

43. In the highly dynamic, open, and profoundly heterogeneous frontier society of Urabá, we are in a completely different context than the one of the 'eternal', Andean world of small peasant communities, that was in part the theatre of *La Violencia*. For a classic description of this 'closed' world, see Fals Borda (1979). The author Mario Vargas Llosa, speaking about symbolic reinterpretation of violence in Peru, also refers to traditional peasant communities, but we should take into account that the Indian element is much stronger here then in the Colombian situation: 'There is the political violence and its derailment, especially from *Sendero Luminoso*. From there was born the counter-revolutionary violence from the police and the army, and that has been nearly as terrifying as the terrorism. We also see social violence, related to poverty, misery, ignorance, isolation, that has especially struck the peasant communities. Together, all this violence has contributed a lot to the resurrection of still another form of violence, which is the one related to irrationalism, to superstition, and that has been at the source of a lot of suffering and misery for the peasants'. Interview on *Radio France Culture* (1996) for the French publication of his book *Lituma en los Andes*.

Bibliography

Abbink, J. (1993a), 'Famine, Gold and Guns: the Suri of Southern Ethiopia, 1985–91', *Disasters* 17: 218–6.

—— (1993b), 'Ethnic Conflict in the "Tribal" Zone: the Dizi and Suri in Southern Ethiopia', *Journal of Modern African Studies* 31: 675–83.

—— (1994), 'Changing Patterns of 'Ethnic' Violence: Peasant–Pastoralist Confrontation in Southern Ethiopia and its Implications for a Theory of Violence', *Sociologus* 40: 66–78.

—— (1997), 'Authority and Leadership in Surma Society (Ethiopia)', *Africa* (Roma) 52: 317–42.

—— (1998), 'Violence and Political Discourse among the Chai Suri', in: G.J. Dimmendaal and M. Last (eds), *Surmic Languages and Cultures*, Cologne: R. Köppe Verlag.

—— (1999), 'The Production of "Primitiveness" and Identity: Surma–Tourist Interactions', in: R. Fardon *et al.* (eds), 'Modernity on a Shoestring. Dimensions of Globalization, Consumption and Development', in *Africa and Beyond,* London – Leiden: EIDOS-CAS-ASC.

Aijmer, G. (1997), *Ritual Dramas in the Duke of York Islands: an Exploration of Cultural Imagery*, Gothenburg: IASSA.

Aijmer G. and V.K.Y. Ho (1999), *Cantonese Society in a Time of Change*, Hong Kong: Chinese University Press (forthcoming).

Alvarez de Miranda, A. (1962), *Ritos y Juegos del Toro,* Madrid: Taurus.

Amira, K. von (1922), 'Die Germanische Todesstrafen', in: *Abhandlungen der Bayerischen Akademie der Wissenschaften, Philosophisch-historische Klasse*, vol. 31: 1–415.

Anderson, C.W. (1967), *Political and Economic Change in Latin America: Governing the Restless Nations,* Princeton: Van Nostrand.

Anderson, D. (1986), 'Stock Theft and Moral Economy in Colonial Kenya', *Africa* 56: 399–416.

Apple Daily (Pinguo Ribao), Hong Kong daily newspaper.

Aya, R. (1990), *Rethinking Revolutions and Collective Violence*, Amsterdam: Het Spinhuis.

Babcock, B. (1993), 'At Home, No Women Are Storytellers: Ceramic

Bibliography

Creativity and the Politics of Discourse in a Cochiti Pueblo', in: S. Lavie, K. Narayan and R. Rosaldo (eds), *Creativity/Anthropology,* Ithaca: Cornell University Press.

Ban Gu (1962), *Hanshu,* Beijing: Zhonghua Shuju.

Bateson, G. (1972), *Steps to an Ecology of Mind,* London: Intertext.

Baumeister, R. (1996), *Evil: Inside Human Violence and Cruelty,* New York: Freeman.

Baxter, P. (1979), 'Boran Age-sets and Warfare', in: K. Fukui and D. Turton (eds), *Warfare among East African Herders* (Senri Ethnological Studies 3), Osaka: National Museum of Ethnology.

Beck, B.J.M. (1986), 'The Fall of Han', in: D. Twitchett and M. Loewe (eds), *The Cambridge History of China,* vol. 1, Cambridge: Cambridge University Press.

Bell, Ch. (1989), *Ritual Theory, Ritual Practice,* New York: Oxford University Press.

Benedict, R. (1932), 'Configurations of Culture in North America', *American Anthropologist* 34: 1–27.

Billacois, F. (1986), *Le Duel dans la Société Française des XVIe et XVIIe Siècles,* Paris: Éditions de l'École des Hautes Études en Sciences Sociales.

Bishco, C.J. (1990), 'The Spanish and Portuguese Reconquest, 1095–1492', in: K.M. Setton (ed.), *A History of the Crusades,* 2nd edn, Madison: Wisconsin University Press.

Blanchard, D.C. and R.J. Blanchard (1984), 'Affect and Aggression: an Animal Model Applied to Human Behavior', in: D.C. and R.J. Blanchard (eds), *Advances in the Study of Aggression,* New York: Academic Press.

Bloch, M. (1989), *From Blessing to Violence: History and Ideology in the Circumcision Ritual of the Merina of Madagascar,* Cambridge: Cambridge University Press.

—— (1992), *Prey into Hunter: the Politics of Religious Experience,* Cambridge: Cambridge University Press.

Blok, A. (1972), 'The Peasant and the Brigand: Social Banditry Reconsidered', *Comparative Studies in Society and History* 14: 495–504.

—— (1981), 'Rams and Billy Goats: a Key to the Mediterranean Code of Honour', *Man* (NS) 16: 427–40.

—— (1988), *The Mafia of a Sicilian Village, 1860–1960: a Study of Violent Peasant Entrepreneurs,* 2nd edn, Cambridge: Polity Press.

—— (1989a), 'Charivari als Purificatieritueel', *Volkskundig Bulletin* 15: 266–80.

—— (1989b), 'The Symbolic Vocabulary of Public Executions', in: J.

Starr and J.F. Collier (eds), *History and Power in the Study of Law*, Ithaca: Cornell University Press.

—— (1991) 'Zinvol en Zinloos Geweld', *Amsterdams Sociologisch Tijdschrift* 18: 189–207.

—— (1995a), 'Dietro le Quinte: Compare la Sfera del Privato', in: M. Aymard (ed.), *Storia d'Europa, IV, L'Età Moderna,* Torino: Einaudi.

—— (1995b), *De Bokkerijders: Roversbenden en Geheime Genootschappen in de Landen van Overmaas, 1730–1774,* 2nd edn, Amsterdam: Prometheus.

—— (1996), 'Mafia and Blood Symbolism', paper presented at the Conference *Risky Transactions, Kinship and Ethnicity*, Max Planck Institute for Human Ethology, 23–25 September (1996), Bad Homburg, Germany.

—— (1998), 'Bandits and Boundaries: Robber Bands and Secret Societies on the Dutch Frontier (1730–1778)', in: M.P. Hanagan *et al.* (eds), *Challenging Authority: the Historical Study of Contentious Politics,* Minneapolis: University of Minnesota Press.

Bloom, H. (1975), *The Anxiety of Influence: a Theory of Poetry,* Oxford: Oxford University Press.

Boase, F. (1965), *Modern English Biography,* 6 vols, London: F. Cass.

Bodde, D. (1975), *Festivals in Classical China*, Princeton and Hong Kong: Princeton University Press/Chinese University Press.

—— (1991), *Chinese Thought, Society, and Science: the Intellectual and Social Background of Science and Technology in Pre-Modern China,* Honolulu: University of Hawaii Press.

Bodde, D. and C. Morris (1967), *Law in Imperial China: Exemplified by 190 Ch'ing Dynasty Cases*, Cambridge, MA: Harvard University Press.

Body Gendrot, S. (1992), 'Les Nouvelles Formes de la Violence Urbaine aux États Unis', *Culture et Conflits* 6: 25–47 (Special issue 'Violences Urbaines').

Boehm, Ch. (1987) [1984], *Blood Revenge: the Enactment and Mangement of Conflict in Montenegro and Other Tribal Societies,* 2nd edn, Philadelphia: University of Pennsylvania Press.

Bokenkamp, S. (1996), ' "Declarations of the Perfected" and "Answering a Summons" ', in: D.S. Lopez Jr. (ed.), *Religions of China in Practice,* Princeton: Princeton University Press.

Bourdieu, P. (1977), 'Symbolic Power', in: D. Gleeson (ed.), *Identity and Structure: Issues in the Sociology of Education,* Driffield: Nafferton Books.

—— (1979), 'The Sense of Honour', in: P. Bourdieu, *Algeria 1960,* Cambridge: Cambridge University Press.

Bovenkerk, F. (1991), 'Over Selectiviteit Gesproken!', *Tijdschrift voor Criminologie* 33: 309–21.

Bower, V.L. (1991), 'Polo in Tang China: Sport and Art', *Asian Art* IV: 23–45.

Brink, G. van den (1991), 'Van Gevecht tot Gerecht', in: H. Franke *et al.* (eds), *Alledaags en Ongewoon Geweld*, Groningen: Wolters/Nordhoff.

Brinkgreve, C. and R. van Daalen (1991), 'Huiselijk Geweld', in: H. Franke *et al.* (eds), *Alledaags en Ongewoon Geweld*, Groningen: Wolters/Noordhoff.

Brittan, A. (1973), *Meanings and Situations*, London: Routledge and Kegan Paul.

Bromberger, C. *et al.* (1995), *Le Match de Football. Ethnologie d'une Passion Partisane à Marseille, Naples et Turin*, Paris: Éditions de la Maison des Sciences de l'Homme.

—— and G. Lenclud (eds) (1982), 'La Chasse et la Cueillette Aujourd'hui', *Études Rurales* no. 87/88: 1–421.

Brown, R.M. (1994), *No Duty to Retreat: Violence and Values in American Society and History*, Norman: University of Oklahoma Press.

Brownmiller, S. (1975), *Against Our Will: Men, Women, and Rape*, New York: Simon and Schuster.

Bruner, J. (1990), *Acts of Meaning*, Cambridge, Mass: Harvard University Press.

Burkert, W. (1983), *Homo Necans: the Anthropology of Ancient Greek Sacrificial Ritual and Myth*, Berkeley: University of California Press.

Burridge, K. (1979), *Someone, No One: an Essay on Individuality*, Princeton: Princeton University Press.

Bushnell, D. (1996), *The Making of Modern Colombia: a Nation in Spite of Itself*, Berkeley: University of California Press.

Cahill, J. (1994), *The Painter's Practice*, New York: Columbia University Press.

Cameron, D. and E. Frazer (1994), 'Cultural Differences and the Lust to Kill', in: P. Harvey and P. Gow (eds), *Sex and Violence: Issues in Representation and Experience*, London: Routledge.

Campbell, J.K. (1964), *Honour, Family, and Patronage: a Study of Institutions and Moral Values in a Greek Mountain Community*, Oxford: Clarendon Press.

Camus, A. (1956) [1951], *The Rebel*, New York: Vintage Books.

Caro Baroja, J. (1981), *Los Pueblos de España*, 3 t. Colección Fundamentos 54, Madrid: Istmo.

Cavalieri, P. and P. Singer (eds) (1993), *The Great Ape Project: Equality beyond Humanity*, London: Sage.

Bibliography

Chagnon, N.A. (1988), 'Life Histories, Blood Revenge and Warfare in a Tribal Population', *Science* no. 239: 985–92.

Chambers, I. (1994), *Migrancy Culture Identity,* London: Routledge.

Chejne, A.G. (1987), *Historia de la España Musulmana,* Traduccion de Pilar Vila, 2nd edn, Madrid: Cátedra.

'China: Organ Procurement and Judicial Execution in China', *Human Rights Watch/Asia Report,* vol. 6, no. 9, August (1994).

Chen Cunren (1973), *Yinyuan Shidai Shenghuo Shi* (A History of Life During the Period of Silver Dollars), Hong Kong: Wuxingji Shubaoshe.

Chen Dingshan (1971), *Chunshen Jiuwen* (Anecdotes from Old Shanghai), Taibei: Shihjie Wenwu Zhubanshe.

Chen Guofu and Qiu Peihao (1947), *Zhonghua Guomin Shenghuo li* (Life Calender for Chinese Nationals), n.p.: Zhengzhong Shuju.

Cheong, Key Ray (1990), *Cannibalism in China,* Wakefield: Longwood Academic.

Ch'ü T'ung-tsu (1961), *Law and Society in Traditional China,* Paris: Mouton.

Cina: Nelle Lastre di Leone Nani, La (1994) (Edited by the Pontifico Istituto Missioni Estere), Brescia: Grafo.

Comaroff, J. and J. Comaroff (eds) (1993), *Modernity and its Malcontents: Ritual and Power in Postcolonial Africa,* Chicago: University of Chicago Press.

Corbin, J.R. (1977), 'An Anthropological Perspective on Violence', *International Journal of Environmental Studies* 10: 107–11.

Cossio, J.M. de (1951),*Los Toros: Tratado Técnico e Histórico,* Madrid: Espasa-Calpe.

Crouzet, D. (1990), *Les Guerres de Dieu: La Violence au Temps des Troubles de Religion (1525–1610),* 2 vols, Champs Vallon: Seyssel.

Crummey, D. (ed.) (1986), *Banditry, Rebellion and Social Protest in Africa,* London: James Currey.

Cruz, A.L.A. (1996), *El Poder y la Sangre: Las Historias de Trujillo,* Cáli: Gobernacion del Valle del Cauca.

Cutter, R.J. (1989), *The Brush and the Spur: Chinese Culture and the Cockfight,* Shatin: The Chinese University Press.

Dahles, H. (1990), *Mannen in het Groen: De Wereld van de Jacht in Nederland,* Nijmegen: SUN.

Daly, M. and M. Wilson (1988), *Homicide,* Chicago: Aldine.

—— (1991), 'Anti-science and the Pre-Darwinian Image of Mankind', *American Anthropologist* 93: 162–65.

Davis, N.Z. (1975), *Society and Culture in Modern France,* Stanford: Stanford University Press.

Delgado Ruiz, M. (1986), *De la Muerte de un Dios: la Fiesta de los Toros en el Universo Simbólico de la Cultura Popular,* Barcelona: Península.

Demélas, M.-D. (1992), *L'Invention Politique: Bolivie, Pérou, Equateur au XIXème Siècle,* Paris: Éditions Recherches sur les Civilisations.

Dentan, R.K. (1968), *The Semai: a Non-violent People of Malaysia,* New York: Holt, Rinehart and Winston.

Domville-Fife, Ch.W. (n.d. *c.* 1930), *World Travels,* vol. V, London: Virtue.

Douglas, M. (1970), Introduction to M. Douglas (ed.), *Witchcraft Confessions and Accusations,* London: Tavistock.

—— (1973), *Natural Symbols: Explorations in Cosmology,* New York: Random House.

—— (1991), 'Witchcraft and Leprosy: Two Strategies of Exclusion', *Man* (NS) 26: 549–62.

Douglass, W.A. and J. Zulaika (1990), 'On the Interpretation of Terrorist Violence: ETA and the Basque Political Process', *Comparative Studies in Society and History* 32: 238–57.

Dreyer, E.L. (1982), *Early Ming China,* Stanford: Stanford University Press.

Duclos, D. (1996), *The Werewolf Complex: America's Fascination with Violence,* Oxford: Berg.

Dülmen, R. von (1984), 'Das Schauspiel des Todes' in: R. von Dülmen and N. Schindler (eds), *Volkskultur: Zur Wiederentdeckung des Vergessenen Alltags (16–20 Jahrhundert),* Frankfurt/Main: Suhrkamp Verlag.

Dumézil, G. (1968), *Mythe et Épopée,* 3 vols, Paris: Gallimard.

Dunning, E. *et al.* (1986), ' "Casuals", "Terrace Crews", and "Fighting Firms": Towards a Sociological Explanation of Football Hooligan Behaviour', in: D. Riches (ed.), *The Anthropology of Violence,* Oxford: Blackwell.

Durkheim, E. (1912), *Les Formes Élémentaires de la Vie Religieuse,* Paris: Alcan.

Eberhard, W. (1988), *A Dictionary of Chinese Symbols: Hidden Symbols in Chinese Life and Thought,* transl. G.L. Campbell, London: Routledge and Kegan Paul.

Ebrey, P.B. (1993), *The Inner Quarters: Marriage and the Lives of Chinese Women in the Sung Period,* Berkeley: University of California Press.

Eibl-Eibesfeldt, I. and F.K. Salter (eds) (1997), *Warfare, Ideology and Indoctrinability: Evolutionary Perspectives,* Oxford: Berghahn.

Elias, N. (1978), *The History of Manners: The Civilizing Process,* vol. I, transl. E. Jephcott, New York: Pantheon.

—— (1983), *The Court Society,* transl. E. Jephcott, Oxford: Blackwell.

—— (1986), 'An Essay on Sport and Violence', in: N. Elias and E. Dunning, *Quest for Excitement: Sport and Leisure in the Civilizing Process,* Oxford: Blackwell.

Elvin, M. (1984), 'Female Virtue and the State in China', *Past and Present* 104: 111–152.

Emerson, R.W. (1950), *Selected Prose and Poetry,* New York: Rinehart.

Errington, F.K. (1974), *Karavar: Masks and Power in a Melanesian Ritual,* Ithaca: Cornell University Press.

Estrich, S. (1987), *Real Rape,* Cambridge, MA: Harvard University Press.

Ess, H. van (1993), *Politik und Gelehrsamkeit in der Zeit der Han: Die Alttext/Neutext-Kontroverse,* Wiesbaden: Otto Harassowitz.

—— (1994), 'The Old Text/New Text Controversy: Has the 20th Century Got it Wrong?', *T'oung Pao* LXXX: 146–70.

—— n.d. 'Gewaltsmonopol und Wiederstand in China', unpublished lecture.

Evans-Pritchard, E.E. (1940), *The Nuer,* Oxford: Clarendon Press.

Fairbank, J.K. (1974), 'Introduction: Varieties of the Chinese Military Experience', in: F.A. Kierman Jr (ed.), *Chinese Ways in Warfare,* Cambridge, MA: Harvard University Press.

Fals Borda, O. (1979) [1955], *Campesinos de los Andes,* 2nd edn, Bogotà: Punta de Lanza.

Faure, B. (1991), *The Rhetoric of Immediacy: a Cultural Critique of Chan/ Zen Buddhism,* Princeton: Princeton University Press.

Feldman, A. (1991), *Formations of Violence: The Narrative of the Body and Political Terror in Northern Ireland,* Chicago: University of Chicago Press.

Fernandez, J.W. (1978), 'African Religious Movements', *Annual Review of Anthropology* 7: 195–234.

—— (1993), 'Ceferino Suarez: a Village Versifier', in: S. Lavie, K. Narayan and R. Rosaldo (eds), *Creativity/Anthropology,* Ithaca: Cornell University Press.

Fernandez de Moratín, N. [1777] *Carta Histórica Sobre el Origen y Progresos de las Fiestas de los Toros en España,* Madrid [n.p., Private print].

Feuchtwang, S.D.R. (1982) [1974], *An Anthropological Analysis of Chinese Geomancy,* Taibei: Southern Materials Centre.

Fisher, C.T. (1990), *The Chosen One: Succession and Adoption in the Court of Ming Zhizong,* London: Allen and Unwin.

Flanet, V. (1982), *La Maitresse Mort: Violence au Mexique,* Paris: Berger-Levraut.

Bibliography

Fleisher, M. (1997), 'Kuria Cattle Raiding: a Case Study in the Capitalist Transformation of an East African Sociocultural Institution', Diss., University of Michigan, Ann Arbor.

Foster, M.L. and Rubinstein, R.A. (eds) (1986), *Peace and Wars: Cross-cultural Perspectives*, New Brunswick: Transaction Press.

Foucault, M. (1982) [1975], *Discipline and Punish: the Birth of the Prison*, transl. A. Sheridan, Harmondsworth: Penguin Books.

Frevert, U. (1995), *Ehrensmänner: Das Duell in der Bürgerlichen Gesellschaft*, 2nd edn, München: Deutscher Taschenbuch Verlag.

Fukui, K. and J. Markakis (eds) (1994), *Ethnicity and Conflict in the Horn of Africa*, London: James Currey.

Gambetta, D. (1993), *The Sicilian Mafia*, Cambridge, MA: Harvard University Press.

Geertz, C. (1971), *Myth, Symbol and Culture*, New York: Norton.

—— (1973), 'Deep Play: Notes on the Balinese Cockfight', in: *The Interpretation of Cultures*, New York: Basic Books.

—— (1980), *Negara: The Theatre State in Nineteenth-century Bali*, Princeton: Princeton University Press.

Geertz, H. (1975), 'An Anthropology of Religion and Magic', *Journal of Interdisciplinary Research* 6: 71–89.

Geffray, C. (1990), *La Cause des Armes au Mozambique*, Paris: Éditions Karthala.

Geiss, J. (1988), 'The Ming Dynasty, 1368–1644, Part I', in: F.W. Mote and D. Twitchett (eds), *The Cambridge History of China*, vol. 7, Cambridge: Cambridge University Press.

Gellner, E. (1969), *Saints of the Atlas*, London: Weidenfeld and Nicholson.

Gernet, J. (1959), 'Les Suicides par le Feu chez les Bouddhistes Chinois du Ve au Xe Siècle', in: *Mélanges Publiés par l'Institut des Hautes Études Chinoises* II, Paris: Presses Universitaires de France.

Gernet, L. (1981), 'Capital Punishment', in: *The Anthropology of Ancient Greece*, Baltimore: Johns Hopkins University Press.

Gibson, T. (1986), *Sacrifice and Sharing in the Philippine Highlands*, London: Athlone Press.

—— (1990), 'Raiding, Trading, and Tribal Autonomy in Insular Southeast Asia', in: J. Haas (ed), *The Anthropology of War*, Cambridge: Cambridge University Press.

Gilmore, D.D. (ed.) (1987), *Honor and Shame and the Unity of the Mediterranean*, Washington, DC: American Anthropological Association.

Ginzburg, C. (1987), 'Sacchegi Rituali', *Quaderni Storici* 22: 615–36.

Giraldo, C.A., J.S. Colorado and D. Perez (eds) (1977), *Relatos e Imagenes: El Desplazamiento en Colombia*, Bogotà: Cinep.

Bibliography

Girard, R. (1972), *La Violence et le Sacré,* Paris: Grasset.

—— (1977), *Violence and the Sacred.* transl. P. Gregory, Baltimore: Johns Hopkins University Press.

—— (1983), *Le Bouc Émissaire,* nouv. édn, Paris: Grasset.

Gluckman, M. (1962), *Essays on the Ritual of Social Relations,* Manchester: Manchester University Press.

Goffman, E. (1963), *Stigma: Notes on the Management of Spoiled Identity,* Harmondsworth: Penguin Books.

—— (1967), *Interaction Ritual,* Harmondsworth: Penguin Books.

—— (1971), *Relations in Public,* New York: Harper and Row.

Goodenough, W. (1963), *Cooperation in Change,* New York: Sage.

Gray, J.H. (1875). *Walks in the City of Canton,* Hong Kong: De Souza.

—— (1972) [1878] *China: a History of the Laws, Manners and Customs of the People,* 2 vols, Shannon Island: Irish University Press.

Groot, J.J.M. de (1989) [1892], *The Religious System of China,* 6 vols, Taibei: Southern Materials Centre.

Guerrero, J. (1991), *Los Anos del Ovido: Boyaca y los Origenes de la Violencia,* Bogotà: Tercer Mundo.

Guizado, A.G. (1993), 'La Reforma de la Policia: Realidades Inmediatas y Objectivos Estrategicos', *Analisi Politica* 19: 50–62.

Guzman, G., O. Fals Borda and E. Umana Luna (1963), *La Violencia en Colombia,* Bogotà: Carlos Valencia Editores.

GZMGRB (1952), *Guangzhou Minguo Ribao* (Republican News of Canton), 1927–1950, Canton: Guangzhou Minguo Ribao Zhubanshe.

Haar, B.J. ter (1998), *Creating an Identity: the Ritual and Mythology of Chinese Triads,* Leiden: E.J. Brill.

Haas, J. (ed.) (1990), *The Anthropology of War,* Cambridge: Cambridge University Press.

Haberland, E. (1993), *Hierarchie und Kaste: Zur Geschichte und politischen Struktur der Dizi in Südwest Äthiopien,* Stuttgart: F. Steiner Verlag.

Haeger, J.W. (1975), 'Political Crisis and the Integrity of Culture', in: J.H. Haeger (ed.), *Crisis and Prosperity in Sung China,* Tucson: University of Arizona Press.

Hamerton-Kelly, R.G. (ed.) (1987), *Violent Origins: Walter Burkert, René Girard and Jonathan Z. Smith on Ritual Killing and Cultural Formation,* Stanford: Stanford University Press.

Handler, R. and D. Segal (1990), *Jane Austin and the Fiction of Culture: an Essay on the Narration of Social Realities,* Tucson: Arizona University Press.

Harada Yoshito (1937), *Kan Rikuchô No Fukushoku* (Clothing of the Han and Six Dynasties Periods), Tôkyô: Tôkyô Bunko.

Harper, D. (1987), 'Wang Yen Shou's Nightmare Poem', *Harvard Journal of Asiatic Studies* 47: 239–83.

Harré, R. (1998), *The Singular Self: An Introduction to the Psychology of Personhood,* London: Sage Publications.

Harré, R. and J-P. de Waele (1976), 'The Personality of Individuals', in R. Harré (ed.), *Personality,* Oxford: Blackwell.

Harrell, S. (1990), 'Introduction', in: J.N. Lipman and S. Harrell (eds), *Violence in China: Essays in Culture and Counterculture,* Albany: State University of New York Press.

Harris, R. (1981), *The Language Myth,* London: Duckworth.

Hartman, Ch. (1986), *Han Yü and the T'ang Search for Unity,* Princeton: Princeton University Press.

Harvey, P. and P. Gow (eds) (1994), *Sex and Violence: Issues in Representation and Experience,* London: Routledge.

Heald, S. S. (1986a), 'Witches and Thieves: Deviant Motivations in Gisu Society', *Man* (NS) 21: 65–78.

—— (1986b), 'Mafias in Africa: the Rise of Drinking Companies and Vigilante Groups in Bugisu District, Uganda', *Africa* 56: 446–67.

—— (1989/1998), *Controlling Anger: the Sociology of Gisu Violence,* Manchester: Manchester University Press (1998 edn, Oxford: James Currey).

—— (1991), 'Tobacco, Time and Household Economy in Two Kenyan Societies: the Teso and the Kuria', *Comparative Studies in Society and History* 33: 130–57.

—— (1996), *The Social and Cultural Effects of Agricultural Intensification in Kenya*, Research Report for the ESRC and the Republic of Kenya.

—— (1997), *Praise Poems of the Kuria,* Nairobi: Phoenix.

—— (1999), 'Agricultural Intensification and the Decline of Pastoralism: a Case Study from Kenya', *Africa* 69: 213–37.

Hemingway, E. (1977) [1932], *Death in the Afternoon,* London: Triad/Panther Books.

Henderson, J. (1984), *Tolima: an Evocative History of Politics and Violence in Colombia,* Birmingham: Alabama University Press.

Hennesy, A. (1978), *The Frontier in Latin American History,* Albuquerque: University of New Mexico Press.

Hentig, H. von (1969) [1958], *Vom Ursprung der Henkersmahlzeit,* Tübingen: J.B.C. Mohr.

Hirschmann, A. (1978) [1963], *Journeys into Progress,* New York: Twentieth Century Croft.

Ho, V.K.Y. (1994), 'Cantonese Opera in a Rural Setting: Observations on Village Drama', in: G. Aijmer and Å. Boholm (eds), *Images and*

Enactments: Possible Worlds in Dramatic Performance, Gothenburg: IASSA.

Hobsbawm, E.J. (1959), *Primitive Rebels,* Manchester: Manchester University Press.

—— (1981), *Bandits,* New York: Pantheon.

Hocart, A. (1927), *Kingship,* Oxford: Clarendon Press.

—— (1971), *Lau Islands, Fiji,* Honolulu: Honululu Museum.

Holcombe, Ch. (1989), 'The Exemplar State: Ideology , Self-cultivation, and Power in Fourth Century China, *Harvard Journal of Asiatic Studies* 49: 118–36.

Holden, R.H. (1994), *Mexico and the Survey of Public Lands: the Management of Modernization, 1876–1911,* DeKalb: University of Illinois Press.

Holy, L. and M. Stuchlik (1981), 'The Structure of Folk Models', in: L. Holy and M. Stuchlik (eds), *The Structure of Folk Models,* London: Academic Press.

Howe, J. (1981), 'Fox Hunting as Ritual', *American Ethnologist* 8: 278–300.

Howell, S. (1984), *Society and Cosmos: Chewong of Peninsular Malaysia,* Oxford: Oxford University Press.

—— (1988), 'From Child to Human: Chewong Concepts of Self', in: I. M. Lewis and G. Jahoda (eds), *Acquiring Culture: Comparative Studies in Childhood,* London: Croom Helm.

—— (1989), ' "To Be Angry Is Not to Be Human, but to Be Fearful Is": Chewong Concepts of Human Nature', in: S. Howell and R. Willis (eds), *Societies at Peace: Anthropological Perspectives,* London: Routledge.

Howell, S. and R. Willis (eds) (1989), *Societies at Peace: Anthropological Perspectives,* London: Routledge.

Hsieh, A.C.L. and J.D. Spence (1981), 'Suicide and Family in Pre-modern Chinese Society', in A. Kleinman and Tsung-yi Lin (eds), *Normal and Abnormal Behaviour in Chinese Culture,* Dordrecht: D. Reidel.

Huang Li-hung (1984), *A Complete Book Concerning Happiness and Benevolence: a Manual for Local Magistrates in Seventeenth Century China,* transl. Djang Chu, Tucson: University of Arizona Press.

Hulsewé, A.F.P. (1955), *Remnants of Han Law,* Leiden: E.J. Brill.

Humphrey, C. and J. Laidlaw (1994), *The Archetypal Actions of Ritual: a Theory of Ritual Illustrated by the Jain Rite of Worship,* Oxford: Clarendon Press.

Jackson, M. (1989), *Paths Toward a Clearing: Radical Empiricism and Ethnographic Inquiry,* Bloomington: Indiana University Press.

Jamin, J. (1984), Une Ethnographie de la Violence est-elle Possible?, *Études Rurales* 95/96: 16–21.

Jamous, R. (1981), *Honneur et Baraka: les Structures Sociales Tradition-elles dans le Rif,* Cambridge: Cambridge University Press.

Janes, R. (1991), 'Beheadings', *Representations* 35: 21–51.

Jin Liangnian (1991), *Kuxing Yu Zhongguo Shehui* (Cruel Punishments and Chinese Society), Hangzhou: Jiejiang Renmin Zhubanshe.

Johnson, C. (1982), *Revolutionary Change*, Stanford: Stanford University Press.

Johnston, A.I. (1995), *Cultural Realism: Strategic Culture and Grand Strategy in Chinese History,* Princeton: Princeton University Press.

Jorgensen, D. (1994), 'Locating the Divine in Melanesia: an Appreciation of the Work of Kenelm Burridge', *Anthropology and Humanism* 19: 130–7.

Joseph, G.M. (1990), 'On the Trial of Latin American Bandits: a Re-examination of Peasant Resistance', *Latin American Research Review* 25: 7–51.

Kam Louie and L. Edwards (1995), 'Chinese Masculinity: Theorizing *Wen* and *Wu*', *East Asian History* 8: 135–48.

Kamen, H. (1983), *Spain 1469–1714: a Society in Conflict,* London and New York: Longman

Kapferer, B. (1988), *Legends of People, Myths of State,* Washington, DC: Smithsonian Institution Press.

Kearney, R. (1988), *The Wake of Imagination: Ideas of Creativity in Western Culture,* London: Hutchinson.

Keeley, L. (1996), *War before Civilization,* New York: Oxford University Press.

Kiernan, V.G. (1988), *The Duel in European History: Honour and the Reign of Aristocracy,* New York: Oxford University Press.

Kinkley, J.C. (1987), *The Odyssey of Shen Congwen*, Stanford: Stanford University Press.

Kjerland, K.A. (1995), Cattle Breed, Shillings Don't. The Belated Incor-poration of the abaKuria into Modern Kenya, Diss., University of Bergen.

Kleeman, T. (1994), 'Licentious Cults and Bloody Victuals: Sacrifice, Reciprocity, and Violence in Traditional China', *Asia Major* (Third Series) VII: 185–211.

Knauft, B.M. (1987/88), 'Reconsidering Violence in Simple Human Societies: Homicide among the Gebusi of New Guinea', *Current Anthropology* 28: 457–500; 29: 629–33.

—— (1991), 'Violence and Sociality in Human Evolution', *Current Anthropology* 32: 391–428.

Bibliography

Koch, K.-F. (1974), *War and Peace in Jalémo: the Management of Conflict in Highland New Guinea,* Cambridge, MA: Harvard University Press.

Krohn-Hansen, C. (1994), 'The Anthropology of Violent Interaction', *Journal of Anthropological Research* 50: 367–382.

Kuhn, Ph.A. (1990), *Soulstealers: the Chinese Sorcery Scare of 1778,* Cambridge, MA: Harvard University Press.

Kurimoto, E. and S. Simonse (1998), 'Introduction', in: E. Kurimoto and S. Simonse (eds), *Conflict, Age and Power in North East Africa. Age Systems in Transition,* Oxford: James Currey; Nairobi: East African Educational Publishing; Kampala: Fountain Publishers; Athens, OH: Ohio University Press.

Lai, C.M. (1994), 'The Art of Lamentation in the Works of Pan Yue: "Mourning the Eternally Departed" ', *Journal of the American Oriental Society* 114: 409–25.

Laing, R.D. (1968), *The Politics of Experience,* Harmondsworth: Penguin Books.

Lamley, H.J. (1990), 'Lineage Feuding in Southern Fujian and Eastern Guangdong under Qing Rule', in: J.N. Lipman and S. Harrell (eds), *Violence in China: Essays in Culture and Counterculture,* Albany: State University of New York Press.

Langbein, J.H. (1977), *Torture and the Law of Proof: Europe and England in the Ancient Régime,* Chicago: University of Chicago Press.

Last, M. (1995), Aspects of Chai Grammar, MA thesis, University of Leiden.

Leach, E.R. (1964) [1954], *Political Systems of Highland Burma,* 2nd edn, London: G. Bell and Sons.

—— (1966), 'Ritualization in Man in Relation to Conceptual and Social Development', in: J. Huxley (ed.), *A Discussion on Ritualization of Behaviour in Animals and Men,* London: Philosophical Transactions of the Royal Society of London, Series B.

—— (1969), *A Runaway World? The Reith Lectures,* London: Oxford University Press.

—— (1976a), 'Humanism'. Public Lecture Delivered at the Humanism Society, University of Cambridge.

—— (1976b), *Culture and Communication,* Cambridge: Cambridge University Press.

—— (1977), *Custom, Law and Terrorist Violence,* Edinburgh: Edinburgh University Press.

Le Bot, Y. (1992), *La Guerre en Terre Maya: Communauté, Violence et Modernité au Guatemala (1970–1992),* Paris: Éditions Karthala.

—— (1996), 'Les Temps des Guerres Communautaires', in: M. Wieviorka

Bibliography

(ed.), *Une Société Fragmentée: Le Multiculturalisme en Débat,* Paris: La Découverte.

Le Goff, J. and J.C. Schmitt (eds) (1981), *Le Charivari,* Paris: Mouton.

LeGrand, C. (1980), *From Public Lands into Private Properties: Land-holding and Rural Conflict in Colombia (1850–1936),* Stanford: Stanford University Press.

Lewis, M.E. (1990), *Sanctioned Violence in Early China,* Albany: State University of New York Press.

Lincoln, B. (1985), 'Revolutionary Exhumations in Spain, July 1936', *Comparative Studies in Society and History* 27: 241–60.

Linebaugh, P. (1975), 'The Tyburn Riot against the Surgeons', in: D. Haye *et al.* (eds), *Albion's Fatal Tree: Crime and Society in Eighteenth-Century England,* London: Allen Lane.

Linger, D.T. (1992), *Violent Encounters: Meanings of Violence in a Brazilian City,* Stanford: Stanford University Press.

Lipman, J.N. and S. Harrell (eds) (1990), *Violence in China: Essays in Culture and Counterculture,* Albany: State University of New York Press.

Liu I-ch'ing (1976) (with a commentary by Liu Chün), *Shih-shou Hsin-yü: a New Account of the World,* transl. R. Mather, Minneapolis: University of Minnesota Press.

Liu, J.T.C. (1985), 'Polo and Cultural Change: from T'ang to Sung China', *Harvard Journal of Asiatic Studies* 45: 203–24.

Liu Zongyuan (n.d.), 'Bo Fuchou yi', *Guwen Guanzhi* 9: 387–90.

Liuyue Xue (Snow in June) (1990) [1915–25], Edited in *Xikao Daquan* (A Complete Collection of Opera Scripts), 5 vols, vol. 1, Shanghai: Shanghai Shudian.

Llewelyn-Davies, M. (1981), 'Women, Warriors and Patriarchs', in: S.B. Ortner and H. Whitehead (eds), *The Cultural Construction of Sexuality,* Cambridge: Cambridge University Press.

Lo Guanzhong (1988), *Suihu Zhuan* (Water Margins), Changsha: Yuelu Shushe [Reprint].

Locke, J. (1991), *Two Treatises of Government,* Cambridge: Cambridge University Press.

Lofland, J. (1977), 'The Dramaturgy of State Executions', in: *State Executions Viewed Historically and Sociologically,* Montclair: Patterson Smith.

Lu Xun (1991), 'Yao' (Medicine); 'Shi Zhong '(Publicly Exposed)', in: *Lu Xun Xuanji* (Collected Works of Lu Xun), Beijing: Renmin Minxue Chubanshe.

Lu Yan (1987), You zi (Pomelo), in: Tan Ying (ed.), *Lu Yan,* Hong Kong: Sanlian Shudian.

Bibliography

Lukes, S. (1974), *Power: a Radical View*, New York: Macmillan.

—— (1975), 'Political Ritual and Social Integration', *Sociology* 9: 289–308.

MacCormack, G. (1990), *Traditional Chinese Penal Law*, Edinburgh: Edinburgh University Press.

MacKay, A. (1977), *Spain in the Middle Ages: from Frontier to Empire, 1000–1500*, London: Macmillan.

McAleer, K. (1994), *Dueling: the Cult of Honour in Fin-de-siècle Germany*, Princeton: Princeton University Press.

McFarlane, G. (1986), 'Violence in Northern Ireland', in: D. Riches (ed.), *The Anthropology of Violence*, Oxford: Blackwell.

McKnight, B.E. (1981a), *The Quality of Mercy: Amnesties and Traditional Chinese Justice*, Honululu: University of Hawaii Press.

—— (1981b) (transl.), *The Washing Away of Wrongs: Forensic Medicine in Thirteenth-Century China*, Ann Arbor: Center for Chinese Studies, University of Michigan.

—— (1992), *Law and Order in Sung China*, Cambridge: Cambridge University Press.

McMullen, D.L. (1989a), 'The Cult of Ch'i T'ai-kung and T'ang Attitudes to the Military', *T'ang Studies* 7: 59–104.

—— (1989b), 'The Death of Chou Li-chen: Imperially Ordered Suicide or Natural Causes', *Asia Major* (Third Series) II: 23–82.

McNeill, W.H. (1982), *The Pursuit of Power: Technology, Armed Force, and Society since A.D. 1000*, Chicago: University of Chicago Press.

Malcolm, N. (1998), 'The Uses of Violence', *Times Literary Supplement*, 16 January.

Martin, G. (1996), 'Sociabilité, Institutions et Violences dans les Frontières Nouvelles en Colombie', in: J.-M. Blanquer and C. Gross (eds), *La Colombie à l'Aube du Troisième Millénaire*, Paris: IHEAL.

—— (1997), 'Violences Stratégiques et Violences Désorganisées dans la Région de Urabá en Colombie', *Cultures et Conflits*, no. 24/25: 195–238.

Marvin, G. (1986), 'Honour, Integrity and the Problem of Violence in the Spanish Bullfight', in: D. Riches (ed.), *The Anthropology of Violence*, Oxford: Blackwell.

Marx, E. (1976), *The Social Context of Violent Behaviour: a Social Anthropological Study of an Israeli Immigrant Town*, London: Routledge and Kegan Paul.

Mather, R.B. (1988), *The Poet Shen Yüeh (441–513): the Reticent Marquis*, Princeton: Princeton University Press.

Meggitt, M. (1977), *Blood is Their Argument: Warfare among the Mae Enga Tribesmen of the New Guinea Highlands,* Palo Alto: Mayfield.

Merkl, P.H. (ed.) (1986), *Political Violence and Terror,* Berkeley: University of California Press.

Meuli, K. (1975), 'Griechische Opferbräuche', in: K. Meuli, *Gesammelte Schriften,* vol. II, Basel: Benno Schwabe.

Michaud, Y. (1986), *La Violence,* Paris: Presses Universitaires de France.

Mitchell, T. (1988), *Violence and Piety in Spanish Folklore,* Philadelphia: University of Pennsylvania Press.

—— (1991), *Blood Sport: a Social History of Spanish Bullfighting,* Philadelphia: University of Pennsylvania Press.

Mollier, Ch. (1990), *Une Apocalypse Taoiste du Ve Siècle: le Livre des Incantations Divines des Grottes Abyssales,* Paris: Collège de France, Institut des Hautes Études.

Moore, H.L. (1994), 'The Problem of Explaining Violence in the Social Sciences', in: P. Harvey and P. Gow (eds), *Sex and Violence: Issues in Representation and Experience,* London: Routledge.

Nabokov, V. (1975), 'Commentary', in: A. Pushkin, *Eugene Onegin: a Novel in Verse,* transl. and comment. V. Nabokov, vols I–II, Princeton: Princeton University Press.

Nahoum-Grappe, V. (1995), 'L'Épuration Ethnique: Désastre et Stupeur', in: V. Nahoum-Grappe (ed.), *Vukovar, Sarajevo... La Guerre en ex-Yougoslavie,* Paris: Éditions Esprit.

Nietzsche, F.W. (1990), *Beyond Good and Evil: Prelude to a Philosophy of the Future,* transl. R.J. Hollingdale, Harmondsworth: Penguin Books.

Niida, Noboru (1980), *Chugoku Hòsei Shi Kenkyù* (Research on Chinese Legal History), Tokyo: Tokyo Daigaku Shuppankai.

Nordstrom, C. and A.C.G.M. Robben (eds) (1996), *Fieldwork under Fire: Contemporary Studies of Violence and Survival,* Berkeley: University of California Press.

Nye, R.A. (1991), 'Honor Codes in Modern France', *Ethnologia Europaea* 21: 5–17.

Ortiz Sarmiento, C.M. (1985), *Estado y Subversión en Colombia: La Violencia en el Quindio en los 50,* Bogotà: Fondo Editorial CEREL.

Ownby, D. (1990), 'The Ethnic Feud in Qing Taiwan: What Is this Violence Business Anyway? An Interpretation of the 1782 Zhang-Quan Xiedou', *Late Imperial China* 11: 75–98.

Palacios, M. (1995), *Entre la Legitimidad y la Violencia: Colombia (1875–1994),* Bogotà: Ediciones Norma.

Park, G. (1974), *The Idea of Social Structure,* New York: Doubleday.

Parkin, D. (1987), 'Comparison as a Search for Continuity', in: L. Holy (ed.), *Comparative Anthropology,* Oxford: Blackwell.

Pécaut, D. (1986), 'Guérillas et Violence: le Cas de la Colombie', *Sociologie du Travail* 28: 484–505.

—— (1987a), 'Crise, Guerre et Paix', *Notes et Études Documentaires: Problèmes d'Amerique Latine* 36.

—— (1987b), *L'Ordre et la Violence: Evolution Socio-politique de la Colombie entre 1930 et 1953,* Paris: EHESS.

—— (1989), 'Colombie: Violence et Démocratie', *Politique et Parlementalisme,* no. 940: 59–73.

—— (1994), 'Violence et Politique: Quatre Éléments de Réflexion à propos de la Colombie', *Cultures et Conflits* 13/14: 155–66.

—— (1995), 'Violence et Politique en Colombie', in: Colloque de Cerisy, *Penser le Sujet: Autour de Alain Touraine,* Paris: Fayard.

—— (1996), 'Réflexions sur la Violence en Colombie', in: F. Héritier (ed.), *De la Violence,* Paris: Éditions Odile Jacob.

—— (1997), 'De la Banalité de la Violence à la Terreur: le Cas Colombien', *Cultures et Conflits* 24/25: 159–93.

Pérez Díaz, V. (1974) *Pueblos y Clases Sociales en el Campo Español,* Madrid: Siglo XXI.

Pitt-Rivers, J.A. (1977), *The Fate of Shechem or the Politics of Sex: Essays on the Anthropology of the Mediterranean,* Cambridge: Cambridge University Press.

—— (1983), 'Le Sacrifice du Taureau', *Le Temps de la Réflexion* 4: 281–98.

Pizarro, E. (1996), 'Les Forces Armées dans un Contexte d'Insurrection Chronique ou le Status des Forces Armées dans la Société Colombienne', in: J.-M. Blanquer and C. Gros (eds), *La Colombie à l'Aube du Troisième Millénaire,* Paris: IHEAL.

Pulleyblank, E.G. (1976), 'The An Lu-shan Rebellion and the Origins of Chronic Militarism in Late T'ang China', in: J.C. Percy and B.L. Smith (eds), *Essays on T'ang Society: the Interplay of Social, Political and Economic Forces,* Leiden: E.J. Brill.

Radcliffe-Brown, A.R. (1952), *Structure and Function in Primitive Society,* London: Cohen and West.

Rand, C.C. (1979/80), 'Chinese Military Thought and Philosophical Taoism', *Monumenta Serica* XXXIV: 171–218.

Ranum, O. (1980), 'The French Ritual of Tyrannicide in the Late Sixteenth Century', *Sixteenth Century Journal* 11: 63–82.

Rappaport, R.A. (1979), *Ecology, Meaning, and Religion,* Berkeley: North Atlantic Books.

Rapport, N.J. (1987), *Talking Violence: an Anthropological Interpretation of Conversation in the City,* St John's: ISER Books, Memorial University of Newfoundland.

—— (1990), 'Ritual Conversation in a Canadian Suburb: Anthropology and the Problem of Generalisation', *Human Relations* 43: 849–64.

—— (1993), *Diverse World-Views in an English Village,* Edinburgh: Edinburgh University Press.

—— (1994), *The Prose and the Passion: Anthropology, Literature and the Writing of E.M. Forster,* Manchester: Manchester University Press.

Redfield, J.M. (1975), *Nature and Culture in the Iliad: the Tragedy of Hector,* Chicago: University of Chicago Press.

Riches, D. (ed.) (1986), *The Anthropology of Violence,* Oxford: Basil Blackwell.

—— (1986), 'The Phenomenon of Violence', in: D. Riches (ed.), *The Anthropology of Violence*, Oxford: Blackwell.

—— (1991) 'Aggression, War, Violence: Space/Time and Paradigm', *Man* (NS) 26: 281–298.

Ricoeur, P. (1967), 'Violence et Langage', in: *La Violence: Recherche et Débats,* Paris: Desclée de Brouwer.

Riesman, D. (1954), *Individualism Reconsidered, and Other Essays,* Glencoe: Free Press.

Robarchek, C.A. (1977), 'Frustration, Aggression, and the Non-violent Semai', *American Ethnologist* 4: 762–79.

—— (1979), 'Conflict, Emotion, and Abreaction: Resolution of Conflict among Semai Senoi', *Ethos* 7: 104–23.

—— (1989), 'Primitive Warfare and the Ratomorphic Image of Mankind', *American Anthropologist* 91: 903–20.

—— (1990), 'Motivation and Material Causes: on the Explanation of Conflict and War', in: J. Haas (ed.), *The Anthropology of War,* Cambridge: Cambridge University Press.

—— (1991), '"Agnostic about Consciousness" – Science, Anti-science, and Ratomorphic Psychology', *American Anthropologist* 93: 165–66.

Robarchek, C.A. and R.K. Dentan, (1987), 'Blood-Drunkenness and the Bloodthirsty Semai: Unmaking another Anthropological Myth', *American Anthropologist* 89: 356–65.

Robinet, I. (1989), 'Original Contributions of *Neidan* to Taoism and Chinese Thought', in: L. Kohn and Yoshinubu Sakade (eds), *Taoist Meditation and Longevity Techniques,* Ann Arbor: Center for Chinese Studies, University of Michigan.

Robinson, G. (1995), *The Dark Side of Paradise: Political Violence in Bali,* Ithaca: Cornell University Press.

Roldan, M.J. (1992), Genesis and Evolution of La Violencia in Antioquia, Colombia (1900–1953), Diss., Harvard University.

Rooijakkers, G. (1994), *Rituele Repertoires,* Nijmegen: SUN.

Rorty, R. (1992), *Contingency, Irony and Solidarity,* Cambridge: Cambridge University Press.

Rosaldo, R., S. Lavie and K. Narayan (1993), 'Introduction: Creativity in Anthropology', in: S. Lavie, K. Narayan and R. Rosaldo (eds), *Creativity/Anthropology,* Ithaca: Cornell University Press.

Rosanvallon, P. (1992), *Le Sacré du Citoyen: Histoire du Suffrage Universel en France,* Paris: Gallimard.

Rotours, R. des (1963), 'Quelque notes sur l'Anthropophagie en Chine', *T'oung Pao* 50: 389–95.

—— (1968), 'Encore Quelques Notes sur l'Anthropophagie en Chine', *T'oung Pao* 54: 2–8.

Rowen, H.H. (1978), *John de Witt, Grand Pensionary of Holland, 1725– 72,* Princeton: Princeton University Press.

Ruel, M. (1959), The Social Organization of the Kuria. Mimeo.

—— (1997), *Belief, Ritual and the Securing of Life: Reflexive Essays on a Bantu Religion,* Leiden: E.J. Brill.

Russell, C. and W.M.S. Russell (1968), *Violence, Monkeys and Man,* London: Macmillan.

Saari, J.L. (1990), *Legacies of Childhood: Growing up Chinese in a Time of Crisis,* Cambridge, MA: Harvard University Press.

Sagan, E. (1974), *Cannibalism: Human Aggression and Cultural Form,* New York: Harper and Row.

—— (1979), *The Lust to Annihilate: a Psychoanalytic Study of Violence in Ancient Greek Culture,* New York: Psychohistory Press.

—— (1985), *At the Dawn of Tyranny,* New York: Knopf.

Salazar, A. (1990), *No Nacimos Pa'semilla: La Cultura de las Bandes Juveniles de Medellin,* Bogotà: Cinep.

Salmi, J. (1993), *Violence and Democratic Society: New Approaches to Human Rights,* London: Zed Books.

Sanchez Albornoz, C. (1977), *El Drama de la Formación de España y los Españoles,* Barcelona: Edhasa.

Sanchez, G. and D. Meertens. (1983), *Bandoleros, Gamonales y Campesinos,* Bogotà: El Ancora Ediciones.

Sartre, J.-P. (1957), *Being and Nothingness,* London: Methuen.

—— (1972), *The Psychology of Imagination,* New York: Citadel.

Schafer, E.H. (1951), 'Ritual Exposure in Ancient China', *Harvard Journal of Asiatic Studies* 14: 130–84.

Schild, W. (1980), *Alte Gerichtsbarkeit: vom Gottesurteil bis zum Beginn der Modernen Rechtsprechung*, München: Verlag Georg D.W. Callwey.

Schwartz, T. (1978), 'Where is the Culture? Personality as the Distributive Locus of Culture', in: G. Spindler (ed.), *The Making of Psychological Anthropology*, Berkeley: University of California Press.

Schweder, R. (1991), *Thinking through Cultures*, Cambridge, MA: Harvard University Press.

Seward, D. (1972), *The Monks of War: the Military Religious Orders*, London: Eyre Methuen.

Seyschab, C-A. (1990), 'The 36 Stratagems: Orthodoxy against Heterodoxy', *East Asian Civilizations: New Attempts at Understanding* 3/4: 97–155.

Shen Congwen (1977), *Shen Congwen Zizhuan* (The Memoirs of Shen Congwen), n.p.: Yawen Zhubanshe.

Shorter Oxford English Dictionary (1984), 2 vols, London: Book Club Associates.

Shostak, M. (1993), 'The Creative Individual in the World of the !Kung San', in: S. Lavie, K. Narayan and R. Rosaldo (eds), *Creativity/Anthropology*, Ithaca: Cornell University Press.

Simmel, G. (1950), *The Sociology of Georg Simmel*, transl. K.A. Wolff, Glencoe: Free Press.

—— (1971), *On Individuality and Social Forms*, D. Levine (ed.), Chicago: University of Chicago Press.

—— (1980), *Essays on Interpretation in Social Science*, G. Oakes (ed.), Totowa: Roman and Littlefield.

—— (1983) [1908], *Soziologie*, Berlin: Duncker and Humblot.

Sivin, N. (1995), 'State, Cosmos and Body in the Last Three Centuries B.C.', *Harvard Journal of Asiatic Studies* 55: 5–37.

Slatta, R. (ed.) (1987), *Bandidos: the Varieties of Latin American Banditry*, New Haven: Yale University Press.

Soper, A.C. (1967), *Textual Evidences for the Secular Arts of China in the Period from Liu Sung through Sui*, Ascona: Artibus Asiæ.

Spence, J. and Chin An-ping (1996), *The Chinese Century: a Photographic History of the Last Hundred Years*, New York: Random House.

Spencer, P. (1984), 'Pastoralism and the Ghost of Capitalism', *Production Pastorale et Société* no. 15: 61–76.

—— (1988), *The Maasai of Matapato: a Study of Rituals of Rebellion*, Manchester: Manchester University Press.

Spierenburg, P. (1984), *The Spectacle of Suffering: Executions and the Evolution of Repression: from a Preindustrial Metropolis to the European Experience*, Cambridge: Cambridge University Press.

Bibliography

Stanage, S. (1974), 'Violatives: Modes and Themes of Violence', in: S. Stanage (ed.), *Reason and Violence*. Totowa: Littlefield-Adams.

Stein, R. (1979), 'Religious Taoism and Popular Religion from the Second to the Seventh Centuries', in: H. Welch and A. Seidel (eds), *Facets of Taoism*, New Haven: Yale University Press.

Steiner, G. (1975), *After Babel*, London: Oxford University Press.

Stevenson, D.B. (1996), 'Tsun-shih and the Inscribing of T'ien-t'ai Liturgy', Paper presented at the 'Buddhism in Song' Conference, April, University of Illinois, Urbana.

Stokvis, R. (1991), 'Voetbalvandalisme in Nederland', in: H. Franke *et al.* (eds), *Alledaags en Ongewoon Geweld*, Groningen: Wolters/Nordhoff.

Strathern, M. (1990), *The Gender of the Gift: Problems with Women and Problems with Society in Melanesia*, Berkeley: University of California Press.

Strickmann, M. (1981), *Le Taoïsme du Mao Chan: Chronique d'une Révélation*, Paris: P.U.F.

Sutton, D.S. (1995), 'Consuming Counterrevolution: the Ritual and Culture of Cannibalism in Wuxuan, Guangxi, China, May to July 1968', *Comparative Studies in Society and History* 37: 136–72.

Su Guoyong (1984), 'Shilun Xiqu Guanzhong De Minjianxing Ji Qi Yingxiang (A Discussion on Theater Audiences Popularization and its Impact)', *Xiqu Yanjiu* (Opera Research) 13.

Tambiah, S.J. (1985), *Culture, Thought and Social Action: an Anthropological Perspective*, Cambridge, MA: Harvard University Press.

—— (1990), *Magic, Science, Religion and the Scope of Rationality.* Cambridge: Cambridge University Press.

Tanigawa Michio (1985), *Medieval Chinese Society and the 'Local Community'*, transl. J.A. Fogel, Berkeley: University of California Press.

Tao Xixing (1972), *Qingdai Zhouxian Yamen Xingshi Shenpan Zhidu Zi Chengxu* (Prefectural and County Levels Legal Proceedings and Judicial System in the Qing Dynasty), Taibei: Shihuo Zhubanshe Youxian Gongsi.

Taussig, M. (1988), *Shamanism, Colonialism and the Wild Man*, Chicago and London: University of Chicago Press.

Théry, H. (1995), *Pouvoir et Territoire au Brésil: de l'Archipel au Continent*, Paris: Éditions de la Maison des Sciences de l'Homme.

Thomas, E.M. (1958), *The Harmless People*, New York: Random House.

Thomas, K. (1983), *Man and the Natural World: a History of Modern Sensibility*, New York: Pantheon Books.

T'ien Ju-k'ang (1988), *Male Anxiety and Female Chastity: a Comparative Study of Chinese Ethical Values in Ming-Ch'ing Times,* Leiden: E.J. Brill.

Turner, K. (1993), 'War, Punishment and the Law of Nature in Chinese Concepts of the State', *Harvard Journal of Asiatic Studies* 53: 285–324.

Turner, P.R. and D. Pitt (eds) (1989), *The Anthropology of War and Peace,* Granby: Bergin and Garvey.

Turner, T. (1984), 'Dual Opposition, Hierarchy and Value', in: J.C. Galey (ed.), *Différences, Valeurs, Hiérarchie: Textes Offerts à Louis Dumont,* Paris: EHESS.

Turner, V. (1969), *The Ritual Process: Structure and Anti-Structure,* Chicago: Aldine.

—— (1974), *Dramas, Fields and Metaphors: Symbolic Action in Human Society,* Cornell: Cornell University Press.

Turton, D. (1975), 'The Relationship between Oratory and the Exercise of Influence among the Mursi', in: M. Bloch (ed.), *Political Language and Oratory in Traditional Societies,* London: Academic Press.

—— (1994a), 'Mursi Political Identity and Warfare: the Survival of an Idea', in: K. Fukui and J. Markakis (eds), *Ethnicity and Conflict in the Horn of Africa,* London: James Currey.

—— (1994b), ' "We Must Teach Them to Be Peaceful": Mursi Views on Being Human and Being Mursi', *Nomadic Peoples* 30: 19–33.

Twitchett, D. (1988), 'The Seamy Side of Late T'ang Political Life: Yü Ti and his Family', *Asia Major* (Third Series) I: 29–63.

Twitchett D. and T. Grimm (1988), 'The Cheng-t'ung, Ching-t'ai, and T'ien-shun Reigns, 1436–1469, in: F.W. Mote and D. Twitchett (eds), *The Cambridge History of China,* vol. 7, *The Ming Dynasty, 1368–1644',* Part I, Cambridge: Cambridge University Press.

Unschuld, P. (1985), *Medicine in China: a History of Ideas,* Berkeley: University of California Press.

Uribe, M.V. (1990), *Matar, Rematar, Contramatar* (Controversia no. 159–60), Bogotà: Cinep.

Verdon, M. (1995), *Contre la Culture: Fondement d'une Anthropologie Sociale Opérationelle,* Paris: Éditions des Archives Contemporaines.

Vincent, J. (1989), *Anthropology and Politics,* Tucson: University of Arizona Press.

Waldron, A. (1991), 'The Warlord: Twentieth Century Chinese Understandings of Violence, Militarism, and Imperialism', *American Historical Review* 96: 1073–100.

Wallace, A.F.C. (1970), *Culture and Personality,* New York: Random House.

Bibliography

Walter, E.V. (1969), *Terror and Resistance: a Study of Political Violence with Case Studies of Some Primitive African Communities*, New York: Oxford University Press.

Wang Yongkuan (1994), *Zhongguo Gudai Kuxing* (Torture in Classical China), Taibei: Yunlong Zhubanshe.

Wärnlöf, C. (1998), An Ovahimba Political Landscape: Patterns of Authority in Northwestern Namibia, Diss., University of Gothenburg, Faculty of the Social Sciences.

Welch, H. (1967), *The Practice of Chinese Buddhism,* Cambridge, MA: Harvard University Press.

Whitfield, R. (1993), *Fascination of Nature: Plants and Insects in Chinese Painting and Ceramics of the Yüan Dynasty (1279–1338),* Seoul: Yekyong.

Wickham-Crowley, T.P. (1990), 'Terror and Guerrilla Warfare in Latin America, 1956–1970', *Comparative Studies in Society and History* 33: 201–37.

Wilde, O. (1913), *Intentions*, London: Methuen.

Williams, S.W. (1883), *The Middle Kingdom*, 2 vols, New York: Charles Scribners' Sons.

Woolf, V. (1980), *Orlando,* London: Granada.

Worswick, C. and J. Spence (1978), *Imperial China: Photographs 1850–1912,* n.p: Pennwick Publishing.

Yasunaga Hajime (1981), *Chûgokoku no Go* (Go in China), Tôkyô: Jijô Tshûshinsha.

Yen Chih-t'ui (1968), *Family Instructions for the Yen Clan: Yen Shih Chia-hsün*, transl. Teng Ssu-yü, Leiden: E.J. Brill.

Zhongguo da Baike Guanshu Zongbianzi Weiyuanwei (The Big Encyclo-paedia of China), (1992), Volume on 'Zhengzhi Xue' (Politics), Beijing: Xinhua Shudian.

Zhou Xibao (1984), *Zhongguo Gudai Fushi Shi,* Beijing: Zhongguo Shuju.

Zihai (The Ocean of Characters) (1948), Shanghai: Zhonghua Shuqu.

Zulaika, J. (1988), *Basque Violence: Metaphor and Sacrament,* Reno: University of Nevada Press.

Zürcher, E. (1959), *The Buddhist Conquest of China*, Leiden: E.J. Brill.

Index

age grades 80, 84, 91, 93
aesthetics 18, 88
Aijmer, G., 39, 53
ambiguity xi, 7, 19, 39, 40, 44–5, 77, 97, 143
anthropophagy 19, 156, 160n14
archery 133–4
archetypal meanings 5, 8, 10, 22
Austen, J., 51
authority 15, 72
automatic rifles 16, 81, 91, 94, 106, 108, 156

Babcock, B., 48
bandits 119n7, 174
bao (excessive violence) 123, 130, 143, 144, 145
baoli (exercise of physical force) 143, 145
Bateson, G., 39, 41
beating up (China) 128
beheading 23, 33, 154
Bell, C., 57
Buddhism 127–31, 138
bing (military violence) 123
biology, socio-biology xv, 8, 21n7
Bishco, C.J., 71
blessing 8, 9
Bloch, M., 73, 78, 83
blood 128–31, 156
blood covenant 128–30
blood revenge 125–6, 132
Bloom, H., 40
body, human 34, 87–8, 129
Britain 21n10
Bruner, J., 44
bull 10
    bos taurus sp. 58, 73n2
    as symbol 59, 73n3
bullfighting 10, 26, 55f.
    arena of negotiation 61

as Spanish national ritual 62, 63–4
sexual connotation of 36n8–9, 61
Burridge, K., 46, 49

Cahill, J., 135
Camus, A., 54
capital punishment 16, 152, 153
cattle 18, 80, 83
cattle raiding 82, 88, 94, 101f., 105, 109, 115
Chambers, I. 45
China 11, 16–7,
Christianity (Christian societies) 17, 63,
clientelism 166, 175
cock-fighting 134–5
code 3, 4
cognition 20n1, 45, 52
Colombia 11, 17, 18, 162
communitas 46, 50
comparison xii, xv, 2, 9
Confucius (Confucian) 124–7, 131, 133, 138, 140
consciousness 43–4, 50
contract killers (*sicarios*) 185
creativity 40–1, 42, 44, 46, 49
cruelty xvi, 162, 171, 182
cultural approach xiii, 178
cultural semantics 18
culture xii, 27, 79
'culture of violence' xvi, 78, 164, 178

Daoism 126, 129, 138
death 12, 14, 72, 155
decapitation, see: beheading
demonological 131, 132
discursive order 4, 18
discursive symbolism
Dizi 81–2, 88, 89, 100n3
domination 8, 9, 45, 79
drug economy (Colombia) 164, 191n41

duelling 15, 38n19, 84, 85, 95
Dumézil, G., 58
Durkheim, E., 50, 55

ecology 15, 16, 93, 98
elites and violence (China) 123, 138
emotions 61, 137
Ethiopia 79
equivalence structures 52
ethology (ethological order) xiii, 4, 8
evolutionary-biological paradigm xv
executions 30–1, 37n14, 44, 128, 144,
    145, 159
  as theatre 153–4
  commoditized 155
existentialism 42
exorcism 13, 146

Feldman, A., 184–5
Fernandez, J.W., 48
fertility 60, 62
feuding 95
Flanet, V., 177
form and meaning 41, 48–54
form of life 40, 44
Freud xiv
frontier 70–1, 103, 169, 176
'full blood' ideology (Spain) 64–5, 72

Geertz, C., 23–4
Germany 15
Girard, R., xiv, 31, 56
Gisu (Kenya) 117
globalization 90, 98, 99
Goffman, E., 27
grammar 18, 20n1
gratuitousness 43–4, 51
Grey, J.H., 147–9, 158n5
groups, social
guerrillas 170, 174–5, 179, 181
guns, see: automatic rifles

habitus 89, 90, 91, 105
Harris, R., 45
heroism 16
Himba 18
Hobsbawm, E., 170
Hocart, A., 58
holism xvi, 2

homicide compensation 85, 86
honour 25, 32, 34, 35n5–6, 67, 78
humiliation xi, xv, 33
hunting 14–5, 26, 32, 37n17

iconic symbolism 1, 3, 4, 5, 6, 14, 17, 18
imagery 3, 7, 10, 82–3
imaginary order 3, 4, 7, 8, 18
imagination 40–1, 43–4, 51
impunity 168, 178
initiation 14, 84, 95
individual 13, 14, 17, 40f., 46
insults 25

Johnson, A., 124
judicial procedures and law 12, 168

Kapferer, B., 20n1
Kenya 13

language 3, 4, 45
language-game 42, 45
La Violencia (Colombia) 170–2, 188–9
Leach, E., 45, 46
Lévi-Strauss, C., 14
Lewis, M., 124, 125
life force 15, 17, 18, 78, 83, 156
Linger, D.T., 84
Liu, J., 134
luan (chaos) 123
Lukes, S., 56

mafia (Sicily) 28
mafia-like organizations (Colombia) 166,
    179
martyrdom 5, 14, 17
masculinity 13, 31, 85, 115
massacres 162, 171, 172, 183, 189n26
mazeway 52
Mencius 138
Mexico 177
military orders (Spain) 68–9, 72
missions 99
Mitchell, T., 59, 60, 61
modernization (modernity) 13, 16, 99, 173
morals xii, 9, 131, 158

narrative 40, 44
Netherlands 14

Index

Nietzsche, F.W., 41, 42
norms 16, 96, 124, 143
Northern Ireland 23, 32

'Old Christians' (Spain) 65, 67
ontology 4, 20
operational perspective 2, 5

pain 1–2, 4, 6, 8
para-military (Colombia) 166, 179, 181
Passion, the 5
penalties (punishment) 12
play 51, 61
playing 135
plural ontologies 9, 20
poetry 40, 41
political polarization (Colombia) 166, 172
polo 134
power 16, 57, 113, 131
pragmatics 4, 7, 8
predispositions xiii, xiv, 9, 44
punishments 136, 137
purification 83

rape 27, 36n8, 171
Reconquista 63
refinement, see *wen*
religion (religious system) 14, 18
'resource competition' 89
reproduction 82
Riches, D., xi, 41, 141
ritual 37n16, 46, 55–6, 62, 72, 81, 86,
    124, 150
  of initiation 84
  political 10
  psychological mechanisms of 57
  religious, 55
ritualization 24, 29, 30, 58, 96
Rorty, R., 42
rule-breaking 45

sacrifice 18, 31, 83, 92, 129, 131
Salazar, A., 185
sanction 12
Sartre, J.-P., 43
(self)mutilation 130, 131, 136
semantics 2, 8, 10, 13, 15, 18, 19, 123,
    145
Seward, D., 69

shamanism 130
Shostak, M., 48
Simmel, G., 32, 35–6n7, 49
slaughtering of animals 142
Soper, A., 135
Spain 55f., 66
social control 55, 56
social structure 40–1, 45–54
sport 15
state 9–10, 92, 144, 148, 157
St Bernard of Clairvaux 69
Strathern, M., 54
suicide 126, 130–1, 137
suffering 5, 8, 11, 17
symbology 2, 17, 20
synthesis 2

terror 30, 162, 82, 190n36
theft 103, 105
torture 136, 137, 152, 162, 171, 182,
    189n23, 190n36, 191n42
tourism 16
'tradition of violence' 164, 183
transcendence 42, 43, 47, 48
Turner, V.W., 46
Turton, D., 80
Twitchett, D., 127

van Ess, H., 133
vengeance, 12, 179
videos 16, 99, 100
violation xi, 33, 40, 42, 44–5, 48, 51,
    53–4
violence xi, 41, 43, 56, 50–54, 162
  communicative aspect of xi, xiii, 24,
    28, 97
  constituent aspect of xii, xiv, 1, 4
  contestedness of xi, 97, 98
  definition of 78, 123, 141, 161
  'democratic' 40–1, 51, 53–4
  every-day 173
  generalized 179
  'horizontal' 163
  'nihilistic' 40–1, 51, 53–4
  'senseless' 24, 29, 31
  theorizing of xiv, 161

Wallace, A., 52
war (warfare) 1, 8, 11, 14, 19, 22, 68, 88

Index

weapons, carrying of (China) 133
wen (refinement) 123, 124, 137
wealth 16, 67, 80
'will to power' 42

writing 45, 49–50, 54n2
wu (martial) 123, 124, 136, 137
Zulaika, J., xiii, 30, 37n13
Zürcher, E., 130